BIRTH STORIES
The Experience Remembered

BIRTH STORIES
The Experience Remembered

edited by
JANET ISAACS ASHFORD

THE CROSSING PRESS/Trumansburg, New York 14886

Book and cover design by Jane Twentyman MacDonald
Cover illustration by Nancy Hom
Typesetting by Martha J. Waters

Printed in the U.S.A.

Library of Congress Cataloging in Publication Data
Main entry under title:

Birth stories.

    Includes index.
    1. Childbirth--Psychological aspects. 2. Mother
and child. 3. Mothers--Interviews. I. Ashford,
Janet Isaacs, 1949-
RG652.B57 1984 618.4'092'2   84-17017
ISBN 0-89594-150-3
ISBN 0-89594-149-X (pbk.)

Acknowledgments

Versions of "Uremic Poisoning" by Jean Chisholm Isaacs, "Chinese Herbs" by Florence Scriven Munro, and "Saddle Block and Forceps" by Alice Munro Isaacs first appeared in *The Whole Birth Catalog* by Janet Isaacs Ashford (Crossing Press, 1983).

The original version of "A Clean White Room" by Lolly Hirsch was published, under the title "Lura's Birth," in *Proceedings of the First International Childbirth Conference* (Cloonan Middle School; Stamford, Connecticut; June 2, 1973) published by New Moon Communications. A tape recorded reading of "Lura's Birth" has also been broadcast on Pacifica Radio stations in California and on WBAI, Pacifica Radio in New York City.

"Surrendering My Baby" by Lee Campbell first appeared in *Understanding the Birthparent*, published by Concerned United Birthparents, Inc. (CUB) in 1977.

"For My Husband's Mother" by Ellen Bass has appeared in *MS.* (February, 1983), and *Our Stunning Harvest* (New Society Publishers, 1984).

"Poem for the Broken Cup" by Kate Jennings is reprinted by permission from *The Hudson Review*, Vol. XXXV, No. 2, (Summer 1982). Copyright © 1982 by Kate Jennings.

"Stillbirth" by Barbara Crooker has appeared in *Connections, Childbirth Alternatives Quarterly, The Whole Birth Catalog* (Crossing Press, 1983), and *Mother Poet* (Mothering Publications, 1983).

"The Lost Children" is reprinted by permission of the Poetry Society of America. It was originally published in *The Poetry Review*, Volume 2, No. 1, Fall, 1984. © 1984 by Barbara Crooker.

"The Birth of Willow" by Martin Paule first appeared in *The Circle News*, a publication of The Birthing Circle, Burkittsville, Maryland.

"For Alva Benson" by Joy Harjo has previously appeared in *Akwasasne Notes* (Spring 1983), published by the Mohawk Nation, Rooseveltown, N.Y. 11217.

Contents

Introduction

What is it like to give birth? During my first pregnancy I pondered, wondered and worried about this. I was intensely curious to know what sort of experience I would be going through, and I felt strongly that in order to have a fulfilling birth experience I should be as well-prepared as possible. I read books on obstetrics and learned about the mechanics of birth, but I also wanted to hear women describe what it feels like to give birth. Because I lived far from old friends and family and had no one else to talk with about birth, I came to rely on the community of women who speak to us through the printed word. I eagerly read as many "birth stories" as I could find, searching them out of the books on childbirth education. Reading birth stories helped me learn how to give birth.

Much has changed for me since those early wondering days of my first pregnancy eight years ago. I have given birth to two children, both at home, and have come to work as an activist in the "alternative childbirth movement," publishing a newsletter and a consumer resource book on childbirth.[1] I have learned a lot about birth. But I have not forgotten my time as an expectant mother and my great need for knowledge then. This anthology of birth stories has come out of my desire to repay my debt to those whose words helped me and to pass that gift along. I have gathered stories which I hope will be especially helpful to two groups of women: those pregnant for the first time, who are wondering what labor and birth will really be like; and mothers who may have been traumatized by an unhappy birth and wonder if anyone else has shared their experience.

For First-Time Mothers

Women in their first pregnancies are usually eager for information about labor. Through reading birth stories we see more clearly how each individual birth is unique, grounded by the biological base of the "normal," but varying slightly here and there. Yet with all the variation, it is impressive to see how the biological "underpinnings" of birth keep shining through, in spite of the differences in personality and circumstance of the mothers. Labor always seems to assert itself and proceed in more or less the same way. Among the women who were conscious during labor and birth we read similar phrases again and again, as they describe the gradual, often sporadic onset of labor, the settling in and attempts to find a comfortable position and pace for established first stage labor, the painful intensity of late first stage and transition, the determined effort of pushing, and the surprising, almost-bursting sensations as the baby's head crowns and is born. Learning about the reliability of the labor pattern was very comforting to me in my first pregnancy. I have learned that our bodies know what to do and that our job in labor is often just to "get out of the way."

In reading over these stories, several other points seem to come up again and again. First of all, it's clear that experienced birth attendants (midwives, labor coaches, childbirth educators) know many techniques to help a laboring mother relax, be more comfortable, progress more easily. These include simple things like changing position, soaking in a hot bath, going for a walk, sitting on the toilet to push, drinking "laborade," using certain herbal teas, applying hot compresses to avoid a tear in the perineum, rubbing, touching, hugging, kissing, saying the right thing at the right time, offering love and affection, making a joke, being always there. The use of these things in childbirth is usually learned through experience, but even a first time mother can help herself by building up a store of "tricks" to try during labor.

The many ways in which emotions affect the progress of labor are clear from these stories. Fear, distress, anger, and apprehension all can slow down labor contractions. At the same time, words of hope, encouragement and affection can help labor progress. We also see that transfers of any kind (from home to hospital, from room to room, from bed to bed) are disruptive. They introduce an element of stress which is not inherent in labor itself. As a corollary to this, we find that many stories reveal the mother's apparently natural impulse to find a place which is safe, warm, wet, secluded, dark, and private for labor. The usual conditions of hospital birth—bright lights, lack of privacy, impersonal treatment, arbitrary time-tables, stressful interventions, unfamiliar surroundings—are in conflict with many of the mother's natural impulses and needs.

After reading twenty or thirty birth stories, a woman will have built up in her mind a complex composite picture of "birth." This will be helpful during her own birthing, as she remembers how other women coped with what she is now experiencing. But although reading about other women's experiences is an important part of preparation for childbirth, it is not enough by itself. Through giving birth myself and attending the births of friends, I've learned things which I could not have learned otherwise and which cannot be adequately described in words. First time mothers need to keep in mind that:

1. Written descriptions of labor can never be as strong as the ex-

perience itself. Labor will be very much more intense than anything you read.

2. Labor is painful. Sometimes the writers in this anthology are very honest about describing their pain; and sometimes you have to read the pain "between the lines." The "breathing" techniques taught in childbirth preparation classes do not lessen the pain but simply help us to get through it without losing control of ourselves. If you are planning to go through labor without drugs (and this is the safest course, both for you and your baby) then you need to prepare yourself seriously for the pain and learn ways to cope with it. Remember that a caring, labor support person can be just as effective as a drug.

3. If you plan to give birth without certain medical interventions which are now considered "routine," make a "birth plan" before labor starts and make sure your doctor and hospital understand and will respect your wishes. Otherwise, your birth may be managed very differently from what you hoped, something which happens commonly in these stories.

It is difficult to describe birth to a woman pregnant for the first time. No one likes to think that she will have a "hard time" and expectant primaparas often try to shield themselves from the bad parts of other women's tales. I know this was true in my case, and so I was shocked by the intensity of labor when it finally came. Nothing can take the place of personal experience, and witnessing a birth is the best preparation for giving birth. But short of that, I hope that these birth stories will provide as much "experience" as can be conveyed in a book.

For Those Whose Births Have Been Unhappy

Perhaps now is a good time to pause and consider why it is important to have a "good birth experience." I take it for granted that the mother's emotional needs in childbirth should be considered as important as the physical aspects; indeed, the two cannot be separated. Yet many physicians and even some mothers believe that the "medical management" of a birth should take precedence over everything else. Two simple facts remain, however: the mother's emotional state during labor affects how her body works; and the way in which she gives birth—actively or passively, with satisfaction or frustration—affects the way she feels about her self afterward and how she relates to and cares for her baby. We see this relation between the emotional and the physical again and again in the stories in this anthology. Birth is a vital life experience. It is stressful but rich with opportunity for proving ourselves, meeting the challenge, and developing confidence and competence. Passively letting someone else "do" the birth for us means losing the opportunity for tremendous personal growth and also puts us in danger of great emotional damage.

But what if our desire for a good experience conflicts with the baby's need for a safe delivery? To put it bluntly, there rarely is a conflict. What's good for the mother's self-esteem is almost always what's best for the baby's health. For instance, if the mother is treated impersonally and becomes apprehensive, this can slow the progress of her labor, which may be physically harmful to the baby. Yet mothers are often intimidated by cautions to "do what's best for the baby" into giving up their important emotional needs and desires.

Many things can happen to make a birth unhappy. Sometimes the source of the sadness and comes in the form of a damaged or dead baby or one who must be given up. In this anthology there are stories about stillbirth, an anencephalic baby, miscarriage, and a baby given up for adoption. The sense of sadness and loss in these stories speaks for itself. The losses of childbearing are never forgotten, the pain never completely dulled. We are captive to our own natures, which make us love and be attached to our offspring. As mothers, we never forget. We search restlessly for our lost young. Over time the restlessness becomes less, but is never entirely gone.

In reading about maternal loss, I have learned two things: first, that a period of grieving is important and should not be denied either by the medical profession or the woman herself. Second, I've learned that no gesture of kindness is ever wasted. It is striking how much a simple word or touch of kindness can mean to a mother in grief, whether over a lost baby or the loss of a good birth experience.

Sometimes a birth is an unhappy experience even when the baby is born alive and healthy. This can happen because a birth is not just the expulsion of a baby but is a vitally important psychological experience for the mother. Each woman comes to birth with her own unique psychological "task" to accomplish and if she is frustrated in her birth work, there will be repercussions.

We have all had dreams of being unable to run or even walk fast enough to get away from whatever is chasing us or toward whatever it is we reach for. Where do these images of powerlessness come from, these metaphors for delay, impediment, frustration? Birth might be called a living metaphor and to suffer frustration in birth is to give bad dream material to the mind. It can be said that the goal of birth is to "push out." It is a difficult and painful process to get the cervix open and then to push the baby through the layers of resisting tissue into a position in which one last push will send its whole body flying out. That's the push we wait for. What happens if that last push is thwarted: by forceps, by drugs that paralyze the lower body, by unconsciousness and the knife? How many times must we then try to push the baby out in our dreams? This frustration disturbs me on behalf of the women who have felt it. It is like a collective burden of frustration which we all carry as women.

Many of the things which thwart women in birth are described in these stories: withholding of information, insensitive medical personnel, painful or distracting procedures, unwanted drugs, lack of one-to-one support in labor, arbitrary rather than personalized care, loss of personal control, unwarranted use of medical technology. It is ironic that at the same time women's knowledge and expectations of birth are increasing, the use of medical technology and intervention is at an all-time high. We can see, through these stories, that in many ways the experience of giving birth has improved through the past seventy years but in many ways it has gotten worse, as birth becomes less and less a personal experience and more and more a medical event.

It is fairly clear, from reading these stories, what elements are held in common by the more positive birth experiences, even those with complications:

1. Recognition of pregnancy and birth as important work, worthy of respect and warranting careful preparation.

2. Maternity care which recognizes the mother as a unique individual and can adapt to her special needs.

3. Constant, loving support from family, friends, and birth attendants who respect and love the birthing woman.

In some of the stories, all these conditions are met and these births shine with good feeling.

Childbirth in Culture

In addition to being personally helpful for women, I hope these stories will also serve as source material for those interested in understanding more about our society and how birth is practiced in it. There are many ways of learning about ourselves. The anthropologist Franz Boaz said that any single artifact—a tool, a picture, a piece of clothing—can teach us about the whole culture from which it arises. Childbirth, with the many artifacts and beliefs used in its management, certainly provides opportunities for learning about our own society. Childbirth reflects our views about women, how we deal with sickness, pain and death, our ideas of the role of medicine and science, and our views on morality, autonomy, and individual rights and responsibilities. The birth of a baby represents the convergence of many cultural threads and vividly expresses the complex interplay of beliefs and circumstances influencing the mother, her partner, her helpers and the culture around her.

I also hope that this collection of birth stories will become part of the effort to reclaim woman's history and voice and restore her unique experience to a more proper position of importance. For some of the writers, this anthology has provided an opportunity to discover their personal female family history, by recording the birth stories of their mothers and grandmothers. Jean Chisholm Isaacs ("Uremic Poisoning"), Florence Scriven Munro ("Chinese Herbs"), and Alice Munro Isaacs ("Saddle Block and Forceps") are my paternal and maternal grandmothers and mother, respectively, and my birth story ("Doing it Myself") is also included. Lily W. Dinerstein ("Childbed Fever"), Helen Dinerstein Henkin ("A Happy Surprise"), and Louise Henkin Wejksnora ("Unexpected Forceps") are grandmother, mother and daughter. Sadie Harris Crissey ("My Sister Jen, The Doctor") and Jennifer Crissey Fisher ("Toxemia and an Induced Labor") are grandmother and granddaughter. Sharon Glass interviewed her two grandmothers and mother for her story, "Birth in My Family." In addition, Sonia Margulis included an account of her brother's birth in 1913 along with the story of her daughter giving birth ("A Grandmother Welcomes and Remembers") and Marcie Rendon includes descriptions of the births of her grandfather, her mother, and herself along with the story of the births of her own children ("A Native American Birth Story"). It is good to have these multi-generational voices in the anthology.

Who Are the Writers?

The birth stories in this anthology are all first-person, non-fiction accounts of birth, most of them written by the mother and some by the baby's father or grandmother. The stories represent a diverse group of women with different childbirth philosophies. The births they describe take place over a range of seventy years, in a variety of settings with a variety of attendants. In this respect the anthology is unique among books on childbirth preparation. Both my publisher and I felt it was important to present as broad a sample as possible. The stories in this anthology were gathered by publishing notices in a variety of childbirth and women's health publications and by passing the word among childbirth activists I know. Most of the writers are white, middle-class women and many are involved in some way in childbirth reform, but the women represented include Polish and Russian Jewish immigrants, a Native American, an urban black woman, a young teenager, a lesbian mother. The writers work at a variety of occupations, including teacher, artist, statistician, women's health activist, midwife, family farmer, childbirth educator, homemaker, bank teller, home-businessperson, writer, antique dealer, secretary and photographer.

The stories in this anthology assume a familiarity with common childbirth terms like "cervix," "dilation," "contraction," "episiotomy," but there is a glossary at the back of the book. You will also find at the back a section of notes which provide more information on some of the medical details and other events described in the stories. I did not want to interrupt the flow of the narrative with lengthy explanations or footnotes, but some points demand clarification, especially in cases where the medical treatment given may not have been the best or the only kind available. More detailed information on the medical statistics of the group of births is presented at the end of this introduction. A bibliography of works for further study is also included at the back of the book. It includes citations for collections of non-fiction birth accounts, fiction and poetry on birth, and books on the sociology, psychology and history of birth practices.

Although many of the writers praise their birth attendants, the names of all doctors and hospitals have been changed, except in those stories which describe people and places of very long ago. Also, in order to protect their identity and often precarious legal standing, midwives are referred to only by first names.

Medical Statistics

Included among these stories are many examples of unusual or abnormal births, somewhat more than would ordinarily occur in a random sample. I have included these in order to show as many examples as possible of what can happen in birth. But I don't want to alarm expectant mothers unduly about the possibility of birth complications, which are really quite rare. To get an idea of how representative our group of births is, I made a careful tabulation of various parameters (place of birth, type of attendant, maternal and fetal complications, medical intervention) and compared the incidence of these in the anthology with their incidence in the U.S. population as a whole. I used statistical information from three sources: a popular obstetrics textbook for physicians, a textbook on obstetrical nursing, and a con-

sumer guide to maternity care, all published since 1980. The results of
my survey are as follows:

Total Births:

In this anthology—43
In the U.S. in 1980—3.47 million

Place of Birth:

In this anthology there are twenty-five hospital births (58.1%) and
eighteen out-of-hospital births (41.8%), which include twelve at
home, five in a doctor's office/home, and one in a free-standing birth
center. This compares with an estimated rate of about 98-99%
hospitalization for birth today, with about 1-2% of births taking place
at home, in doctor's offices, in birth centers, in other locations, and in
transit to a hospital. The very high rate of out-of-hospital birth in our
sample reflects the fact that we are covering a 70-year period during
which the hospital was not always the common place for delivery, and
also the fact that I have purposefully included several "alternative"
births in order to provide some examples of how birth is managed in
different settings.

Type of Birth Attendant:

Of the forty-three births described in this volume, thirty-three
were attended by physicians (76%), of whom twenty-eight were
trained in the obstetrics speciality (eighteen male, ten female) and
seven were general practitioners. Of the remaining ten births, five
were attended by lay midwives, three by the baby's father, and two
by nurse-midwives. This break-down roughly parallels the national
experience today, in which about 1% of births are attended by nurse-
midwives, 2-3% by lay midwives, under 20% by general practitioners, and the rest by obstetricians. Our percentage of female
obstetricians, however, is probably much higher than the national
average.

Maternal Complications:

In our group there are two cases of toxemia and two cases of
postpartum hemorrhage, producing rates slightly lower (4.6%) than
the national average for these complications (about 5% for each). Our

rate for puerperal fever (one case) and miscarriage (two cases) is lower than the national average and our rate for probable marginal placenta previa (one case) is higher.

Fetal Complications:

Our group of forty-three births includes two stillbirths, which makes our infant mortality rate 4.6%, four times higher than the national rate of 1.17% in 1981. In our two cases, one death was caused by anencephaly, a birth defect that occurs in about 1-2 of every 1000 births, and one by probable placental insufficiency (rate unknown). Other "complications" include one set of twins (making our rate twice the national average of 1%) and three cases (6.9%) of iatrogenic (doctor-caused) prematurity brought about by induction of labor early for toxemia (two cases) and elective repeat cesarean section (one case). The national rate for premature births (most of which are spontaneous) is 6-7%.

Medical Intervention:

Because of the high percentage of out-of-hospital births in our sample, our group's rates of medical intervention are quite a bit lower than the current national averages. The following national statistics are cited from various government sources by Diana Korte and Roberta Scaer in their book, *A Good Birth, A Safe Birth*.

Type of Intervention	Anthology Rate	National Rate
Induced labor	10%	12%
Episiotomy	15%	85%
Oxytocin augmentation	2.5%	20-30%
Forceps delivery	12.5%	25-33%
Electronic fetal monitoring	12.5%	60-70%
Cesarean section	6.9%	17.9% (1981)
Analgesia/Anesthesia for birth	55%	80%

According to Korte and Scaer, the highest rates of medical intervention occur in standard hospital maternity units, followed in decreasing order by hospital "birthing rooms," in-hospital "alternative birth centers," free-standing birth centers, and home births.

Through statistics like those above it is possible to get at least a rough picture of the way in which these stories parallel those of the greater population medically. But it is much more difficult to know about the emotional aspects of the births. We know that many women are unhappy with their birth experience, even when the result is a healthy child. But to my knowledge there are no statistics available on these aspects of birth, sometimes called the "soft" outcomes (as opposed to the "hard" and more easily measurable outcomes of death or disability). I have tried to create a balance of "good" and "bad" experiences, including many stories which are too complex to be easily labelled. I think the stories ring true, in all cases. Taken together, I hope that this collection of birth stories will help all women and society, as we move toward more positive birth experiences for ourselves and our families.

Uremic Poisoning

JEAN CHISHOLM ISAACS

1915, Pittsburgh, Pennsylvania

My first pregnancy was pretty serious and both the baby and I came very close to dying because of uremic poisoning which developed early in the seventh month. That situation doesn't seem to be prevalent today, but in 1915 it was something for which doctors were constantly on the lookout.[1]

My mother's youngest sister, who was expecting in December 1915, died of uremic poisoning in September, after my experience. She was married late. She was 35, a graduate of Vassar. She had an obstetrician who allowed the condition to continue too long before taking steps to end the pregnancy and clean out the uterus. The doctor finally did take the baby, a girl who weighed two pounds, but Aunt Mabel went into convulsions and died. The baby lived five days.

I was firmly set against going to a hospital to have my baby. There had been several cases in the news about that time, in which nurses were accused of being careless in handling the infants. The mothers were never sure they had the right baby. But my family doctor convinced my husband and my parents that I must go to the Magee Hospital and have the pregnancy terminated. He told them that I was so full of poison that if I had one convulsion it would be fatal. He did not tell me this, but rather persuaded me to go to the hospital for "treatment."

We had figured that the baby would be due about the middle of April. I entered the hospital the afternoon of March 3. My doctor drove me and my mother to the hospital in his Ford touring car. My feet, legs, hands and face were so badly swollen, I had to wear my grandmother's underwear and old-fashioned shoes with garters that had elastic in the sides.

Magee Hospital was the first maternity hospital built in Pittsburgh. At the time I was there it was housed in a very large mansion belong-

ing to some wealthy Pittsburgh brothers named Magee, who gave the building plus several acres of ground and money for the new building then in progress, in memory of their mother who had died in childbirth with the last child of a large family. As soon as I got to the hospital, the head doctor examined me and, without telling me what he was doing or why, inserted instruments which began dilation.[2] This was done about 5:00 P.M. and I went into labor around 7:00 or 8:00, though I did not know what was happening. As far as I knew I was just getting "treatment," but by 9:00 P.M. they took me downstairs to a small room and then I lay on a hard cart while a nurse kept taking my blood pressure. I had a severe backache.

The head doctor came in about 10:00 P.M. and I asked him what was going on.

"Jean, don't you know you are in labor?" he said. I cried very hard.

"Doctor, I can't have this baby now; I haven't been married nine months till the 16th of March. People in the church are going to talk about us.

"Well, there's nothing can be done about it now. Just send the people to me. Anyhow, you are allowed two weeks with the first."

In the meantime the hospital had called my husband John and my parents and my family doctor. They arrived at the hospital about

11:00 P.M. The nurses told me that my family members were outside the delivery room, but they were not allowed in. My doctor was allowed in, but he was not permitted to have any participation in my care.

For two hours I suffered Hades. Because of the high content of uremic acid and my high blood pressure, the doctors said I couldn't have enough ether to put me out, only little whiffs. The baby's head was visible, but it was wedged sideways and face forward. Finally I heard my own doctor say, "Hurry! She's getting too weak. Never mind the baby, save her!" So the obstetrician used instruments and grabbed the baby wherever he could and pulled. You can well imagine I was badly lacerated.

I could just barely see the doctor hand the baby to the nurses, who began to walk away with him. But I was alert enough to know that the baby did not cry.

"Something's wrong," I cried out, "That baby didn't cry. Do something." The doctors said something to the nurses and my doctor moved over beside me and took my hand.

"It's all right, Jeannie," he said. I was aware of some activity in the corner where the nurses had gone with the baby and then after a bit I heard a faint cry.

"Oh, Jimmy, your mother's awful sick!"

"How did you know it was Jimmy?" the doctor asked.

"He's always been Jimmy." I had always felt I would have a boy and had planned to name him after my father. My doctor told me that the obstetrician had thought the baby was dead. The baby was nearly black and did not seem to breathe, and after the way he was simply pulled out they thought he could not be alive. If I hadn't called out, the nurse would just have put him in a small basket and done nothing. Jim still has a large scar up on the front of his skull and another behind an ear just at the base of the brain where the instruments grabbed.

The doctors knew I was badly torn internally by the forceps delivery, but my blood pressure was still so high they decided I'd have to have repairs later. When Jim was two years old I went to another hospital and had it done. The surgeon told me there was not much of the neck of the uterus left and I had fifteen stitches in the vagina and hemorrhoid repair also. He said he didn't see how I could carry another baby, but two years later almost to the week I was back in the hospital and my second son, John, was born with no complications. He was small-boned and plump. My third son, Bob, was born at home with my mother and my family doctor in attendance. I had no anesthetic with either one.

I don't know whether my story will be of any value to readers now. Obstetrics has greatly improved since 1915.

4

Childbed Fever

LILY W. DINERSTEIN

1919, New York City

During 1918 we had the flu, a very famous flu, and pregnant women died like flies. It was reported that the large proportion of pregnant women among the dead was sad.[1] At that time there were no automobiles. We lived in New York City, on a street where funeral processions passed, and you'd hear the horses clomping up and down. I was pregnant with Herbert, my first child, and I did have the flu but everything was alright with me. I gave birth. That was nothing unusual for a 22-year-old. It was a little hard in the beginning, but it wasn't anything unusual, and Herbert was a very nice baby. He weighed about seven pounds.

Herbert was born in 1919, in a private hospital. The war was still on and I suppose that's why I got infected with childbed fever in that miserable little private hospital where there were many wounded soldiers and the conditions weren't what they should have been.[2] As a result I was sick in bed for six months. After the first three months at home, I went to the seashore in New Jersey and recuperated there. My sister Nancy and Herbert and I all moved to the seashore and my husband Sam came out on weekends. At that time he owned and ran a store near our apartment in the city. An obstetrician, not the one who delivered the baby, had sent me to another doctor out in Jersey and told him that they were to take my blood and make a serum out of it and inject me with that. So I survived the fever and got well.

Nancy took care of me and Herbert like a devoted grandmother, even though she was the younger sister. She took care of Herbert from the minute he was born until he was six months old and then she continued to live with me until her marriage. She loved both my children, but Herbert she practically brought up. Maybe he would have died if there had been no one there to give him the proper care. I did breastfeed him, even with my illness. The obstetrician said, "Yes, you try to have a good diet and that will be good for your baby." He was really an advanced man, John Osborne Pollack, who took care of me when I was very sick. I was finally cured of the childbed fever. I must have had a very good constitution.

In our neighborhood there was a clinic run by the city and I thought it was just as well to take the baby there as to that doctor I didn't like who delivered him and caused the infection. So when I came back from Jersey and felt better, I took Herbert to the clinic.

When the young doctor examined him, he said, "Mother, do you know that this baby has a heart murmur?" Well, if I didn't drop dead at that clinic, I won't ever drop dead.

"Are you sure?"

"If I were you," said the doctor, "I wouldn't worry very much." Well, he could say that because it wasn't his baby. My doctor, the one who delivered Herbert, hadn't told me, perhaps because he thought I was too sick to be told something like that. I came home from the clinic and my husband saw that I didn't look too well.

"What happened?" he asked, and I burst out crying and told him what the doctor had told me. Well, my husband didn't feel so good, because evidently the delivering doctor hadn't told him either. What a stupid old ignorant doctor he was.

We started to think about where we should go to get special care for Herbert. An acquaintance advised us to see a pediatrician, Dr. Laws, at Long Island College Hospital which was at that time a very good hospital. All the good men were there. So naturally we went and when Dr. Laws examined Herbert he said, "It's true that he has a murmur, but it is a congenital murmur, so it isn't the same as acquiring a murmur. This is how his body knows how to live. He might grow up and be a ball player." My having the flu when I was pregnant must have been the reason the baby had the murmur. Dr. Laws said that was the result.[3] Herbert was under his care until he was about thirteen and he grew up okay.

When I became pregnant again, Dr. Pollack, the doctor who took care of me when I was sick, was overjoyed. But he said to me, "You go to my colleague Dr. A.A. Beck. He's very good and I'm too old to be awakened at night to come to the hospital." So then it was Dr. Beck who took care of me. Herbert was about three years old when I became pregnant again and this pregnancy was considered most unusual. The doctors were very surprised and pleased that I became pregnant again after having had the childbed fever.[4]

I went to Long Island College Hospital to have my second child,

Helen. Because I had gotten sick in that little dump of a private hospital, we couldn't be too careful. I had a private room and I had nurses and I had everything to make sure that I would be all right. Dr. Beck was really very proud of me. And then when Helen was born she was a lovely baby. Dr. Beck came in and looked at me and was very careful, so that nothing should happen. While I was in the hospital my husband would bring Herbie and they would stand outside where I could see him from the window. Herbie looked so sad and I felt so sorry. But of course, after what happened the first time we just had to be careful.

The men who cared for me were dedicated doctors. Dr. Pollack was very friendly and very nice. When I became pregnant with Helen, he just looked at me and said, "Mrs. Dinerstein, you're such a lucky woman, I can't tell you."

Editor's note: Lily's birth story and that of her daughter Helen—"A Happy Surprise" by Helen Dinerstein Henkin—were collected by Lily's granddaughter, Louise Henkin Wejksnora, whose own birth story, "Unexpected Forceps," is also included in this volume. About her family's birth stories, Louise says, "All the births described took place in New York City. My four grandparents were Russian-Jewish immigrants. My Grandma Lily's mother, Chaya, died young in Russia and her husband then came here and brought his four children. Chaya had two sons, then two daughters, and since they came three or four years apart in a non-contraceptive culture, she may have had the menstrual irregularity that my grandmother, mother, sister, and I all have. My paternal grandmother died in 1961 so I could not get her story. My paternal grandfather, the oldest of ten children all born at home in the shtetl, came to the United States and became a physician. A family doctor, he had a preponderance of obstetric cases and though he delivered babies at home, he personally preferred to work in the hospital. It was he who delivered me and my sister. Both of my parents are committed to hospital birthing, a concept I've slowly grown away from.

Chinese Herbs

FLORENCE SCRIVEN MUNRO

1921, Los Angeles

After we were married, my husband Jim and I talked it over and decided it would be very nice if we had a little baby. That's really the way it started. So I was pregnant when he went away to the service in World War I.

I had been told nothing about childbirth by my mother or by my older sisters. There were tests for pregnancy in those days, but I didn't have any checking done; I just knew when I was pregnant. Jim and I were living in my parents' big house in Plainfield, New Jersey, with my sisters Emmy and Clara. My brother Walter and his wife Hazel lived with us too, with their children. Hazel was with me and she told me everything I needed to know, because she had had children. My first baby was born while we were still living back East. It was a very large baby and broke its shoulder in delivery, so it passed on.

After that we all moved to California and that's where Alice was born. Because I had had such a hard time with that first baby, I was almost afraid to have another one. Then my mother talked to a woman who told her about a Dr. Shaefer, who was said to be a very good person for bringing in the babies or anything like that. So I saw Dr. Shaefer and I took her course. I went every Tuesday, or maybe it was every other Tuesday, and I got everything from Dr. Shaefer. She had some sort of liquid stuff that she got from China and this was supposed to help your whole insides work very smoothly so you wouldn't have many hard labor pains. She was a homeopathic doctor. She said I should eat plenty of greens, salads; and I got the herbs from her, I don't know what they were. I felt pretty fair during the pregnancy.

Jim had bought a car, and one day he and my brother Elmer and I went for a ride. When we got back I wasn't feeling very well. I decided to go up and see Dr. Shaefer to see how I was getting along. In the afternoon of the next day, we went up to her office and Dr. Shaefer examined me and said, "You're almost ready for labor pains." So she told me I should stay there. Jim was with me and Dr. Shaefer also had a nurse. We were at her home up in the mountains, in the hills somewhere above Los Angeles. She had a couple of rooms set up for having babies.

Dr. Shaefer and the nurse both went to bed. Jim said he'd stay with me and Dr. Shaefer said she'd just be in the next room and the nurse would be in the other room. So Jim stayed there with me and after a while I told him I was beginning to feel some pains. And then I said, "Jimmy, you'd better get the doctor right here because the baby's coming!" I knew it was coming myself. But the baby came before the doctor and nurse got there. Of course, they were right there in the house and Jim was right there. So Alice was born and they fixed Jim on a cot so he could stay for a few nights. He stayed right there. The nurse took care of the baby. They gave it to me sometimes, but the next day I got a terrific headache, something terrible. They were afraid my milk wouldn't be good for the baby. But I could give it a little, and they also had milk there. I did nurse the baby some and I guess I did all right.

The next day I saw a mouse coming out of the room they were keeping the baby in and I said, "You take that baby out of there and put her in here with me." So they did put Alice in with me, not in my bed, but in a baby bed. Eventually Jim had to go back to work, so my sister Emmy hired a cab and came up to get me and the baby and brought us home to our place on 58th Street. She'd never done anything like that before in her life; she wasn't that brave. Emmy helped me at home and she was just crazy about Alice and took her over, as much as she could. I wanted to continue nursing Alice but I didn't have enough milk, so Dr. Shafer gave me a formula that was very good.

I don't remember very much about my next baby that died. I went completely out. Who was my doctor? I guess it must have been Dr. Shaefer again. The baby was only seven months when it was born—it was premature. They tried to keep it from being born and I ruptured something awful. The baby lived for an hour or an hour and a half. I was terribly ruptured and was taped up. This was an awful sticky tape, not just a binding, and when they pulled it off I felt as though all my skin was coming with it. I never had anything so terribly hurtful.

With my next baby I was in the hospital and I had a different doctor, Dr. Blathowick. Jim had done a masonry job for this doctor and also the woman next door to me had used Blathowick and she said,

"He's wonderful!" Already I was seeing Dr. Shaefer and I was along two or three months, but I told her I'd better have a doctor closer at hand and I went to see Blathowick. His brother was also a doctor and he made a good examination of me in all ways and said I was okay and everything was all right.

When it came time, Jim took me to the hospital and the people there said, "It isn't time yet."

"Well," I said, "I simply have an awful lot of pain. I think the waters broke."

"Oh, no, that couldn't be," they said.

"Well, I certainly do think something like that happened," I said.

Then the nurse came in and examined me and said, "The waters broke! Get her in the delivery room right away."

Jim was there with me that time too. They put a cap on him and he stayed right there with me all the time. They wouldn't let him get near me; they made him stand way over there, but he was in the room. When the baby was coming I said, just as I did before, "Well, seems like the baby's about here."

The doctor said, "You'll have to have some stronger pains." I didn't feel too much pain with this baby, for some reason. But the doctor said, "You have to if you want to have your baby." I was older, forty-one, and of course he knew it. So I tried to bear down hard and finally the baby was born. The doctor held him up and said, "It's a boy and he's in good shape." Then he patted him until he gave a little yell—you know, the way they do—and then he handed him over to the nurse and went off.

Later on the nurse cleaned me up and got me in bed, and put little Arthur where they put the babies, all in one place. She wouldn't let me touch the baby in the delivery room. I didn't have any anesthesia for this birth. I was wide awake for both births. Arthur was born on Alice's sixth birthday. Alice was staying with Emmy and she had her birthday party there. I was in the hospital for a week.

When I came home my cousin Bertie came to take care of the baby while I rested. But the doctor thought I should get someone else who had more experience. So I talked to Jim and we decided to put the baby in the crib beside us and have Alice sleep in the bed with us. I got a nurse to come the next day to take care of the baby, because I wasn't going to take any chances. Emmy came too and helped to bathe the baby. I myself thought it was best to try to breastfeed, but again I couldn't; I didn't have enough. I wasn't able to get the formula from Dr. Shaefer, but at the end of 57th Street there was a family that kept goats and I got goat's milk for Arthur.

After Arthur was born, Jim and I decided that since we now had one boy and one girl, that would be enough children. I got a book on birth control, written by Margaret Sanger, and we used that advice.

(Editor's note: This story was transcribed from an audio tape made of my grandmother by my mother, her daughter Alice. My grandmother was responding to a list of questions I'd sent, asking about her birth experiences. She was about ninety years old at the time the tape was made.)

My Sister Jen, The Doctor

SADIE HARRIS CRISSEY

1922-37, Western New York

For my first pregnancy, in 1923, my doctors were my sister, Jennie Harper Harris, and my father, John Thorne Harris. Jen had a three-bed maternity hospital in her home, which was a 22-room Victorian house in Tonawanda, New York. It was right across the street from my own house. Jen was the obstetrician and Dad helped her. He was a general practitioner, but people always said he was a good obstetrician because he had such small hands.

Pregnant women were doing a lot of dieting at that time to keep their weight down. One day a week we were supposed to eat only light food and concentrate on milk with a teaspoonful of something added for calcium. Of course, we cheated a bit.

With Kermit, my firstborn, Dad and Jen were both there. The labor took overnight, about twelve hours, from 11:00 P.M. to the next morning. They didn't give anything for pain during the labor, just chloroform toward the end for the birth itself. But I was given pituitrin to make the birth go faster.[1] Dad wasn't too fond of giving chloroform because he thought it might be harmful to the baby, but he did use it.[2] When I was getting the chloroform, I noticed that the seams of the wallpaper didn't match. I thought, "I must remember to tell Mother that." When I looked later, the seams were perfect!

I was sick during the labor and vomited. Jen and Dad had a hard time because the cord was around the baby's neck. After the baby was born, I looked into my father's big brown eyes and said, "I wanted a brown-eyed baby." Jen said, "You should have thought of that before you married a blue-eyed husband."

My husband Earl was there during the labor and birth. Jen always tried to encourage the men to be in the room. One of them fainted. Some wouldn't go in at all. But Earl stayed the whole time. He was pleased to have a boy. I was expecting a girl and planned to name her

Kay, my middle name. We'd already received gifts with "K's" embroidered on them. So Jen and her friend Ruth decided to think of a boy's name which started with "K." They called up the stairs to me, "Is Kermit all right?" I was miserable with an abscessed tooth and said, "Name him anything." So they named him Kermit.

At that time you stayed in the hospital for two weeks and didn't get out of bed at all for three days. The babies were kept in a nursery and brought in to the mothers. I started out breastfeeding Kermit. But he was so fussy that we took him to a specialist in Buffalo who told me that the baby wasn't getting enough nourishment. So I added supplementary bottles and he was completely on the bottle soon after that. They had babies on schedules at that time, every four hours, and I was afraid something terrible would happen if I broke the schedule; so I would hold off feeding him until it was time. Perhaps I didn't have enough milk because of not nursing often enough.

By the time of my next birth in 1924, Jen had given up the maternity hospital. She told the local hospital that as soon as they put in a maternity ward she would like to give hers up. She still had most of the equipment at her house though, so I just went over there to have John. I never thought about going to the hospital. It wasn't the thing then to go to the hospital to have a baby. That was for the next generation.

Just before the labor began, I was asleep and I dreamed that the little kid next door kicked a football; only I realized that what I'd actually had was a kick in the side from the baby and the water broke. I'll never forget that trip across the road to Jen's, with a dress on and leaning down to pull up my stockings. Jen was on vacation, so Dad took care of me alone. When he was giving the chloroform I said, "There's a red ten on a red jack." Then I laughed. I had been playing double solitaire with my twin sister and had tried to fool her by putting a red ten on a red jack. Somehow it came into my mind with the chloroform. Dad said, "Here, here, Sadie, get down to business. This isn't a card game!" John was big, nine pounds and twelve ounces. He was delivered with forceps. I heard Dad say, "He's got shoulders like an elephant." It was then that I knew I had another boy.

Foster's birth, my third, I remember best because I had him at home, in my own bedroom. There is not much to tell though, because it was such an easy birth and quite fast. The labor began at noon and the baby was born during the afternoon. Dad was out of town at a football game, so only Jen was there. When she came she said it wouldn't be too long, so she stayed right with me. She was always very nice and sympathetic when a woman was in labor. However, I had a little chloroform and evidently asked for more, because I remember Jen saying to Earl, "Boy, she really likes her chloroform, doesn't she?" and I was really mad at them for being facetious when I was going through such a trial.

David was born twelve years later when I was 42 years old, in 1937. We were living in Albany then, but I went home to Tonawanda to have the baby. Earl had to stay in Albany, so he didn't see the baby until a few days later. Jen did the delivery; Dad had died by then. My mother said the reason I had all boys was that my reasons for wanting a girl weren't proper. She said I only wanted the fun of dressing her! I enjoyed my boys.

(Editor's note: This story was transcribed by the author's granddaughter, Jennifer Fisher. Her birth story, "Toxemia and an Induced Labor," also appears in this volume. She adds this note: "My great aunt Jen was not married and had no children. It was unusual for a woman to become a doctor in those days, though as a matter of fact there were two or three other women in Jen's class. She got her M.D. degree at the University of Buffalo and did her one-year internship entirely in obstetrics at the Woman's Hospital and Infants' Home in Detroit. She had wanted to be a doctor from kindergarten on, because her father was a doctor, as was a half-uncle. I don't know whether it was a factor or not, but the two sons born to Jen's father died in early childhood, one of meningitis and one of diptheria. Perhaps Jen, as oldest daughter, filled what might otherwise have been a son's role. Jen's father, my great-grandfather, received his M.D. cum laude from the University of Buffalo.)

Birth In My Family

SHARON GLASS

1920s-60s, New York City and Los Angeles

The birth of my first child at home has sparked my interest in the ways childbirth practices have changed over the years and in efforts at childbirth reform. Shortly after my daughter's birth in 1981, I visited my two grandmothers and my mother to learn how they had given birth. I found that my family's experiences were fairly typical of birth practices in the United States from the 1920s through the 1960s, a time when hospitalization for birth became the norm rather than the exception.

Both my grandmothers came from similar backgrounds in Eastern Europe. My maternal grandmother was born in Warsaw, Poland, in 1902. Her family ran a small grocery store. Helen emigrated in 1920, met my grandfather Joseph in New York City, and married him in 1925. She had three children. She now lives in a nursing home, severely stricken with Parkinson's disease. Questions about her birth experiences are from another world now, and she rapidly grew tired and impatient with me. We sat and held hands and before I left she leaned towards me, whispering of her love for her first great-grandchild, my daughter.

My father's mother Celia was born in 1905, in the town of Ostralanka, Poland. She was the daughter of the town's Kosher butcher and was, therefore, considered to be middle-class, because they usually had enough to eat. She came over in 1921, part of the wave of two million Jews who emigrated to the United States between 1880 and the 1920s, forced out of Eastern Europe by religious and political repression and persecution. My grandfather sent for Celia from the old country and they married when they could afford their own apartment in New York. She had two children and now lives in a comfortable home in Hollywood. We talked at my father's house, alone after

dinner. Celia spoke freely in her Yiddish-accented English, gesturing
when the English words would not come easily.

"At the time I was raising my children," said Celia, "there was a terrible depression. People were put out in the streets because they didn't
have money to pay the rent. Evictions were common. There were
long lines for bread. There was no unemployment compensation, no
social security then. It was a very tough time. If somebody had a job,
he was shivering when he went to work, in fear that the employers
would say that business wasn't good and he was fired."

Children were desired but economically it was difficult, and most
pregnancies were unplanned in my family. Money was scarce. Helen
worked until she was six months pregnant, as a dressmaker in a
woman's home, a long bus ride away. "It was hard," she said. "I
vomited every day." Celia worked until she was three months pregnant for $8 a week making kitchen curtains in a sweatshop. If she
worked overtime, she brought in $12.

"We lived in an apartment in New York City," said Celia. "We
didn't even dream of having a house. We were so poor we were barely able to pay the rent. One time we were almost put out because we
didn't have money to pay for the rent. Your grandfather lost his job
and we didn't have enough to buy food for the children. We always
had a lodger from the day we were married, to help pay the rent.
Probably all my married life we had a lodger. I cooked for him,
washed, and took care of him. This extra income was not for luxuries,
you understand, but for necessities."

Despite their outside jobs, pregnancy did not mean that my grandmothers did less work at home. "I did everything. I was laying with
my big belly on the kitchen floor and washing it," Celia told me. "I felt
miserable when I became pregnant. I was too young. I was seventeen
when we married and I became pregnant three months after. We were
too young really, just too young. We weren't educated enough. You
worked or you couldn't eat. There was no time to educate yourself. It
wasn't an easy life at all. It wasn't easy."

Birth control was not widely available then.[1] Celia knew of the
diaphragm but could not use one. My grandfather used condoms,
"But when it burst or didn't work, what could you do? I got pregnant."
Abortion was illegal and dangerous, yet both my grandmothers and
my mother were forced to have illegal abortions at some point in their
lives.

For my grandmothers, pregnancy was not a topic one discussed
very freely. This was a carry-over from the old country, where in my
great-grandmothers' communities one did not acknowledge pregnan-

cy until the baby was virtually due to be born. In the old days, prenatal care was provided by practical nurses or midwives for the ones with money, or else not sought. Babies were born at home.

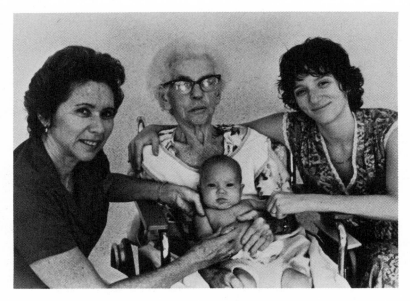

Helen said that, in her neighborhood in Warsaw, "We were a poor people and the doctors wouldn't even think of taking us in the hospital." With difficult births the doctor was called in, but usually only midwives were involved. Helen told me that usually in Poland you saw the midwife three times: at the birth, and on the first and third days following. "It was altogether different when I had my children," she said. "I had a doctor's care when I was pregnant and it cost $50 for everything."

My grandmothers' prenatal care was similar to that of today, with scheduled visits and routine physical examinations. But there was very little education about childbirth itself. "When I asked the doctor, 'How will I know when I'm in labor?' he said, 'Nobody has to tell you, you'll know,' " said Helen. "He didn't tell me anything about pregnancy or labor. He didn't educate me at all."

Celia didn't receive any prenatal care for her second baby, as the hospital was located up a steep hill. She did not have the strength to push her first baby in the buggy all the way up the hill and there was no money for a taxi, so she did not go.

I asked my grandmothers about their nutrition in pregnancy and if there were any particular foods they were told to eat or avoid. Both said their doctors limited their pregnancy weight gain to fifteen pounds. Helen said she drank a lot of milk, but as for avoiding foods, she said, "Nobody thought of food you weren't supposed to eat or didn't want. You were glad to have food to fill your stomach. We were poor people."

My grandmothers both felt very isolated during their pregnancies. English was slowly picked up and often family and friends were far away. "I was alone," said Celia. "I had no parents; I had nobody. Your grandfather worked fourteen to sixteen hours a day. I had nobody to complain to, good or bad. I cried a lot. I was very lonely."

Although home birth was still common in the 1920s and 30s, it was rapidly becoming less so and neither woman considered it. Celia's older sister had her children at home out of fear of hospitals, but Celia did not want to.

Neither Celia nor Helen knew much about the process of labor and birth. But they had both heard enough "horror stories" to know that they wanted to be "knocked out" for as much of it as possible. The situation in many hospitals at that time made this desire very understandable. Celia described the hospital in which she delivered: "There were twelve to a room; it was dirty, a horrible place. The conditions were very bad and no visitors were allowed except the father. They made me stay in bed when I was in labor. They shaved me and gave me an enema. They wouldn't allow me any food or drink, not even a little water. Oh, I was dreaming about water. No one stayed with me. I was alone, all alone and scared." Helen said, "Nobody thought of having husbands with you in labor. 'Men don't belong in there'—that's what was said. Men get off too easy. They don't understand the pains you go through."

Childbirth at this time was dangerous, due to poor conditions in home and hospital, disease, poverty, poor nutrition, lack of birth control, and generally low standards of public health. After World War I, maternal death was the second leading cause of mortality among women aged fifteen to forty-five, after tuberculosis. Birth was a frightening experience for many women, clouded not only by fear of death and pain but by lack of education and preparation. "Twilight Sleep," a combination of morphine, scopolamine (an amnesic), and ether, became popular in the 1920s as a way to avoid the pain of labor and almost the whole experience of birth. The combination of painkillers with an amnesic drug worked to dull pain as well as obscure the memory of the birth. Though the woman might be conscious and even delirious during labor, afterward she would not remember what had happened and might think she had been asleep. I suspect that Twilight Sleep was used with my grandmothers. "I wasn't particularly worried about labor," said Helen, "but maybe that was because I made up with the doctor that I had to have pills instead of pain. At the last part of the labor, I got some pills and went to sleep and when I woke up they showed me a baby they were holding by the legs, the head hanging down, and that was your mother." Helen was fortunate, as she woke up in time to see her baby right after birth. "I remember how Tamar was put on my stomach after they scrubbed her. And I thought that was the most marvelous thing the earth could produce, the most beautiful thing. We were so enthused, especially your grandfather. He's crazy about babies. There is nothing as precious as a baby."

Celia described her birth experience: "At that time if you didn't have stitches, it was called 'natural.' Well, I had my first child natural. When I gave birth to your father, the doctor put me to sleep in the last stages. I wanted to be put to sleep because I couldn't bear it. I woke up and felt my stomach and felt I was empty. I was lying on a bed and the first thing I did was feel my stomach. The baby wasn't with me."

The babies were kept in the nursery during the entire ten to fourteen days of one's stay, except at feeding time for the breastfeeding babies. Celia told me, "I wanted to be with the baby to comfort me. When they were ready to take him away I'd say, 'Let him be a little while longer,' but they had a certain time even if he wasn't finished nursing. For them it was a routine."

But being in the hospital was also a time to rest and recuperate after the birth. This was important for my grandmothers, who were not of a class that could afford hired help during the postpartum period. Helen said, "I was satisfied to be in the hospital for ten days. Everything was normal and I accepted what was dished out to me. I didn't ask any questions." Helen was fortunate to be in a very pleasant, clean Seventh Day Adventist hospital, with better conditions than the one in which Celia delivered.

Celia and Helen were helped to breastfeed by hospital personnel. But when Helen did not seem to be producing enough milk, her baby was given a bottle with no further ado. Bottle feeding was becoming increasingly common at that time. Both women were also helped by their in-laws on their return home, but their lives were difficult and mostly they raised their children on their own. "After my second child, Manny, was born I had two abortions," said Celia. "I didn't want any more children; it was too hard for me. It was not like now when everything is push-a-button. I had to wash diapers in two pitchers. We lived on the fourth floor of a building without an elevator so I'd have to bundle up one child, take him down and put him in the carriage and ask somebody to watch him, then go back upstairs and do the same with the other one. Sol helped me but he was working all the time. He'd wash the floor or bathe the children, but if the kid would make wet or something he would say, 'Celia, Celia, come over here, take him, take him!' "

But although Celia spoke of the difficulties of her childbearing years, she felt she had a better time of it than her mother in Poland: "My mother had nine children. Before she was through with one, she was starting another. We don't know how easy we've got it here. We should appreciate our life more."

My mother Tamar is a first generation American, born in California in 1931. She went directly from her parents' home to the house of her husband and had four children in twelve years. Divorced after twenty-seven years of marriage, Tamar has now entered into the wage-earning labor force for the first time. She has had a tough time of it and shadows of worry and bitterness line her face. As I sat talking with her, I thought back to a time two years before, when she called me on the phone, crying. She had just read a newspaper article about a couple's lovely home birth and was crying in anger and sorrow for the loss of her childbirth experiences. My mother had her first baby in 1952 when she was twenty years old, and her last in 1964. None of them were planned except the third, and that one was planned only by her (she "forgot" to put in her diaphragm).

Tamar considers herself to be middle-class, a step above her mother's generation, but money was always a concern for her and her husband Murray. In 1953, shortly after the birth of their first child, they bought a house in Los Angeles, with a loan from their parents. "It was difficult," said Tamar. "We ate a lot of spaghetti and hamburger for quite a while. It was financially a difficult time because Murray wasn't settled in a particular job. He made a big point of saying he didn't trust that I was thrifty enough, and I felt I was. So, that led to some troubles we had about money. Our parents helped us out; they would buy presents for the children, like clothes."

Tamar had regular prenatal care for each of her pregnancies. For the first three children, the doctor and hospital bills came to between $100 and $150 for each. The last birth was with a more expensive obstetrician and cost $450. The prenatal routines were more or less the same as in the preceding generation and so, unfortunately, was the lack of education in childbirth preparation. "I never asked many questions," said my mother. "I didn't know what to ask. The doctor either didn't care or else assumed I knew things. Probably he didn't care. Part of the reason I had such a difficult time in labor was that I wasn't prepared in any way and the doctor didn't help in any way. There were no classes available then. The doctor assumed that I knew what I needed to know because he didn't mention anything."

In the 1950s, as before with my grandmothers, it was not common for people to question their doctors' advice. Women were still being told to limit their weight gain in pregnancy and nutritional information consisted of the prescription of a vitamin supplement and mention of the four basic food groups. Tamar said, "I felt that people in the medical profession knew what they were doing. They were considered like gods. We just never questioned them. They said, 'Take this and you'll be okay,' and we took it."

Even when Tamar attempted to educate herself and have "natural" deliveries, she was thwarted by the system. "When I was pregnant with my third child, I started reading a lot about exercises and the idea of not using drugs in childbirth—Lamaze. I wanted that kind of delivery but the doctor was quite conventional and the hospitals were not equipped to deal with it."

My mother's labor experiences were difficult. "With my first baby, the bag of waters broke first and the doctor felt it would be a 'dry' birth, which would be bad.[2] It was a very difficult labor, starting and stopping. They gave me cod liver oil and the student doctors kept doing rectal exams to determine my progress.[3] I was so sore. I was scared, all alone in a room, and no one was allowed to be with me. I felt pretty awful. I just wanted to go to sleep and so they did put me to sleep. I woke up after it was all over. I didn't know anything about the delivery. I was told I had a son, but I didn't see him for many hours. It certainly crossed my mind, when I did see him, that he wasn't my baby. I didn't feel any immediate feelings of maternal love. It was so difficult. I had a postpartum depression that lasted six weeks. If anyone talked to me at all, I'd start to cry. I mean that if someone came in and said 'Hi' to me, I'd cry. I attribute this to the way the whole thing was handled. I didn't know anything about birth and I had no support.

"The second time there was a nurse present during my labor and she was helpful. When they put me under I fought to stay awake. I floated in and out of consciousness and saw the baby on my belly, a big leap forward from the first time.

"The third time, with you, I had a relatively easy labor. The doctor poked his head in the door and said, 'It will still be a while,' and left. But soon I called to the nurse, 'The baby is coming!' She said, 'Oh, no he's not,' and she clamped my arms down, blindfolded me, and strapped my legs together, because the doctor wasn't at the hospital. It seemed like forever I was this way, but it was probably about an hour. I could feel the baby push, gather herself and push. I opened my mouth to scream and they clamped the ether cone over my mouth. I choked. I thought I'd go mad. It took me about a year to recover.

"With the fourth one, I wanted to be induced because I was very uncomfortable. I couldn't sit, stand, or lie down. I was happy to hear it when the doctor agreed to induce me, but I was totally unprepared for what the drug did. I went from not being in labor at all to being in heavy labor. I had a headache from the spinal anesthesia for the first week."[4]

Tamar had difficult times in her postpartum recoveries. She had little support while in the hospital after the births. "I wanted to nurse the baby but nobody in the hospital was at all cooperative. Nobody wanted to show me how. They said, 'Oh, it's easier to use formula.' They gave my first baby a bottle even though I wanted to breastfeed him."

Tamar felt somewhat secure in the hospital though, because the staff were responsible for taking care of her baby for the four to five days she was there. "I was scared to go home because I didn't know how to take care of the first baby. I was apprehensive. I didn't enjoy the hospital, but I did feel safer there as the baby was mostly in the nursery."

Unlike my grandmothers, however, once Tamar did go home she was financially able to engage a nurse to live in for the first six days after her return. She said, "The nurse took care of the baby and I was in bed, my mother taking care of me!" My father's role during this time was basically as provider for the family. When I asked Tamar what he did otherwise, she succinctly and somewhat sarcastically said, "He took a lot of pictures."

When my turn in the cycle came, my husband and I chose to give birth at home, attended by lay midwives. We feel this is a safe alternative for healthy mothers and babies. We rejected the often unnecessary interventions practiced in the hospital, which can transform birth from a normal life event into a pathological operation, sometimes quite literally an operation considering the very high cesarean section rate now. When a complication involving the placenta did arise after Wenona was born, we were thankful to have a hospital for care. But we believe that hospitals are best used for emergency situations and birth usually does not fall under that category.

I'm glad we were able to have a natural labor and birth at home, without medication or intervention. My husband was by my side for the whole labor and we stayed out in our sunny backyard for most of it. Our midwives attended us in pregnancy and birth with loving care. Hearing of my foremothers' pregnancy and birth experiences makes me feel fortunate to be in a generation which has more education and choices in birth. I also realize that it is because women in the past had bad childbirth experiences and struggled to make things better, that we now have the alternatives available today. I hope that my daughter and all our daughters will have even more education and choices available to them if and when they choose to bear children.

A Labor Saving Device

JOAN JOFFE HALL

You know what a hassle
it is to go to the movies, the circus,
a basketball game? Get your hat and purse,
unlock the triple lock door,
open it, step out, close it, triple lock it—
forgot your gloves?—unlock, enter,
get gloves, out, close, lock the lock lock lock,
press the elevator button, down, out,
walk, dodge dogshit, subway buy token,
squeeze by the turnstile, ride
the jiggle jiggle jiggle down to the Garden,
crowd the line, buy the ticket,
pant up to seat, clean seat, off gloves and coat,
and the game circus movie
hasn't even begun?

They could start a service:
pick you up at your dining table,
knock you out, do your door thing,
lug you through the subway,
plonk you in your ticketed seat, painless,
just like TV, and all over New York
people will be carrying other people
slung over their backs on the way
to the movies game circus.

That's just the way I had a baby.

Saddle Block and Forceps

ALICE MUNRO ISAACS

1949, Los Angeles

I wanted children very much. My husband Jack was content with life as it was—no complications. And besides he liked having me work. I was working as an elementary school teacher then and have done that all my life. Jack liked being able to buy a new car every couple of years and I myself was interested in acquiring furniture. But after we had been married for two years, I insisted that on our third anniversary, May 9th, 1948, we stop using contraceptives. Jack agreed and I became pregnant quite quickly, within the first month.

I had been told very little about childbirth by anyone. When I was a child, I was told nothing. I actually believed that babies came down in a special room in the hospital directly from heaven. It was quite a shock to me when I found out it just wasn't that way. It turned me into an atheist for some period of time when I realized there was no direct connection between heaven and earth.

I knew I was pregnant when I missed my first period, because I was always so regular. So when I missed my second period, I went to the doctor and had a test done and sure enough, I was pregnant. I went to a doctor who was part of a group practice at a clinic. I guess I chose her because she was a woman, although she was not married and had no children. Her office was near my mother and dad's house. In the beginning I went for prenatal visits once a month, then twice a month, then once a week. Generally I saw the same doctor. This clinic had its own pharmacy, which I believe is illegal now in California because it was really an opportunity for doctors to rake in the money. All my prescriptions and vitamin pills were handed to me directly by the doctor and we were not billed for anything until after the baby was born. I had been told how much it would cost for the prenatal care and delivery and I was too naive to question anything else. When the bill finally came and all the prescriptions were included, we had a tremendous shock. It was about double the amount we had been originally quoted.

I didn't have any sisters and I didn't have any friends who had had babies yet, so I had no one with whom to share ideas. I read articles in magazines, but I guess they were all pretty superficial. It never occurred to me to question the doctor's authority in any way.

During the first three months I was quite sick to my stomach and so I went to the doctor once a week and got a shot in the arm for nausea. I haven't the slightest idea what was in the shots. Around the third or fourth month I had some cramps in my legs and was told to take more calcium. Also, early in the pregnancy I became constipated and began taking something regularly for that, as the doctor directed. As for diet advice, they just kept telling me not to eat too much.

As the pregnancy went on I felt better and better. After the first three months I was quite healthy and happy and I had a sense of well-being right up to the delivery.

Jack's Grandma Emma gave me my first baby gift, a pink and blue knitted carriage cover that she made. I made kimonos for the baby and embroidered them and bound them with ribbon and made ribbon ties. These later turned out to be very impractical because the satin ribbon was forever coming untied as the baby kicked about. People gave me baby showers—friends, relatives, the other teachers at the school where I taught. There were a lot of lovely things waiting for the baby. I had a crib, a basinette, a "bathinette," a high chair and a carriage before the baby was born. Grandma Jean, Jack's mother, loaned me a rocking chair.

When my due date came and went with no labor beginning, we went up to stay at my parents' house. My mother was worried about my being alone at home because Jack was going to school two or three nights a week at U.S.C. At that time my folks lived near downtown Los Angeles, not far from U.S.C. and the hospital where I was to deliver.

It was difficult to stay with my parents because I had nothing to do but sit around and wait. This waiting went on for two weeks. Finally, one morning I told the doctor that I was getting awfully tired of waiting. She told me to go home and take a small bottle of castor oil. She said if it was time, the castor oil would make the labor begin.

I waited all day and nothing happened. Jack came home from work and we all had dinner and then he left for school. It must have been around 6:30 P.M. and I can remember sitting at the dining room table and then getting up to carry some dishes to the kitchen. I got as far as the kitchen door when I felt this warm rush of water. Then every step I took there was more. Mother got me a bath towel to put between my legs and then Mother and Dad took me up to the Methodist Hospital.

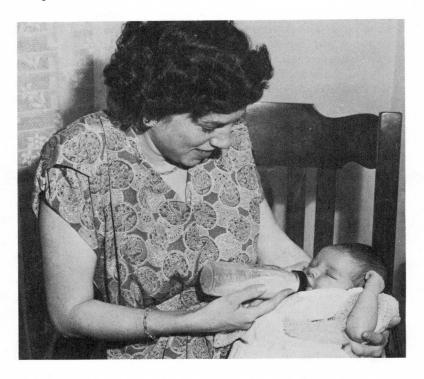

   I can remember walking up quite a flight of stairs and into the front door of the hospital. It never occurred to me to go to the emergency entrance. I don't think I had ever been in a hospital in my life before, even to visit someone. When I told them the water had broken they immediately got a wheel chair. I said I could walk, for I had no labor pains yet. But the nurse told me that I had to sit. If I walked, there might be a danger of the cord coming down first. I sat. The nurse took me in an elevator upstairs to the "prepping room." There I was shaved and given an enema. I told her that I had had castor oil earlier, but she said that didn't make any difference. Everyone was shaved and had an enema. She asked me about my pains but there were none yet.
   Next I can remember being taken into a small and dimly lit room. It was a private labor room. There I was put into a bed. Finally, I was beginning to feel some contractions. Soon Jack arrived. My dad had gone over to U.S.C. and called him out of class. Jack was with me for

what seemed a very short length of time, when a nurse came in and told me she was going to give me a shot. She said it would either make me go ahead and have the baby or put me to sleep. Jack was told he had to leave. I don't know what was in the shot and I don't really understand the nurse's statement about what it would do. But Jack and I didn't question anything that any medical person said, so he went downstairs and waited and I did go to sleep.

I have vague recollections of someone telling me to wake up and push. They called me by my first name. "Alice, you have to push if you want to have a baby. Wake up and push." I was so annoyed that I gave a big push to stop them from bothering me. They said that was good. Then they wheeled me into the delivery room. It was intensely bright after being in dim light and the brightness helped to wake me up. They got me onto the delivery table and turned me on my side. The doctor was there and gave me a spinal injection—a saddle block. A saddle block was a new kind of thing at that time and they considered this to be the best thing to do and so that's what I had said I wanted.

The spinal made me lose all feeling in my lower torso. The doctor quickly did her job, but I didn't have the vaguest idea what she was doing. I know I had an episiotomy and the doctor used forceps to take the baby. I felt no pain during the delivery. I could feel the pressure of the baby being expelled, but no other feeling. I was not fearful. I felt okay. I really wasn't worried about it, I don't know why.

The baby was born about eight or nine in the morning, after about twelve hours of labor. But most of the night, the whole labor, is just a blank to me. Whatever they gave me just wiped it out.[1] When the baby was first born the doctor said, "Oh, it's a little boy," but then she said, "No, it's not, it's a little girl." I know the baby cried immediately because I was listening to hear that. They held her near me so I could see her for one brief instant. Then she was whisked away from my sight and they began kneading my stomach to loosen the afterbirth. I wasn't allowed to touch the baby in the delivery room.

Next the doctor began to talk to someone about the stitches she was putting in. I remember her saying, "Now feel this. Feel how smooth this is. It has to be just this smooth." I understood that the other person, a young man, was a resident or intern who was learning to do the job. No one addressed me and I remember I had the feeling of being so much meat on the table.

Later they took me to my hospital room and moved me into my bed. I was told to stay flat so that I wouldn't get a headache from the spinal. Jack came up to see me then, after he had seen the baby in the nursery. He had spent the whole night in the father's waiting room downstairs, drinking coffee and trying unsuccessfully to concentrate on his school work. He said, "That sure took a long time."

"You have no idea!" I answered.

I was able to see my baby pretty soon after that, I think, and I was told to undress her and look her over and make sure everything was okay. I remember they pointed out the fact that they had used forceps and that the marks on either side of the baby's forehead would go away.

My room held four mothers, but the two pairs of us were back to back so that I never saw two of the women although we could talk to each other around a partial partition which separated the room into two halves. The young woman next to me had just had her first baby, a boy, the day before.

We were all kept in bed for three days. On the third day we were able to sit up and "dangle" our feet. We were not allowed to be up out of bed until the fifth day, which was the day we were to go home. My baby was brought to me several times a day for a brief time. She was beautiful! Janet weighed eight pounds, four ounces, so she was nicely rounded with wispy dark brown hair and dark eyes.

I remember I was told to have my husband bring a pillow to ride home on. Believe me, I needed it. The stitches hurt. I was awfully un-comfortable and quite disillusioned. Here the birth was all over and I was still having pain from the stitches. I had never expected this. We went home to my mother and dad's, where we planned to stay for a week. I was nursing the baby, which I continued for six weeks. But she was fussy and they told me I didn't have enough milk and would have to supplement with formula. So then I thought, if I have to go to the trouble of making up the bottles I may as well not breastfeed too and so Janet was completely on the bottle.

The first night at home, when Janet cried around two in the morn-ing, her dad promptly got up and changed her diaper. He didn't seem to have the least bit of trouble doing it. One would have thought he had done it many times before. Then I knew he was really very pleased with becoming a father. He has always been very proud of Janet and her accomplishments through childhood and adulthood. When Janet was little she demanded that she have at least one story every night. Her dad was almost always the reader while I was clean-ing up in the kitchen. I was delighted with Janet. She was a pretty baby and a bright little girl and the center of much attention. She was the first grandchild for my parents and the only one nearby for Grand-ma Jean. Janet gave us so much joy that three years later we decided to have another baby. And so her brother Douglas came to be.

A Happy Surprise

HELEN DINERSTEIN HENKIN

1951, New York City

I had been told that I couldn't have children because I menstruated very infrequently and my cycles were anovular.[1] My husband and I had been trying for three years, unsuccessfully, and I had all kinds of examinations by various specialists. They said, "You won't have any children." I wanted to adopt a child but my husband did not, so since adoption requires two we decided that we wouldn't. Because we would no longer have to save our money carefully for the future, we decided to buy a new car and to take a trip to Bermuda during Christmas. We had a great vacation in Bermuda.

When we got back from Bermuda, I didn't feel all that well. I felt all right except that my breasts became very sensitive and I assumed that was because my period was very late—as usual. Then that sensitivity passed. I noticed that I was getting a little rounder, but I thought that was because I was eating too much, so I cut down on the amount of food I ate. I was also feeling sort of draggy, but I thought that was because I was depressed that I couldn't have any children. This went on through January, February and March and then April came around.

My father-in-law, who was an obstetrician, had read about some new hormones, or some new treatment for sterility and thought that it might be a good idea if he tried that on me. On my way to his house, coming from work, I was wearing a long, loose-fitting coat and standing in the subway and a woman who must have been about fifty offered me her seat. I was mortified. The only reason a woman of fifty would offer me a seat was if I was pregnant, and to think that I looked pregnant without even being able to have a child was just too awful. I thanked her and didn't take the seat and went on to my father-in-law's feeling pretty rotten. He then told me about this new drug and he said, "But before I give you anything, I really should make sure, because I wouldn't want to give you this if you were pregnant. He examined me and said, "Relax, relax!"

"I am relaxed," I said.

"My God, it must be the fourth or fifth month."[2]

There was then enormous consternation. For one thing, they thought that I might have a pseudo-pregnancy, since I was so eager to become pregnant. The other problem was that I had been treated with radiation while I was pregnant—at least it would seem that the period of time was while I was pregnant. The radiation treatment had been, ironically, for my infertility. It was difficult to know, because of my irregular menstrual periods, exactly when the baby was conceived. So the question arose, should they abort the pregnancy? After much consultation with various radiologists (and taking into account my other symptoms: that I immediately began to feel life; my belly popped out; and so forth) it was decided that the point at which the radiation had been given was not at a time when it would affect the fetus, so far as they knew about radiation at that time, and also that it had not been in a large enough dosage to have had any effect.[3] And so it was decided to let the pregnancy go through.

My father-in-law didn't believe in severe weight restrictions. I wasn't supposed to spend my days in front of the refrigerator gaining eighty pounds, but he told me to satisfy my appetite and I did. I must say I felt very well all through this pregnancy. I continued working at my job as a statistician until a month before the birth. We moved into a larger apartment and we took a vacation, figuring that it would be our last vacation for a while. When we came back I began getting ready, fixing up the room for the baby. I went shopping with my mother and we selected furniture, but my mother was superstitious. She said that the furniture could not be delivered until after the baby was born. We selected and ordered the whole layette, but it was kept there in the department store waiting and the sales people seemed familiar with this kind of madness.

On August 27 I went shopping with my husband's cousin's new wife, to get them a wedding present. We walked miles through the city and bought the wedding present that she selected and I felt very tired and went home. The next morning, about 5:00 A.M., I woke up and I felt new sensations. I felt just different, slightly as though I had menstrual cramps, which was of course impossible, so I thought this must be labor pains. I woke up my husband and told him that I thought I was in labor. He was very sleepy, but being a lawyer, he cross-examined me. He said, "Have you ever been in labor before?"

"No."

"Then how do you know you're in labor now?"

"Well, I don't really know, but I think I'm in labor."

"Well, when you're sure, wake me up," he said and turned over and went back to sleep.

I thought to myself, "Well, I may be really in labor, because this is a different sensation," so I started to time these "cramps" and I found they were about seven or eight minutes apart but they were really very mild. I decided I should pack my bag, which I did, and then I took a shower. I remembered that the hospital staff were most likely going to put me on a table with my feet up in the air, so I examined the soles of my feet, which didn't look so great, since I'd been walking around barefoot all summer. I got out a basin and some chlorox and cleaned my feet. I timed the pains again and they were about five minutes apart. I decided it really was time to do something about this, so I woke my husband up again and said, "Norman, I really think you have to get up, because I'm having these contractions five minutes apart and I really think we should do something about it." At that point he got up and we called his father, who was to be the obstetrician. We went to his apartment, which was near the hospital. When we got there he looked me over and said, "You are in labor and you really should go to the hospital and I'll follow." So my husband took me and when I came in they said to me, "Oh, you'll be here all day." I said to my husband, "There's no reason for you to hang around here all day." He got me some magazines, as I remember, and then I think he went back to his parents' apartment to wait.

They took me to a room and as I went through the hall I could hear other women screaming and cursing their husbands for making them go through this and I couldn't really understand it. I wasn't comfortable, but it wasn't at all intolerable. They shaved me and prepared me but at that time they didn't give you IV's and my father-in-law didn't believe in much anesthetic. He felt that it was better for the baby and the mother if you had as little anesthetic as possible. I really didn't need it. The nurses examined me again and said, "Oh my, you're fully dilated!" This had happened very quickly. I think it had happened by the time they were finished preparing me. When they announced this, my father-in-law came rushing in and said, "Oh my, she's fully dilated!" I can remember them all yelling "Fully dilated!" and they wheeled me very quickly into the delivery room where I was told to push.

At the very last minute they gave me some nitrous oxide and I came to in the delivery room with everyone saying, "Oh, you have a wonderful little girl."[4] I saw the baby and she was a very nice little girl with a head full of black hair. I was pleased and I said, "Is everything perfect?"

"Yes," they said. The baby was small, five pounds even, and it was thought that she was born at the very beginning of the ninth month.

The rest is sort of hazy, but I do remember I was wheeled back to my room and the first thing I did was to call my mother, who didn't know that I had gone to the hospital. I guess it was about 10:00 A.M. by the time the baby was born, but it all seems telescoped. I don't remember really laboring for any length of time. But I do remember calling my mother.

"Hello, Ma."

"Yes?"

"I'm in the hospital."

"Oh?"

"I had a baby girl," I said, and then there was silence. "Ma!" There was still silence. So I hung up and called my aunt Nancy who lived in the same building and said, "Nancy, go upstairs and find my mother. I just called to tell her I had a baby girl." Well, it seems my mother had fainted dead away. At any rate, there was much jubilation over Louise's birth, because I had really thought I would never have a baby and I was very, very excited.

I was planning to nurse my baby and they brought her to me to be nursed, but I didn't have much milk. Then I guess they just brought me some pills. I didn't know they were something I wasn't supposed to be taking and I took the pills. They were the ones they were giving uniformly to women at that time to dry up the milk. I assumed that it was just something the doctor had prescribed that I was supposed to have. But it turned out it was the milk suppressant, so I had no milk. Then once I didn't nurse my first baby, I didn't nurse my second.

When Louise got to be a little more than a year old, I thought we should really start on the second one because it took so long to conceive the first time. I decided that the worst that would happen if I conceived at that point was that the two children would be two years apart. Well, they were two years and one month apart, and it may even have been that we conceived immediately, because I expected my second baby at the beginning of September and she was born September 24 and was quite large, over seven pounds.

Since I had such an easy birth with my first, I thought that it might be very quick with the second. We lived in Queens and Grandma Lily, who was to care for Louise while I was in the hospital, lived in Brooklyn. We made arrangements that my cousins David and Sonia, who were close by, would come to stay with Louise if I had to go to the hospital during the night. Then we'd call my mother and she would come. Sure enough, I woke up again at 5:00 A.M. and said, "Norman, this is it." This time he didn't stop to argue. He called Sonia and David and they said, "OK, we're on the way." I knew that when I got to the hospital they wouldn't feed me and I was hungry, so I got up, got dressed, got my suitcase which was all ready, and I made myself some coffee and had some fruit and rolls. I was sitting happily munching on my breakfast when my cousins came storming into the apartment and said, "What are you doing just sitting there?!"

Norman came and by this time the pains were coming every few minutes, so we rushed to the hospital. Norman was hoping the police would stop us because we were going through the red lights, but nobody stopped us and I got to the hospital. They took one look at me and rushed me right upstairs to the delivery room—they never had time to prep me—and my father-in-law, who had been called, got there barely in the nick of time and Alice was born immediately. She was in a big hurry but she was just fine. I think from the time I woke up until Alice was born was maybe an hour, maybe an hour and a half.

They were very busy in that hospital that morning, so after they finished with me they all rushed out to the other room and left me lying on the delivery table. They had moved the stretcher-cart next to me, but then they left me lying there and it was uncomfortable on the delivery table. I wasn't feeling really knocked out because I had no medication at all with Alice and it was such a short labor, so I just moved myself over to the cart. When they came back and found me on the cart they got very excited and said, "Oh, you shouldn't have done that." I guess they were afraid I might have fallen or something. But I felt fine. I was very glad to have two little girls.

A Clean White Room

LOLLY HIRSCH

1953, Long Island

Eighteen years ago today, in the very early morning, I gave birth to Lura. It was one of the best experiences of my life and, like all experiences, had good parts and bad parts. I tell the bad part for emphasis in my battle with the field of gynecology. But, in my mind and heart, the good part is by far dominant.

She was our third child.

I very much wanted this baby. I'd had the first two children during the war, with Elliott in the Army and me staying home with my parents and living in the rigid, fishbowl existence of a Midwest parsonage.

When the war ended we were caught in the upheaval of trying to create a new life, Elliott and me and two children. He graduated from college and I tried suicide, then received psychiatric counseling which taught me to "adapt" to housewifery and motherhood.

Now we were in our own home on Long Island, in a little Cape Cod house in the fastest growing area in the country, a neighborhood of young families struggling to achieve the American Dream.

I tried going back to school, making the tremendous effort to matriculate when I was twenty-four. This was one of many things I've done before it was the "thing to do." But "going back to school" was a disaster. I was considered "old" and felt freakish among the nineteen-year-olds. I felt guilty about the expense, guilty because the house was neglected. I found the instructors boring.

I tried organizations: church, PTA, garden club; but it was a dull world of dull women.

So, I wanted another baby. I thought that if I had a baby in our own home it would be different. I'd had the first two with Ell at war and with my mother and father playing the roles I had been taught the "husband" should play. But Ell wasn't the husband I'd been led to expect. In order to enjoy the American Dream he had to work. He went to his job in the city and left me alone. He confided in me less and less. Even when he did, I couldn't understand what he was talking about because I had no similar job experiences to relate to his.

Ell also wasn't the father I'd been led to expect. My father had always been home, a preacher in his study. He'd been there for all three meals. But the father of my children was never there. He worked all week, often late into the night, and slept late on weekends. I used to wait and wait and wait on Saturday and Sunday mornings for him to wake up so we could have breakfast together.

I finally decided that the reason Ell didn't like his wife and children was that he had never been through a pregnancy with me and hadn't fully participated in the development of an infant. Maybe if he did, in our own home with no distractions from my parents and with everything his, then he would like us.

What idiocy! He was never home when I was pregnant, probably less than when he was in the Army, for then he had leaves. He obviously wanted no part of the whole experience. He was a horrible husband in comparison with my doting parents.

Autumn was crisp and beautiful on Long Island. The sea and air were blue and clear and crystal. But there was never any sense of sharing my pregnancy. My pregnancy was lonely.

Since that distant time I have learned that this trip through life is a lonely trip. Why is it that we spend so much of our time searching the world for someone to share it with? If we could only know at the very beginning that each of us is alone.

But I started to describe Lura's birth. And it occurs to me that if I went to a hypnotist and it was suggested that I "sit down and record Lura's birth" as if it had happened the day before, my recollection would be different than it is now, eighteen years later. Do I remember correctly?

I remember the house in Oceanside. It was as clean as I could get it in anticipation of the birthing of the third child. I had scrubbed and polished and washed the windows and everything was clean, clean, clean. The basement tile shone.

While my children slept, I took a shower and dressed in my spotlessly clean house in the clean town of Oceanside surrounded by clean ocean air and awaited my husband who was bringing my mother from the airport. She would help keep house when the new baby came.

They arrived and everything felt happy. Yet just nagging under the surface was the unhappiness with Elliott. I yearned to feel closer.

But with my mother there, everything seemed happy.

We ate ice cream and everything was so clean.

Then I started feeling peculiar and knew the baby was coming, but thought that maybe I was being dramatic because my mother had come.

I had taken the natural childbirth course at the Freeport clinic and one of the things I had learned was that there is a natural period of amnesia before birth. Looking back, I see myself going to the bedroom, to the bathroom, feeling restless and not knowing what to do. I didn't seem to know what to pack, what to wear.

Then there was the midnight drive with Ell to the hospital, wishing he and I were closer. I felt miserable sitting next to him, so alone. I can see us in the car, the big station wagon of that era. I can remember the streetlights and his silhouette and the feeling of separateness.

In the labor room everything was super hospital silent and super hospital clean. White draw curtains separated my cubicle from the rest of the room and I was all in white, feeling "cared for" and "safe."

I felt in total control because this time, unlike my other two deliveries, I was knowledgeable. I had attended all the childbirth classes and conscientiously exercised and practiced the ritual of delivery.

Dr. M. had promised me for nine months that he would go along with "natural childbirth," that he knew all about it. He reassured me throughout my monthly, weekly visits.

I was in prime, tip-top health and well cared for. I lay on the white bed in the white robe and felt happy and cozy and safe.

Then Dr. M. came into the room and into my view and held out a huge hypodermic needle saying, "Now I'm going to give you this needle and you're going to feel great! Feel like you've had seven martinis."

I was dumbfounded. I tried to explain to him that I don't like feeling drunk. He had told me for nine months that he would cooperate, that he was trained for natural childbirth. I said gently, "But you said you would do natural childbirth with me."

He shrugged.

I turned to total tenseness like an animal. I had come out of my first delivery with arms, legs and face black and blue from fighting the ether and the straps on the delivery table.

Now, today, these eighteen years later, I feel my nostrils dilating, anger and fury flooding my chest. I feel congestion across my throat. I can't get my breath. Eighteen years later.

He became my antagonist. He stood there, a doctor's form; huge hairy arms holding a huge hypodermic needle, poised to shoot.

We were enemies.

I hated him—loathed him—despised him.

I lay there animal tense.

He said blithely, "Wellll. . .this is your last chance."

I said very carefully, "I want to go through natural childbirth."

It was as though we stood and faced each other in the arena. The clock stopped. The crowd was hushed. He walked over to the window: inhuman, subhuman, nonhuman. He looked at the needle poised against the window screen and looked at me and said with total lack of emotion, interest or regard, "This is your last chance for anesthesia."

I looked at him with incredible hatred. "Shoot!" I said and watched him trigger the plunger with his thumb, shooting the stream of poison out through the window screen.

God, god, god how I hated that man. Jesus christ, how I despised him then and despise and detest him now.

He left.

I lay there turned to stone, totally alone in the whole white universe of hospital and anesthesia and disinfectant.

Alone in the world.

Then I became aware of a nurse in the shadows and knew she had observed the exchange. I was aware of her presence as a caged animal is aware. She walked over to me and patted my arm lightly and said, "Don't worry. You'll be all right."

And now eighteen years later I start to cry tears of sorrow for that girl, that woman I was, for that aloneness in that hospital. I cry thinking of that nurse who tried to help me for she was the one human being who was with me and she was a woman.

And I cry and cry here at my typewriter for those two women who were alone together in that male pigs' hospital in that Long Island suburb in New York.

Because I was beautiful. She was beautiful. We were both smart and sensitive and we were human beings together and the rest were all pigs. The doctor was a pig and Elliott had brought me and left me there alone and both these men were subhuman.

I had been good. I had kept our world clean and orderly. I had only yearned for friendliness. I had yearned to be treated like an intelligent, warm human being on the verge of giving birth to a new human child. Those men tried to dehumanize me and make me into a nothing, a non-functioning zero, but now these many years later I know they failed. I am still me.

For it was then that the beautiful part transpired. I was alone and recently trained in natural childbirth. I knew what was happening to my body and it was incredibly beautiful. My body performed just as the teaching had said it would perform. It was a cathedral of perfection. Muscles going into a pattern, reforming, regrouping and then forming another pattern of rhythm and universal accord—in the rhythm and pattern of the celestial movement of planets and stars and meteors—all was in rhythm, all was in tune. Nothing was discordant. All was profound beauty, the pattern and music of Nature. My body was a heaving symphony of movement. My hands on my abdomen caught the rapture of surging tidal waves. My brain luxuriated in my aloneness with this physical self that was ME, heaving and moving and contracting and relaxing and pushing and sighing and waiting and moving again in the primeval rhythm of all living, pulsating heavenly and earthly beings.

It was sheer, unadulterated pleasure. Sheer ecstatic joy.

I was glad I was alone. I wanted no others to take these moments from me and distort and destroy them with their sounds, their touches, their interpretations.

This was all mine!

The goddesses of the Universe gave these moments to me. I didn't have to share them with a husband, or a doctor or a nurse.

As I lay there with my hands on my abdomen, the nurse came in to look at my progress.

I smiled happily, conspiratorially.

She took a glance, then looked more carefully and, shocked, rushed out.

She and Dr. M. ran back in and both started working to get me from cot to wheeled stretcher, from wheeling, reeling stretcher to delivery table.

And at some point, with my back arched, head and neck flat on the cot, with my whole birthing area high up in the air and exposed,

half way between stretcher and table,

suddenly—

pphhhht!

The doctor made a quick slash, opened up my delivery and the baby was out high in the air.

I was unbound, free and empty on the table and he laid my baby on the cold counter.

Then he pressed upon my abdomen and hurt me terribly and I asked him, "What are you doing?"

He was forcing out the afterbirth.

He hurt me physically but I didn't mind.

Because I could see the baby lying there: beautiful, perfect, a girl. The doctor's hostage.

She had a great big clamp on her umbilical cord. She moved her head around and around to focus on the bright light overhead. She was wide-eyed and incredibly beautiful, just looking, looking, looking.

I held polite conversation with Dr. M. He seemed to be friendly and we seemed both to have forgotten the earlier episode. The nurse avoided my eyes as she busied about.

Then suddenly at my labia there was a sharp, searing pain and I questioned, "What are you doing?"

He answered, "Sewing you up."

I had had episiotomies with each of my other two children and still had not learned that in a good birth, there is no need for tearing or slashing, so I good-humoredly thought this to be part of his game. I didn't know until months later that he could have given me a local anesthetic.

He stitched and with each stitch came a jabbing pain and I got so I was tense and tightened my teeth when I anticipated his needle, and he stitched on and on and I questioned him through clenched teeth about how many more and he kidded about wanting to make me tight for my husband.

We joked.

I look back at myself: young, stupid, polite girl.

Eventually he turned from me and went to my baby. Her hand was clenched tightly on the clamp and he wanted to release her hand and take care of her cord. He took her tiny hand and forceably unclenched it.

She looked up at him and started yowling. She opened up and really howled. Nothing would pacify her. She knew him to be a bastard.

He fiddled with her cord and I think he put silver nitrate in her eyes.

Eventually they wheeled me out. Ell was outside and he bent over and kissed me. It was a dark, dusky corridor and I couldn't see him well.

The doctor came swaggering out and stood there like a big hot shit and made cracks with Ell. Ell was with me and didn't respond to the big shit.

He was with me this one time.

I said, "We have a little girl. You get to name the girls."

(He'd named the first girl for his first girlfriend.)

He said, "I'm going to name her Lura Grace."

My given name. I thought I was going to cry. I didn't think he liked me. He was going to name this beautiful baby girl after me. I still cry now eighteen years later.

Surrendering My Baby

LEE CAMPBELL

1962, Massachusetts

It seems strange, but I was happy about being pregnant. I had been going with the father since the eighth grade and we had recently been reunited after a short time of separation. Simply put, I loved Tom very much and felt that our child was an extension, an affirmation, of this love. But Tom was scared to death by the pregnancy, and could not project it into the future to its final culmination in the birth of a new human being. Certain that his mother would never permit our marriage, we did make vague plans to elope to a southern state which permitted young marriages without parental consent. I was seventeen.

Against Tom's wishes, I told my parents about the pregnancy, needing their support and help. I expected them to welcome the idea of marriage, for they were very fond of Tom, who was like a member of the family. But instead, they put additional pressure on Tom and insisted he tell his parents, something he predicted would mean disaster. He was right. A phone call brought the stunning news that Tom had denied paternity and I was then forced—out of anger, revenge, love/hate, and practical financial need—to file a paternity suit against him. Our school friends chose sides and I was very much the loser.

I had to make a quick decision about whether to surrender my baby for adoption, in order to determine the court settlement. My parents told me that though they loved me, they had to protect my four younger siblings from the stigma of my unwed pregnancy. They could not offer any support for keeping and raising the child. Utterly beaten, I agreed to surrender my baby.

It was an interminable pregnancy, during which I tried to cultivate a remote, detached attitude about the child who swelled my body and moved in waves within me, sticking a foot out here, and thrusting an arm out there. This effort took about all the day-to-day resources I could muster and left little reserve of strength to combat the rush of overwhelming love which followed his early birth. The baby, being small and close to incubator weight, was allowed to be with me for almost continual feedings. I have never forgotten the shivers of exquisite joy his presence brought me. I have only to close my eyes—many long, full years later—to see his tiny Indian-red face topped with a mop of downy black hair.

Following my return to my parents' home, and the baby's admission to a foster home, I attempted most assiduously to regain my former detached attitude toward Michael, as I had begun calling him in my heart. I did make a few feeble attempts to discuss with my mother my feelings of painful separation, but I was rebuffed. No one was equipped to deal with my feelings. I also made an attempt to see Tom, but it seemed he was already engaged to another girl.

My social worker and I began a two-month game of sliding the surrender papers across the desk to each other. I summoned the courage to insist to this woman, who intimidated me greatly, that I be allowed to see my son in his foster home. With her assurances that I was only making the inevitable more difficult, I did see him there twice and twice took him from the foster home to care for him in the homes of friends.

My social worker did not hide her waning patience and she implied that I was interfering in my son's proper early adoptive placement. Clearly, I was in the way. No other options were ever ventured. Feeling that I had no help available, I finally did "surrender." Gaining access later to what had been written about me, as guaranteed under the Freedom of Information Act, proved to be revealing. In a letter from my adoption worker to the worker at the home for unwed mothers, the former admitted: "It was touch and go for a while as to whether she would release him and finally she decided to do so." Yet, in her official records filed with the probate court, the adoption worker stated flatly, "Lee had no maternal feelings for the child and felt that keeping him would not be in tune with her lifestyle." In another letter to the home, this same adoption worker discussed the completion of my financial arrangements and concluded her letter: "On the lighter side, the baby is lovely and should be excellent material for adoption."

I have dealt with Michael's surrender in a number of vastly different ways. For ten years I blotted out everything, then remembered, and acknowledged, then channelled my concern for him by having the adoption agency notify the adoptive parents of my willingness to provide information. I have been active in adoptee groups and founded a support group for birthparents, called CUB, Concerned United Birthparents.[1] Because of the agency's eleven month battle with me over my Consent to Inform, I was forced to look for another, more willing intermediary, and in the course of this search I learned Michael's new identity.

Knowing Michael's identity has provided relief, but of course my relationship with him has been forever changed. During the first three years of knowing his name, I did not see him or interfere with the adoptive relationship in any way. Then when he was nearly sixteen, a friend of mine who is herself an adoptive mother wrote a letter on my behalf to his adoptive parents. His parents met with me and soon offered Michael the same opportunity. While I do not begrudge the happiness Michael has brought to his adoptive family, his parents remain threatened by me. I find this sad, although his parents do enjoy a good relationship with Michael's birth-father. Fortunately, Michael, my other two sons and I continue to have a strong rewarding relationship.

Looking back, it angers me that I was denied options to raise my son. If there had to be a separation, I wish I could have known my son's early life. If the adopting parents had always been encouraged to consider the reality of my existence, I don't think they would need to deny me to the extent they have. I find it difficult to justify society's lack of emotional recompense and its negation of me in this, the ultimate sacrifice of my life. I'm not sure that I regret the basic concept of adoption; it is, rather, that I regret that there is so little place for me within it.

For My Husband's Mother

ELLEN BASS

Those months I carried Sara
I'd think of your mother,
the woman who carried you
though she could not
keep you.

　　　This woman
we do not know, this girl
whose life was changed
in ways we'll never know,
who wanted or did not want
who loved or did not love
who chose or did not choose
but, willing or reluctant
carried you.

Easily, like the grass that sprouts the pasture green
after first fall rains; or in great pain,
volcanic, slow,
the creaking
cracking of the earth, she
birthed you.

We do not know her name
or what she thought as her fingers soaped her taut
belly in the bath,
as your kicks reached her
first uncertain, then
definite, firm rabbit thumps.

We do not know if she could
keep food down, if
her legs cramped,
if she grew dizzy in the grocery
had to drop her head between her knees
to keep from blacking out.

We do not know if she held you in her hospital bed,
if her breasts were bound to keep the milk from
letting down
or if they drugged her and she woke
only to the new softness of her belly, like dough.

We do not know
what friends or family criticized her, if they
sent her out of town and brought her back
as though she'd been on holiday.

We know only
there was a woman who gave you
the food of her blood
the bed of her flesh,
who breathed for you.

We do not know
if anyone ever
thanked her.

Birth with "La Partera"

BARBARA CHARLES

1971, New Mexico

I was living in New York when I became pregnant for the first time. After an obstetrician confirmed what I already knew, I began to plan how and where I was to have the baby.

A woman friend had told me about the Catholic Maternity Center in Santa Fe, New Mexico. It was a free-standing birth center, across the street from a hospital where patients could be taken in case of an emergency. It was staffed by nurse-midwives, who allowed their patients to walk around or take a shower during labor. The midwives promoted natural delivery, and let the mothers go home after twenty-four hours, provided everything was normal. The woman who told me about her experience at the Center gave me the idea that she had been allowed to do whatever she wanted during labor, as long as it was safe. What she liked most about the experience was that she was allowed to be her own person. She was able to express herself, in her own style, while participating in one of the most important events in life, giving birth. This kind of birth appealed to me too and I dreamed of its becoming a reality in my own life. My hopes became the basis of a personal search that was to be a major turning point in my life.

My husband, Joe, and I bought a truck and moved to New Mexico. We had travelled a lot in the past few years, so subletting our apartment and moving across the country was not a big deal. Joe is an artist and I am a registered nurse; both of us were in a position to find work wherever we settled.

We found a very comfortable adobe-covered log house to live in. It was on the outskirts of a protected wilderness area twenty-five miles from Santa Fe. Soon after we arrived, I learned that the Catholic Maternity Center had been closed for over a year. But since I was only about twelve to fourteen weeks pregnant, I let the matter drop and concentrated my energies on getting a job. I applied for a nursing staff position in obstetrics at the hospital in Santa Fe. But the director of nursing knew I was pregnant and would not permit me to work in the maternity ward of the hospital. She didn't want me to see "what goes on up there, especially since you are pregnant." This attitude reinforced my already negative opinion of conventional hospital-based obstetrics and contributed to the intensity of my search for an alternative. At this point I couldn't clearly describe what I was looking for; it was more a feeling than anything else. But I did know that I didn't want a conventional hospital birth.

I was assigned to the Cardiac Intensive Care Unit as evening charge nurse. There I met a very pleasant and caring general practitioner as he made rounds. He volunteered to deliver my baby in the hospital in "the old-fashioned way," but he recommended that I receive prenatal care from the obstetrical group across the street from the hospital. I knew that this doctor was sincerely trying to help me, but I wondered whether the arrangement would work out.

I made an appointment with the obstetrics group and bungled along under their care for the duration of the pregnancy. The doctors were always in a hurry and scheduled so many women to be seen at one time that I really felt it was an imposition to ask more than one question at each visit. I finally learned that the best resource person was the office nurse and got most of the information I needed from her. I never had the courage to discuss with the obstetricians my plans to be delivered by the general practitioner.

The actual moment of reckoning came at a visit when I was about thirty-six weeks pregnant. The doctor brought up the subject of the delivery, after an uncomfortable pelvic exam during which he told me that my pelvis was "borderline" in some respects and that it was possible I might fracture my coccyx during delivery.[1] But that concern paled in comparison with his response to my request for a drug-free delivery. He leaned against the wall next to the examining table, and with his arms folded across his chest and a look of disbelief and disdain on his face, retorted, "Now why would you want to expose yourself to such pain when I am here to give you safe, sound analgesia and anesthesia?"

As I left the office, my mind was reeling from the enormity of the realization that I was now without a viable birth plan. I had wanted to believe that it would work out with the G.P., or that even if it didn't work out, the obstetrician I was seeing would support me in my decision to have an unmedicated labor and delivery. I felt betrayed, alone and afraid. So I began the search for an alternative all over again, but this time I had a clearer idea of what I wanted. I had to find someone I could trust to help me with the birth of my baby.

I located a young physician who did deliveries at his home in the mountains, a short distance from Santa Fe. My friends, Bernarr and Kiki, took me there in their bus. We had to travel over several miles of deeply rutted roads to get to the doctor's place. It took a few hours of driving. Finally we walked up a steep driveway to a large one-story adobe house at the top of an incline. The mountains were all around us and the view was spectacular. It was very isolated, but seemed peaceful. I tried to look at the positives.

A woman greeted us at the door. Inside we met two or three pregnant women, who were seated at a large wooden table in an oversized kitchen, apparently the main room of the house. They were ready to deliver any day and were staying at the house until the time came. An unfamiliar, impersonal air permeated the place and I felt awkward and out of place. The doctor emerged after about half an hour and gave me an orientation to the facilities, which included a small building in the back of the big house, where deliveries were done. I was taken into a simple, sparsely furnished room with a bed, a wood stove and a rocking chair. The doctor explained that birth is a natural process and that my body would "tell you what to do." He would be there just in case I needed him. He didn't believe in "interfering with nature."

I thanked the doctor and we climbed back into the bus to begin the precarious descent down the steep mountain road. I was disappointed by the visit and felt frustrated and even somewhat helpless. I didn't want someone controlling every aspect of my labor and delivery, but the idea of managing everything on my own, with a mystical doctor hovering somewhere in the background, wasn't exactly what I had in mind either.

Some time later Bernarr and Kiki took me to visit friends of theirs in the little town of San Miguel, about half-way between Pecos, where we lived, and Las Vegas, New Mexico. A woman they knew had just had a baby, delivered by a lay midwife. The arrangement was that everyone went to the midwife's house to be delivered. She would not do deliveries in your home, only in hers. I went to see this woman, Jesusita Aragon. She was sixty-three years old and told me that she had learned the art of midwifery from her mother, who had also been a midwife. She had delivered her first baby when she was thirteen and she was very proud that she had "never lost a mother or a baby yet" in her fifty years of practice.[2] Jesusita's native language was Spanish, but she spoke English well enough for us to converse. We sat in rocking chairs in her living room and rocked and talked.

In response to Jesusita's questions, I told her that I had been receiving prenatal care but didn't want a hospital delivery. She asked about my pregnancy and health. I told her I had not had high blood pressure or other complications during the pregnancy. I had gained about thirty pounds and was physically very active. In fact, I felt great! After listening to me, Jesusita agreed to do the delivery. In turn, I had many questions for her. I learned that she was licensed by the State of New Mexico Public Health Department, which would require that a birth certificate be filed. Jesusita instructed me to come to her house when I was in active labor and she told Joe that he should park the truck facing the street, in case we needed to transport either me or the baby to the hospital. I could see the hospital from the end of Jesusita's driveway. Now I knew why she only conducted deliveries at her house.

Now that my search for a birth attendant was ended, I began to unwind a bit. Having finally arranged the place of delivery and the person who would deliver the baby, I was able to turn inward and take care of so many aspects of my inner life that needed to be put in order before the baby came. I took long walks along the Pecos River, putting on heavy leather boots that came up to mid-calf, to guard against the lazy rattlers which lace the trails in New Mexico. I swam in the water, made icy cold by the springs that feed into the river from the mountains that surround it. The air was crisp and sweet. The sky was incredibly blue. I began to find my essential self. To this day, New Mexico is very special to me and I hope that someday I will go back there to live.

My labor began at five minutes to midnight, according to the Big Ben clock on the stump of wood that served as our night table. I was just turning in after a long day of visiting with friends, who shared in celebrating my twenty-ninth birthday. I was tired.

At first I felt a sensation similar to that of menstrual cramping. Then it went away. Five minutes later it came back again. I really wasn't sure what it was; indigestion, maybe? If you've never experienced uterine contractions it's very possible not to recognize them when they come, no matter how well versed you are on the subject. There is also often a tendency, as was true in my case, not to believe that labor is really happening to you right at that very moment.

For the next twenty minutes or so the contractions came with amazing regularity every five minutes. I was surprised, because I had expected labor to be erratic, with irregular contractions in the beginning. Nothing seemed to fit the picture I had in my mind, yet I knew one thing for sure: the contractions were continuing to come at regular five-minute intervals and they were definitely getting stronger.

I got up and shuffled into the baby's room, where I had stored my bag, all packed and ready to go. Between contractions, I managed to get downstairs to the bathroom, for on top of everything else I felt the urge to have a bowel movement! I used the toilet only to find that I still felt I had to go. This was a "sign," I knew, and though the contractions had only just started and were still five minutes apart, the intensity was picking up. I knew that I had to alert Joe, who was in his studio room painting. We had to get to Jesusita's as soon as possible.

Joe is nearly totally deaf. He has about ten percent of his hearing in both ears combined. He wears a hearing aid, but half of the time it isn't working right. He can read my lips very well, so it didn't take long for him to figure out what was happening. Joe backed the truck up close to our porch and assisted me into the front seat. We were both excited. The time had come. It was now after 1:00 A.M. We started off down the deserted highway to Las Vegas, some forty miles away.

We had not driven more than fifteen or twenty minutes when I discovered that I could no longer manage the pain with Lamaze breathing. I had not realized that the contractions would be so strong. They were so powerful that I was not able to sit upright. I rode the rest of the way half lying down on the front seat of the truck, urging Joe with frantic hand signals to please drive a little faster.

We pulled into Jesusita's driveway sometime around 2:00 A.M. She appeared sleepy-eyed at the screen door and ushered me into a plain room with a double bed and a crucifix on the wall. I could see another woman in a bed in the next room. She was recovering from a delivery earlier in the evening. I was so glad to be there. I felt safe in what I later called Jesusita's Maternity Motel.

I implored Jesusita to hurry as she made up the bed with fresh sheets and layers of plastic and cotton padding. I could not wait to get into the bed. Finally it was ready and Jesusita helped me into it. Oh, those clean sheets felt so good! She examined me and announced with surprise that I was six to seven centimeters dilated. It was no surprise to me! The contractions were incredibly strong and seemed to be coming closer and closer together. The worst was about to come.

I vomited bile-colored liquid. Then, when my stomach was empty, I got the dry heaves. My back was killing me! Every time I had a contraction it felt as though an explosion was tearing through my muscle and bone. I moaned and writhed around and didn't want anyone to do anything except put pressure on my back during contractions. The Lamaze breathing didn't help one bit. The contractions were coming so close together that I could not seem to get on top of them no matter how hard I tried.

"Oh, God," I prayed, "What am I doing here? Why am I not in a hospital?" The nurse's part of my brain, that knew about medical pain relief, insisted on being heard. Yet the greater part of me knew that I was exactly where I wanted to be and that everything would be fine.

To cope with the pain I took my mind, well-trained from years of studying yoga, and went straight up out of my body. I flexed my right big toe into a rigid knot and held on for dear life through each contraction, breathing slowly and shallowly. I have since learned that every laboring woman has her own personal style of coping, in addition to or in spite of what she has learned in childbirth education classes. My way was an out-of-body experience coupled with a cramped big toe.

Finally Jesusita told me I could push. It was 3:45 A.M. I had had a short labor, though it felt agonizingly long. My sense of time was totally distorted. But I knew that the greatest part of the pain was over. I was eager to get it over with now and I focussed all my attention on pushing. I grunted and squeezed down with my abdominal muscles as hard as I could. Jesusita urged me to push harder and coached me on how to improve my pushing. But even though I was sitting nearly bolt upright, with three pillows behind me, I was amazed at how hard it was to push! The baby felt like a small sapling, coming out branches first.

I continued to push with resolve. The baby was coming down. Jesusita's encouraging words were all that I needed. Joe, who had been supporting my back during the pushing, went to the bottom of the bed in order to see the birth. I could feel the baby's head swell the pelvic outlet. But I also felt tremendous pressure on my pubic bone. It hurt and didn't feel right. The head felt too big. I thought I was going to tear. I reached my hand down to feel what was happening; why was it burning so much? Jesusita quickly removed my hand and told me not to touch there. She urged me now, with irritation in her voice, to push as hard as I possibly could!

I couldn't. I felt myself holding back, suspended in time. I made half-hearted attempts, but I couldn't push because I was afraid of tearing. It was awful to be stuck like this and I felt guilty. I had to push, but I couldn't bring myself to do it.

I had to make up my mind. The baby was nearly fully crowned. Her head, Joe told me later, was almost out when I panicked. So many things were going through my mind. I was aware of some part of me that wasn't ready to have the baby. After some minutes (I think it was minutes, though it seemed much longer), Jesusita leaned over and shook me. She looked me straight in the eye and ORDERED me to PUSH. She told me that if I didn't push, something would happen to the baby.

That snapped me out of it. My fears were focussed in a new direction. I knew I had to push. I took a deep breath and pushed so hard that the baby literally flew out, like a cork out of a champagne bottle.

"It's a girl." What a relief! Jesusita bulb-suctioned the baby and I heard her cry. She clamped and cut the cord, then wrapped the baby in a soft blanket and let me hold her. Shortly after, I had one more contraction and the placenta came out. Jesusita took the baby into the warmth of the kitchen, where there was a fire going in the woodstove. She weighed the baby—seven pounds five and a half ounces—bathed her, then gave her back to me to examine, telling me to count all of her fingers and toes. Then she rewrapped the baby and placed her next to me and said she was going back to bed. Joe lay down on the bed next to us and covered up with a blanket. Joe couldn't hear, but the baby made little cooing sounds the rest of the night. I kept raising up to look at her. She sounded like a little turtledove.

At 9:00 A.M. Jesusita woke me up to check on me. She assisted me to the bathroom and stayed with me until I finished urinating. She massaged my uterus and I expelled a few big clots of blood. I padded back to bed and Jesusita's husband, who had a good fire going in the woodstove by this time, took orders for breakfast. I polished off two eggs, toast and tea, and a short while later sat up in bed and wrote out a check for fifty dollars, Jesusita's total fee.

I got dressed and we drove back home to Pecos in a light misty rain. By noon I was cooking lunch in my own kitchen, with friends dropping by to help out with the housework and supper. It was great to get back home so quickly. Jesusita called me a week later to ask me the baby's name for the birth certificate. I told her we called the baby Pajarita, our "Little Bird," but that her official name was Andrea Rain Tui. Jesusita didn't understand that I meant Pajarita as a nickname, so she put all four names on the birth certificate. Now we call our daughter Paja (Pa-ha) for short.

There are always risks associated with birth, but for me the risk was less with Jesusita than with birth in a hospital. Today Jesusita is seventy-five years old and still practicing midwifery in Las Vegas, New Mexico. She once said, "You know, midwives never grow old. They just keep on going." I am grateful to Jesusita for helping me to find what I had been searching for—an alternative birth in my own style.

Walking Out of the Hospital

JEANNINE PARVATI BAKER

1974, Sonoma County, California

The birth that I will share with you has attuned my awareness as a midwife more than any other experience I've had. The home birth experience has made me more spiritual than any other rite-of-passage. I imagine that only death could be as strong a testimony as birth is to the spirit.

In part, I became a midwife because of this birth experience with my twins, my second pregnancy. Up until then, I'd been a friend, labor coach or "monitrice" at many births. I was fascinated by birth and devoted to helping my sister women give birth in joy, peace, trust, and with their families bonding in love.

Being pregnant with my twins provided an opportunity to learn all I could, as we expected that no one would help me have a home birth. Because of the twins I was labelled "high risk," even though I knew full well that they would deliver just perfectly. My health was optimum and there was a lot of love in my life. Yet, I was a "category," not a unique person anymore, and it was difficult to gain medical help. At the time of this pregnancy, there were few professionals who would risk attending a home birth of twins. Also, one of my twins was in a breech presentation, a "high risk" condition in itself, but especially so when coming first before a head-down twin. It was feared their chins might lock. Actually, an obstetrician friend of mine called me one morning (while I was eating breakfast hotcakes) to tell me that if I delivered a breech first and its chin locked with the second twin, he might have to decapitate them both to get them to deliver without killing me! However, I knew in my heart that my babies and I stood a safer chance at home with trusted friends, than with paranoid professionals educated way beyond their intelligence. In fact, I resolved to trust Heavenly Mother (or whatever divinity was on call the night I birthed my twins) and let go of reliance on anyone other than myself and Her to give birth.

As it was the early 1970s, there was not much community support for unattended home birth. I was more interested in doing what was best for my twins than in "setting trends" and so rather than try to persuade medical professionals to attend, I asked some close friends to help me deliver. We had meetings before the birth and here we all spoke our fears and desires and affirmations for a peaceful delivery. I delegated tasks to my friends so that the father of our babies and I could spend those first few precious moments just being with the babies. We all meditated as a group and grew in trust of one another.

I feel it was the nature of my twins as much as our need as parents which brought together that friendship circle. The twins are remarkable for bringing people into my life and they began right away. Some wise voice within guided me to extend myself to others preparing for their births, and from the start my pregnancy seemed to be less for me personally and more for our community. I felt a shift from experiencing myself alone to being with others and caring about others passionately in a way unknown before. I was alone-among-others and still felt one hundred percent responsible for my own birth. I trusted that the coming birth would happen as it was meant to be.

The night I went into labor, my husband said to me, "Let's go to the movies, because soon the babies will be here and we won't be able to go out together again for a while." I knew the babies were very close to coming, but since my husband rarely asked me for a date, I accepted. We saw *The Three Musketeers* and as I already felt quite pulled inwards to focus on the twins, I really don't remember the movie except for all the bloodshed, which I hoped was not portentous. I do remember the breech baby kicking my cervix, like peddling a bicycle during the film! After the movie, we came home and my husband went to sleep. Our daughter, Loi, four-and-a-half, slept by us. I stayed up and practiced my prenatal yoga as I had never done before. My flexibility and concentration were at their best. As I retired, I whispered to my sleeping family that tonight the babes would be born. I was happy.

I awoke probably less than an hour later in a puddle of liquid. "Funny," I thought, "to begin a labor with my bag of waters breaking." I got up and sloshed my way into the bathroom and then filled up the toilet bowl with more amniotic fluid, or so I thought. What a shock, when I turned on the light, to see the bowl filled with blood! More was gushing from me and I stuffed a towel between my legs and waddled back to the bedroom. Turning on the light brought a gruesome sight—there was blood everywhere, from the bed all along our white wall-to-wall carpet to the toilet, and now the towel I was wearing was soaked also. "That movie!" I thought, "Now there's blood all over the place!" I woke my husband and we decided it would be best to get medical help, as this wasn't something he felt he could handle alone. I had previously had a suspicion that my placenta might be marginally placed over my cervix.[1] In fact, I had agreed to take the long drive next morning to San Francisco for a sonogram test, which could show where the placenta was situated. I had prayed my labor would begin before that grueling drive and the medical test. Now it had, but I was bleeding more than I had ever seen or heard of as normal.

I called an obstetrician friend of mine, who agreed to meet me at the local hospital. We called a neighbor to come sit with our Loi. As we left the house, my neighbor stuffed into my pocket some herbs to stop bleeding. We were admitted at about 2:00 A.M. with no contractions yet started. I was bleeding enough to have soaked another bath towel by that time. However, despite the bleeding, I did not feel weak. I felt a lot of love for all the people I met at the hospital. Even the coldness of the sterile conditions didn't bother me. I asked the nurse to check me and see if my placenta was the cause of the bleeding, but she said she couldn't do anything like that as such examination and diagnosis is the doctor's province. In fact, I had to submit to a battery of tests before the doctor would even come.

Meanwhile I had been drinking lots of bayberry bark and shepherd's purse tea—the herbs given to me by my neighbor.[2] A cup of hot water was the only thing I asked of the hospital. I steeped the herbs in the water and after I drank a cupful or two, the bleeding subsided. I was feeling great and contractions began slowly, rapidly gaining in strength. They were completely painless if I concentrated and surrendered to them. My breech baby was still riding high and did not apply any painful pressure on my cervix. I spent three hours dilating and I could feel I was entering transition even before the doctor arrived to check me out.

But instead of my obstetrician friend, in walked his partner, the same doctor who had called me during breakfast with the image of decapitating babies' heads. When I asked where my friend was, the partner said it was his turn for night duty. I told him that a special agreement had been made between myself and my doctor friend, yet he was adamant that it was his turn! I burst into tears. This was another "sign of transition," and also, as I have been realizing lately, a deep purification. I cried out my disappointment. I was very attached to the idea of having my friend come to meet me at the hospital if need be, as his attitude was very supportive for breech delivery and I knew that not many other doctors felt comfortable in delivering a bottom-first baby, whether at home or in the hospital! But I stopped crying. My trust and faith returned, knowing that this doctor standing in front of me would try his best too. He examined me and said the placenta was fine. I asked him why the copious blood flow had happened and he said he didn't know why. I felt that now I could carry on without worrying about my placenta. I had been visualizing the placenta migrating away from the opening of my cervix steadily for three hours and that, coupled with my herbal teas to stop hemorrhage, was all that was done to help me.

At that point I asked the doctor if a vaginal birth was possible. He ordered an X-ray, which I didn't want. I had been X-rayed as a fetus during my mother's labor and have always had that extra fear of radiation exposure. This was a fear I didn't want to pass on to my children. However, the doctor insisted and, because I also wanted information, I yielded. This is my only regret in the story. I was wheeled into the X-ray room and I concentrated on surrounding myself in white light to protect my babies from the radiation. After the X-ray, the technician took a long time to come out of his lead walled room, so I got off the gurney and walked back into the labor room. Back in the labor bed, I heard a flurry all along the hallway—"Where is she? She has disappeared!!" Finally I realized they were talking about me! No one had ever seen a woman in transition with twins walk back!

Some time after the twins' birth, I asked for a copy of those X-rays and a doctor told me that there was no way the hip bones of the woman pictured could vaginally deliver those babies. He would have C-sectioned the parturient! Luckily, the doctor who was helping me in labor read the X-rays differently. He said a vaginal delivery was possible. So I seized the moment and asked if our daughter could come to the labor room and watch the birth of her siblings. "No way, it's against all hospital policy" was the answer. I was very close to full dilation at this point and feeling a little spaced-out. Yet the vision of my family being together at the birth was strong. I then informed everyone that we would be leaving the hospital. It was more important to me to be with my daughter than to have the help of these kind professionals.

They thought I was joking. Even my husband did! Yet I was getting up and getting ready to leave. To try to change my mind, the doctor said, "Mother Nature has given you a signal, by all the bleeding, to stay in the hospital." I told him that I was in touch with Mother Nature and she was telling me to go home to my daughter. Next, the doctor went into conference with my husband in the hallway and all I could hear of that conversation was my husband's testimony as to how strong-willed I am. The doctor then called several "witnesses" and made a loud statement, loud enough so that I could hear, that the patient was leaving against his better medical judgment. He brought in a paper for me to sign, which basically said that I relieved the doctor and hospital of all blame if I died as a result of leaving the hospital. I signed it eagerly. In one last heroic try, the doctor placed his arms in the door on either side and his feet squarely at each corner of the exit-way and said, "Jeannine, over my dead body will you leave!"

My reply, equally as desperate with the drama now unfolding, was "That could be arranged, Doctor!" With that, we left.

As we walked out of the hospital, the doctor called out to me say-ing that I would drop those babies out of me before we even made it home. I could feel that there was no pressure yet on my cervix and, though fully dilated by now, I knew we would make it home to deliver. The doctor then said, "How long to get to your house?"

Both my husband and I said "Twelve minutes." This was a family joke. We always said "twelve" when asked for a number we didn't really know.

"I'm going to follow you," the doctor said. I hadn't an argument left in me at that point.

We arrived home just before dawn and found that our neighbor had made up the birthing bed, lit candles and incense, and called our friends to arrive as previously planned. But try as he might, he hadn't been able to get hold of the only midwife in our county, who had reluctantly accepted the possibility of being called if we had no one else to help. The doctor, with his nurse, arrived looking sleepy. "Ex-actly twelve minutes!" he said, looking at his watch. He asked where the spare bedroom was and promptly fell asleep.

It felt so wonderful to be home! The soft lighting was a relief after the glare of the hospital and the fragrant smell of incense was more comforting than that of antiseptics. My daughter lay peacefully sleep-ing next to me as I began to feel the pressure of the first twin's descent. It took a couple more hours for the breech babe to rotate into posi-tion. The doctor awoke at one point and asked if I wanted him to turn the baby manually, to help it come out sooner. My feeling was that my baby knew best how and when to come. No thank you. My yogic breathing kept me open, soft and peaceful and I had still no pain!

As the rosy-fingered dawn crept upon us, I could feel Oceana, my first twin, slide into my birth canal. Now the urge to push came on strong and I roared her down my birth canal. In between my loud pushing sounds, I would say, "How wonderful! It feels so good!!" If I hadn't recorded that on tape, I might even doubt it myself. Yet to this day, it was the only painless labor and delivery I've been graced in having.

Oceana's little feet poked out of me and I reached around, in my hands and knees position, to feel her warm and kicking. Pushing out a breech baby was very different from the vertex (head first) delivery I had experienced four and a half years before. During this pushing time my daughter Loi woke up, not during my roaring, but just when Oceana was delivering. Loi integrated remarkably well what was happening—the room was filled with people, there was the foot of her sister sticking out of her mother, and she took all this in her stride. During a contraction my attention would focus, as in a tunnel, on the task at hand and in between contractions I played hostess, film director, audio technician, and mother to my Loi. When the doctor asked Loi whether she would like to have a sister or a brother she replied that either the baby is a boy or a girl. She said this very phenomenologically and without a hint of preference.

The birth process itself taught me how to deliver a breech. Once the breech baby's head entered my birth canal, I felt I could get some traction by pushing on it from within with my abdominal muscles. The baby slid right out. There she lay beneath me (I was still on all fours, holding onto my husband's body for leverage) and the room filled with violet colored light. The baby was indeed quite purple. The doctor said, "There she is Jeannine; now get your baby going." Since I had been at births with this doctor, he knew my capability and allowed me this greatest privilege, of being the one to massage and cuddle my baby into breath. When she began her sputtering we were all quite moved and I was in bliss.

"My baby, my baby," I kept crooning over and over. There are only a few times my voice sounds like that—when having orgasms, when birthing babies, and when praying.

"We still have another one in there, don't forget," the nurse's efficient voice reminded us. And no sooner said than I felt a wave of expulsion take me over.

"Oh, here it comes!" With the help of my friends I turned over to a seated pose, holding my first twin in my arms as the second one came into my birth canal. She was coming so fast! What a rush I felt and ecstasy filled me to the brim.

"Don't spurt her out, don't spurt her!" The doctor's voice came through to me and I only pushed once to have her on my perineum, a gush of waters about her now crowning head. I breathed slowly and delivered her into one arm in a matter of seconds, stretching easily and painlessly. There was our Cheyenne, all pink and crying from her quick entrance. The room filled with coral colored light and I scooped her up next to her sister and held them both close to my breasts. The second twin arrived just seven minutes after the first. The sun was streaming in and it was a warm clear day.

True to my "Three Musketeers" form, I then began a good post-partum hemorrhage and delivered the placenta amidst more than the usual amount of blood. The doctor said, for the last time, "Mother Nature is giving you a sign to return to the hospital." I merely asked for my herb teas, all handy now at home, and stopped bleeding in a few minutes.

"Well, you were right once about Mother Nature," said the doctor, "so I guess I'll just have to trust you again."

What a marvelous lesson for him, to learn to trust the birthing woman as being the one who knows best what is going on!

Infertility
and Adoption

ABBY JOAN SYLVIACHILD

1975, The Midwest

We have always been planners. We planned our educations, our travels abroad, our garden rows, and our childbearing. We planned to get pregnant when things were just right. We thought that having a child would be another accomplishment we could complete by choice, like the new house or job or degree. But the supposedly simple act of getting pregnant can sometimes turn out to be much harder than we think. Months and menstrual periods go by without any sign that our bodies are aware of our longings, dreams and hopes. Our bodies betray us by being beyond our control. Like so many infertile couples, our feelings began with surprise and shock, then led to disappointment, denial of the reality, anger, isolation, depression, guilt, appeasement, then finally grief and mourning for the biological child never-to-be. Finally we came to some resolution as we planned, again, to reach our goal of parenthood another way.

My own reproductive history started out without a hint of the sadness to come. I had a positive pregnancy test after three cycles without birth control. Everything was fine until eight weeks past my last menstrual period. I stained; but my obstetrician wasn't too worried. Light staining of blood is fairly common in the first months of pregnancy. But ten days later, contractions woke me at 4:40 A.M., a night when it was eight degrees below zero outside. We made the hurried long trip to the hospital, were installed in a room on the labor and delivery floor, and a decision was made to do a D & C (dilation and curettage). Even then, I was so caught up in the mechanics of my medical care that I didn't think this miscarriage was too unusual or that it was, in fact, the beginning of a very long quest for children. After all, I was "only" twenty-nine; I hadn't had "trouble" getting pregnant; and I was too scared to think about the "what if's." But it was a loss: a lost pregnancy, a dead fetus. Our baby died. The pain stayed inside long past the time when the contractions ceased. It was a miscarriage of what was to have been, what would have been, our child.

A year passed. I began to read about infertility, furtively, because I wasn't yet identifying myself as infertile. I began to chart my Basal Body Temperature (BBT).[1] In the beginning, BBT's give you a positive sense of knowing what your body is doing. But by the end, the thermometer is a hateful daily reminder of all the disappointments—month after month, year after year, doctor after doctor. The thermometer began to tell us when to make love, and making love became a "project" of sex on days eleven, thirteen, fifteen and seventeen or ten, twelve, fourteen, and sixteen.

While using the thermometer is at least a private affair, our cycles, temperatures, and times we had intercourse became public information at the doctor's office. This information is used to schedule office visits, when cervical mucus is measured, endometrial lining is biopsied, semen is analyzed. What most of us consider a very private part of our lives becomes a part of medical treatment. And despite the knowledgeable physicians who are Board Certified Reproductive Endocrinologists (the official term for infertility specialists), most infertile people have to cope with the dreadful and constant feelings of infertility by themselves, because the specialists are not interested, don't themselves know how to cope with these powerful emotions, don't have the time in a busy office and surgical schedule to even find out how we're coping.

One out of every six couples of reproductive age is infertile and at last there is an organization for us, RESOLVE, Inc., a national, nonprofit, grass-roots organization giving information, support, referrals, and counseling to people with infertility.[2] In the forty-five local chapters around the country, people like me can find others to talk to about the effects of infertility on their personal lives, and we can compare notes on diagnostic tests, treatments, and doctors. Through RESOLVE I found out that I was not "crazy" for crying every time I got my period and that it was not "unbalanced" to have feelings of jealousy and anger toward every pregnant woman I saw, whether among my family, friends, or strangers on the street. Through RESOLVE I learned that what seems an obsession to others—perhaps even to our husbands—is just the way this life crisis behaves: infertility takes over our lives entirely until we resolve it. I found out that not being able to look at or be in the same room with anybody else's baby or small child is also "normal" for infertiles. And I discovered that while fifty percent of us will be helped to achieve a successful pregnancy and give birth to a baby, many of the rest of us will be able to build our families through adoption. Through RESOLVE I learned what my options were.

Infertility can become the center of a couple's life. It is only when the difficulty of the treatments and the small percentages of success seem not worth the trouble, and when we realize that we want to have a child with or without a pregnancy, that the option of adoption becomes the next and very positive step. Many couples refuse to consider adoption when they are in the thick of their infertility work-up. They think that even considering adoption means that they are giving up on their infertility. But it is possible and even common for couples to look into adoption and continue their medical treatments at the same time.

In our case, after the miscarriage and another fifteen months of "trying," I had a year of infertility investigation—monthly office visits, tests, hormone medications—with a very old-fashioned, dogmatic, and sexist specialist (who had been highly recommended) and then switched to a more modern but hardly feminist one. For another year I endured a few dozen more blood tests, endometrial biopsies, post-coital cervical mucus exams, a diagnostic laparoscopy with an hysterosalpingogram and a D & C, and then major abdominal surgery for endometriosis.[3] At each stage and with each test, I'd hope that they would find something specific that was treatable, rather than just "normal infertility." At least with a diagnosis of endometriosis, there was solid information available and known percentages of success.

After these three years we were reaching the limit of our ability to be infertile and childless (we thought). There is a six to twelve month optimum time in which to get pregnant after conservative surgery for endometriosis. At about that time we became very serious about adopting a child. We investigated every available piece of information and learned about the various routes of adoption open to us.[4] In the U.S.A. we could choose between public or private agencies or independent, also called private, adoption. We could also adopt abroad through an international adoption agency, perhaps in Mexico, Central or South America, or in Asian countries like Korea or India. By then we were in a hurry, so we tried everything. We started a home study locally for a Korean child, put our names on every agency list in the state, and went to every adoption information meeting and agency orientation that we could. We also started "putting out the word" that we were hoping to adopt a baby. We began to tell everyone we knew, and had our families and friends do the same, and we followed up all the leads we heard about, no matter how strange. Within two months we heard that someone knew someone who knew someone who knew a pregnant woman who was considering adoption for the baby. From that phone call on we were so exhilarated at our chance to be parents, and so frightened that it might not work out, that we could hardly concentrate.

The elevator ride up to the nursery floor of a small community hospital was the most intensely exciting moment of my life. I was about to meet my newborn daughter. After three and a half years of doctors, tests, temperature charts, drugs, surgeries, X-rays, a miscarriage, and the depression, sadness, and loneliness of being among dear friends with children, I was at last becoming a parent.

Although the events leading up to my daughter's being placed in my arms are certainly not the usual pregnancy-labor-and-delivery ones, I went through many feelings and emotional stages, some common to all expectant parents, as I waited for our first child. I wondered if the birthparents would follow through with their plans to let us adopt this baby. I was scared that they would change their minds. I wondered when this baby would be born, since not knowing an exact due date meant not planning anything, not even telling anyone about the possibility.

Sometimes I wondered happy, lazy thoughts—as I weeded my vegetables more vigorously that summer than any summer since—about the baby's sex, size, and looks. I wondered in a worried way about the baby's health, since I had no control over the nutrition, vitamins, toxic substances, or other things affecting this pregnancy. Along with that, I also worried about the birth itself, hoping it would be spontaneous, non-traumatic, and unmedicated. I worried about Apgar scores and about fingers and toes like everyone else does. Things I didn't worry about, things I took for granted and assumed, were that I would love this baby, that she would be my own child, that we would be a family forever.

An 8:30 A.M. telephone call saying, "It's a girl, very big, very healthy," was our first information about our daughter. It came when she was about fifteen hours old. A day later we told her four grandparents that, if all went well, we'd have our baby girl in two more days. We chose my grandmother's name for her but didn't dare to buy a single baby item until the papers were signed. It would have been too cruel to look at tiny new baby things in our home if the adoption hadn't taken place.

The morning of that exciting day, we were up and dressed early to go to the county court house. There we were interviewed about our ages, address, marriage, and state residency. The birthparents had had a parallel experience before us. We had a quick hearing in front of a judge who asked us if we were aware that adoption meant our taking on the "care, custody, and control" of this baby for the rest of our lives. Of course we were aware! That was the whole object of becoming parents by adoption: to be our child's parents. At the time I couldn't believe the judge really asked us that, though I didn't make a peep in the courtroom.

From court we went to the hospital, an easy and familiar drive that seemed to take forever. We stopped only to call our parents. Mine were waiting back East for our call so that they could jump on the first airplane to be with us at this exciting time.

I will never forget riding up that hospital elevator, with our attorney who had to check the baby out of the hospital. Seeing our baby daughter for the first time, in a tiny examining room on the maternity floor, was dreamlike. Here was this *beautiful* baby who was going to me *mine/ours.* I watched the nurse dressing her. I was entranced, though holding back. I don't know why I didn't just pick her up and hug her, but I guess I still felt that maybe it was not going to happen, that something else would happen to keep me from being a "Mommy."

Finally all the paperwork of hospital checking-out was completed and a volunteer brought a wheelchair for me, just the way they do for every other new mom, even though I had walked in there by myself just twenty minutes before. A nurse held my daughter all the way down the elevator and out the front door to the car. Then, at last, she put the baby in my arms in the car and wished us good luck.

We had only one hospital pack of formula, so we stopped at our corner drugstore for our first baby shopping: formula, bottles, nipples, cotton and alcohol for her navel, a box of diapers until diaper service started, and a baby thermometer. We took several instant print photos and mailed them right away to her other grandparents, who would come to visit the very next weekend.

At home we just sat and looked at her sleeping. We couldn't take our eyes off her. We watched her breathing, her face movements, the flexing of her fingers and toes. We were fascinated, falling in love, amazed, and in awe of such a miracle. We also didn't know what to do until she woke up and needed to be fed or changed. We phoned a few more family members and a friend who started calling our other friends to spread the good news.

My parents arrived within an hour of our return from the hospital. We ran out to greet them, hugged and kissed and cried, all four of us stumbling over each other on our way from the taxi to the front door with suitcases and a huge plastic sack of a dozen stuffed animals and toys. One of my dad's customers, upon hearing of his new grand-fatherhood, had collected one of each of his products to take to us. They almost needed an extra airplane seat for the animals!

The baby was asleep on our bed when her grandparents saw her for the first time. They beamed; they exclaimed; they cooed about her beauty, her size, her loveliness, her skin, her hands. We all felt so filled with incredibly good feelings. After she woke up, we all worked on changing and feeding her, with much discussion of the right temperature for the bottle, whether the water to dilute the formula had to be boiled (yes, until she was four weeks old said the pediatri-cian later), and how often to burp her. She helpfully fell asleep after two and a half ounces, so we all could relax again and watch her sleep. This was a most fascinating activity and one which, before the day I became a mother, I had never even known about.

After about an hour, my parents borrowed our car to go shopping for "their baby." Our few borrowed clothes weren't enough. In two hours they returned with just about a full layette: a beautiful white wicker basinette, blankets, little shirts, stretchies, wash cloths and towels, diapers, sheets, pads, more toys, a diaper bag, and a clown mobile with a music box singing a song from my dad's childhood. We washed everything, but in the muggy midwestern summer nothing dried on the line. The next day our baby's grandparents bought a clothes dryer for "their new baby granddaughter."

By supper, we were exhausted. We were all floating on clouds of happiness and incredibly high on this one little baby. We fed and changed her a few more times before we all went to sleep. The first time she woke us at 1:00 A.M., I really didn't know where I was (in the living room on the sleepersofa) or what was happening. Her cries seemed so loud in the otherwise silent house. She seemed so intensely hungry. We tried to get the bottle warmed up as quickly as we could, but she woke her grandparents anyway. My mom took over this feeding and I gratefully snuggled back under the covers for another three hours of sleep. By 4:30 A.M. my arms and legs felt leaden when I tried to move out of bed for her feeding. I wondered how anyone could continue to function after a night of being awake for forty-five minutes every three hours.

In the morning, the most ordinary things seemed changed. Everything was revolving around the baby. My thoughts were: is she up? is she wet? is the formula warm? do we have more pins for the diapers? can the basinette go out on the patio? do we need mosquito netting? How busy we were—all four grown people not finishing our breakfasts without running to look at her, do some laundry of hers, wash and boil her bottles and nipples, call some more friends and family, get referrals for a pediatrician in town for her first visit. And in between, we all smiled at each other as we bent over the basinette to look at her and listen to her breathe, watching her turn her head from side to side, yawn, or sneeze.

That day progressed like a carnival, with telephone calls ringing in with congratulations and friends stopping by to welcome our daughter. They brought with them treasured collections of their own children's outgrown baby equipment and clothes to share. A car seat, stroller, car bed, swingomatics, playpen, high chair, infant seats, baby bath, and changing table arrived until the patio looked like a babyland garage sale, with all the stuff being scrubbed clean and drying in the sun. My friends had saved their kids' stuff for my child-to-be, whenever she would arrive. Before, when I was suffering with my infertility and childlessness, they had agreed among themselves not to talk about their children when I was around. I did not know about their consideration until much later. I felt so much more connected to all of them now that we were sharing this mothering experience and now that they could talk "mother talk" freely with me.

Adoption is another way of building families; for after our child is with us, the same issues of sleeping through the night, parent exhaustion, learning to parent, coping with the first fever, bad diaper rash, ear infections, enjoying, worrying, teaching and learning with our child, and all the other wonderful and frustrating parts of being a family occur whether we have adopted or given birth to our child.

Poem for the Broken Cup
for David and Anne

KATE JENNINGS

The way I winced as my elbow hit it,
then even before it hit the floor
the frenzy of weeping, astonishing

the children, who stared in stunned
silence for fully five seconds before
the baby wailed in fear and David

joined in sympathy while I dried my
eyes and tried to explain to him, to
ease the terror my tears had caused:

Not the cup, I said, though the cup
was lovely, white mellowed these nine
years to cream, with its Potter

pictures of Peter Rabbit, and the
sweet frieze of green leaves on the
handle: not the cup, but it was

yours, I bought it for you four years
before you were born, just at the very
beginning, just when we were starting

to recognize that getting you was going
to take more work than simply making
love: and all those barren years

in Queens, I used to drink my morning
coffee from that cup as though that cup
were magic, as though it could change

things—And I started to cry again,
closing my eyes against his frightened
uncomprehending face: the scalding

realization that even though I have them
now, those two, the scars of those years
are still with me and always will be:

and standing in spilled milk and shards
of china, crying and not even trying to stop,
scaring my children, I cried My cup! The cup!

Doing It Myself

JANET ISAACS ASHFORD

1976, North Aurora, Illinois

Friday, December 3

After a night of sporadic and increasingly painful contractions, I decided to commit myself to being in labor for yet another day. It was the third day past my due date. For the past few days I had had several false starts; contractions would cluster together and then dissipate. I would say to myself, "I think I'm going to be in labor now," and then nothing would happen but more waiting. I tried timing the contractions, but as soon as I got out the watch they would stop. I ended up restless and annoyed, feeling like a watched pot. I tried to rest in bed as much as possible, to be ready for the coming exertion, but the contractions woke me early Friday morning and I was too agitated to sleep any longer.

So far the contractions were not very painful, except when the baby kicked me in the bladder during one. I felt them mainly as aching, pulling sensations in the area of my cervix and sometimes the pulling radiated through to my lower back. There was also some rectal pressure during the contractions, which made me suspect that I had a bowel movement due. Along with the ache, I felt the usual Braxton-Hicks, fist-tightening of my upper uterus and also a new fluttery feeling around my heart, which seemed to signal the beginning of a contraction. The contractions were long, about a minute and a half, and each one was unique, combining sensations in a slightly different way. In all, I felt not very uncomfortable, but not overwhelmed by a sense of well-being.

Until Friday morning I had felt clogged up and stuck in time, as though I could never get this labor to move. But now I could feel a sense of something beginning to change, as though the birth were now visible on the horizon and coming toward me. As the sun came up I sat alone, rocking by the window, and felt myself to be finally in position at the very center of the universe. In my mind I saw an image of deep space, lit by various suns, and then, coming closer, our own round world and on it the big lakes and the state of Illinois. I saw the Fox River meandering through the snowbanks; then our house by the river, then myself in my rocking chair, then the baby inside of me. This progression from large to small gave me a feeling of great pleasure. For a moment I felt perfectly balanced between being connected to everything and yet alone. I felt meshed fast in the fabric of world being, yet driven by the urgency of one particular, special event.

Vic was still asleep. I got up and started cleaning the house again, feeling compelled to put everything in its place. My desire for order was annoyingly compulsive but I could not abandon it. The house had to be straightened up or else the baby could not come out! I knew when our dog was about to go into labor because she scratched and clawed at the rags and newspapers in her box and turned round and round trying to make herself comfortable there. I was doing the same thing.

At noon I took a deep, hot bath and regarded my belly. The baby's feet and elbows visibly rippled my skin as it moved inside of me. It seemed odd to think about a time when the baby would be outside of me and my belly would no longer rise up out of the water. After my bath, Vic put his fingers into my vagina to feel my cervix and said that it seemed to be one and a half to two centimeters dilated. We decided it was too early to call the birth crew. Vic went to the store to buy food for the birth and I lay down to rest. When Vic got back he joined me in bed and we both slept until late afternoon. I was awakened several times by strong, painful contractions, but I slept deeply between them. Then I got up to sit on the toilet and my mucous plug came out! I could actually feel it sliding down my vagina. I looked into the toilet bowl and found a little stringy, bloody mucus floating in the water and a large glob of light brownish-yellow mucus on the paper.

By early evening my contractions were quite strong and well-defined and painful enough that I had to pay attention to them and do slow, deliberate breathing. The contractions were quite far apart though, coming only every ten to fifteen minutes. After dinner I went back to bed for a nap. I slept and my relaxation brought on several painful contractions, closer together. These were hard to handle because I was half awake and not paying attention. I got up again and had a snack. So far, the early labor had not dulled my appetite.

Vic had his stacks of computer print-out paper from work spread out on the table. I found it difficult to imagine how he could concentrate on anything other than me. My contractions were becoming more painful and I was developing a headache. I thought it might be time to call the birth crew, but hesitated in distaste at having them all milling around. I was becoming crabby and discouraged; I thought, how long is this going to last? How much more painful will it get? I had a hard time thinking about the baby or caring about its being born. I brooded over Vic's preoccupation for a while and then told him how I was feeling. He looked surprised and promptly put aside his work.

"I didn't know you were feeling this way," he said, "I didn't know anything was happening."

We sat down and played a few hands of cards and then watched television together. Vic made me a sandwich, which I ate with a small glass of beer. I felt much better. We talked about the day and I said that I was disappointed the baby had not been born yet, after waiting around for it all day, but I was glad that we had a chance to get the house picked up and everything ready. Tomorrow would be Saturday, a day off from work. I was glad we hadn't called the birth crew yet.

Saturday, December 4

Just after midnight I had a loose, expulsive bowel movement which felt good. I seemed to be having the bowel-cleansing, pre-labor diarrhea I had read about. My contractions continued, but they varied so greatly in intensity and frequency that I decided I must be going through false labor or prelude to labor or onset of labor but definitely not *labor* labor. I looked up my symptoms in various books but couldn't come to a definite conclusion. I decided to just go to bed and wait to see what would happen next.

I lay in bed for a few hours, sleeping lightly and feeling very relaxed. Soon I began having strong contractions close together. I had to breathe through all of them, so I couldn't go deeply to sleep. More blood-tinged mucus came out. At 3:30 A.M. I was too restless to stay in bed any longer and got up to sit in the rocking chair again. I wondered if these contractions would go away or continue. After a few hours Vic got up and started recording my contractions on a piece of paper. I asked him not to tell me the times, because it made me too nervous.

At daybreak I ate a light breakfast. My contractions were coming continuously at about four to five minutes, with no lapses. Each one seemed to be longer and stronger than the one before. Vic checked my cervix again and announced that I was about two centimeters dilated and fully effaced. It became necessary for Vic to help me with my increasing discomfort by pushing on my lower back during each contraction. It became clear that this was labor.

The moment we acknowledged the fact of being in labor, I felt a rush of adrenalin through my blood and my stomach filled with butterflies. I got up and paced around the room between contractions. I felt as though I had actually walked out the door and was already halfway down the street on the beginning of a great journey.

"This is it now, isn't it?" I said to Vic, "I'm going to start getting the supplies ready."

With great pleasure I went to the bedroom and took down the neatly wrapped packages of brown paper and string. I opened the one filled with sterilized sheets and made up the bed. Then I took a last, hot bath and while I was soaking Vic brought me a cup of hot tea with lemon, honey and brandy. I felt warm and relaxed. I combed my wet hair and plaited it into a single long braid down my back. I opened the package containing my blue and yellow birth gown and my blue knee socks and put them on with delight. Then I climbed up onto the bed.

Sitting up at the edge of the bed, leaning forward and hugging onto Vic, I breathed slowly and carefully with each contraction while Vic pressed my lower back with both hands, his arms around me. The pain at this point was about as strong as a bad case of menstrual cramps, the sort that two aspirin tablets and a nap would relieve. I felt I was able to handle it well, especially since the worst pain lasted only a few seconds and between the contractions there was no pain at all. We continued like this for about an hour and a half. I felt very safe and comfortable with Vic's arms around me. I buried my face into his chest and shoulder during the bad part of each contraction, and felt his soft beard against my cheek. The rest of the time we looked at each other and talked.

"Do you think we should call the birth crew now?" asked Vic, after a while.

"Oh, yes, I suppose we should. What time is it?"

Vic looked at his watch. "It's eleven."

"Okay. You go call. I'll stay here."

Vic went into the living room to the phone. He called Walt and Pat first and talked briefly. I felt another contraction coming. I took a deep breath and leaned forward onto my hands to receive it. It was not so bad, but I liked it better when Vic was with me. I heard him calling the bookstore, where the rest of the birth crew worked. He talked for a while. Another contraction came and I decided to lie down for it. I rolled over onto my side and curled up my knees so that my back was curved. It was a little harder that time to go through the contraction alone.

Vic came back. "Everybody's getting ready to come over," he said. "Do you want to sit up again, against me?"

"No, I think I want to stay lying down. Will you get me a pillow though, for my head?" Vic put a pillow under my head and a blanket over me.

"Did you turn up the heater?" I asked.

"Yes."

"It has to be warm for the baby."

The phone rang and Vic went away again. I had another contraction; it was very painful and I felt myself being drawn down into a different world where Vic's voice sounded very far away.

It seemed like a long time before Vic came back. I asked him to press on my back, while I was lying down. He did and it seemed to help the pain, but sometimes he did not find the right place to push.

Time went by and I became more and more fuzzy and lost. The doorbell rang and Vic went to answer it. It was Rick C., the first to arrive. I heard his voice at the door, sounding excited and shy, but when he came in the bedroom he looked worried at the sight of me, his brow furrowed. I tried hard to say something that would reassure him, but I just couldn't. Why is he looking at me like that? There is nothing wrong with me. I didn't want to see a worried face, it drained my strength. Go away, I thought, and Rick backed out of the room. It was 12:30.

I was now deeply in pain. The bad pain seemed to have come on very suddenly, almost at once. It seemed that only a few moments before the pain had been small, smaller than the size of my head. Then suddenly it was big and it seemed that I had been in pain for a long time. Always. I tried hard to keep my breathing steady and slow, but as the pain of each contraction built up, it kept going and going and went too far and I had to hold my breath and tense up to keep it back.

Each pain began in my cervix. It was small at first, just a dull, achey feeling, but it gained rapidly in intensity until it had become a dense centrifugal force, spreading out, shoving its way through resisting tissue. The area of pain was disk-shaped, about two inches thick. It angled through my pelvic region from groin to lower back, with my cervix at its center. Through this region the pain proceeded thickly, spreading from the center like concentric ripples in a pool of honey. When it reached the edges of my body it threatened to keep on going, to expand beyond my skin. It was the worst pain I have felt in my life;

horrible, awful. I didn't think it would be like this. "It hurts," I said to Vic, and my voice sounded far away and incredulous.

"I can see that it does," said Vic. His voice was very kind and soft, but he couldn't make the pain go away.

The door bell rang again. Vic opened the bedroom door and I heard a confusion of voices. It was everyone; excited, laughing and talking. Vic didn't linger with them, but came back to me. "Shut the door," I said, "They're making too much noise. I don't want anyone to be with me, except you."

The pain kept going. It got worse. The relaxation exercises were useless now. Stupid. With each contraction I wriggled and clenched my fists and held my breath against it. I screwed up my face, oh, ooohhh, my breath coming out in gasps, in small moans. My toes curled under; I couldn't believe it! I had never been in such a bad place before. After each contraction there was a moment of rest before the next one. I lay there exhausted, drained. Then another one would begin. Oh, no! I dread it, I dread it. I was struggling again.

I was still lying on my side. I kept my head low and tucked down away from the light. Where is my mother? I want her to help me. I remembered when I used to be sick as a child and my mother would hold me and make me feel better. She was very big. She could surround me. I wanted to go down, down, somewhere, close to someone's big lap.

"Vic, can you do. . .do. . .something?" I made sentences in my mind but I couldn't speak them. Vic was bending over me. "What do you want me to do?" he whispered.

"Press my back hard," I said, "really hard." He pressed when the next contraction came.

"Like that?"

"That's. . .not. . .no."

"Harder?"

"Yes."

"I can't get into a good position. How about like this?" He gripped my drawn-up knees with one hand and my back with the other and pressed me hard together like a vise.

"Yes, do that." I got through the contraction.

The door bell rang far away. Vic didn't move. The door opened and I heard Walt's voice. Pat! Where's Pat? I wanted to see Pat, Walt's wife. She was the only one who had had a baby before. Maybe she could tell me what was happening. Where am I? I don't know what stage of labor I am in. Walt came into the bedroom and smiled at me, a big smile. What? He's not worried? "Looks like you're coming right along," he said. I felt good. Walt's smiling made me feel very light for a moment. "Where's Pat?" I asked.

"Pat can't come," he said. "Janette got sick and our baby sitter got sick too, at the last minute."

"Oh," I sank down again. It was 1:30.

Another one was coming. "Press hard, press hard!" The contraction was exploding. I thought I might fly apart but Vic saved me. He held me together. We were both struggling now. I could feel Vic's arms trembling when he squeezed me. He was pressing as hard as he could.

Why won't this pain leave me alone? I wanted to scream. When the next pain comes, if it gets any worse, I'm going to. . . But I couldn't. If I opened my mouth to scream I'd be lost. I'd never be able to stop. I'd scream and scream and frighten everyone and things would get out of control and they might take me away to the. . .

The house was very quiet. No one was laughing. I heard whispers in the next room and quiet walking. I was starting to sleep. Something was happening and I was falling, going down, and my uterus was going. . .it was floating! My uterus left my body and floated up to the ceiling. It hovered there in the northeast corner of the room, straining by itself. I could see it contract but I couldn't feel it anymore. It was gone. There was no pain. Oh! My uterus. I must be very still. If I don't move at all I can rest for a while. There is no pain. I couldn't have stood it any longer. My uterus finally left. Vic moved away from me. He didn't press on my back because I didn't ask him to. I must not speak. I am very low, submerged, somewhere. My thoughts are very small. I am resting in a very small place in my brain, right in the middle, away from my eyes and ears. I must lie very still. My uterus kept contracting but I didn't feel it. It went on like that for a while, for seven, eight contractions. I prayed Vic wouldn't talk to me. I was resting. It was gone. I was sleeping.

Crash! I came splashing back up to the surface again. The room was full of light and sound and color. My uterus shot back into my body and the pain came back with it. I have to get out of here! I'm going to get up off the bed and walk around. The pain will stay on the bed and I will stand to the side of it. Will that work? I'm going outside. I'll run out the front door before anyone can stop me and the pain won't be able to catch up with me. I'll run down as far as the library, through the snow. It won't be too cold, if I am running. No? I'm going to ask someone to get me a hammer. Rick? Go downstairs and get me the big hammer, not the ballpeen one, the big claw hammer; it's on the work bench. Bring it up here and hit me in the head with it. Okay? Then I can go down again, where I was before. Where I can't feel the pain.

Vic was squeezing me again. I would make a groan and he would squeeze me. The pain was still going on, endlessly. But then—what is that? I felt something pressing on me inside. It felt like something pushing. It was. . .it was my uterus pushing! Oh! It can't be time for that yet, can it? It feels so difficult. There is so much resistance inside. I can't be dilated yet, can I? My uterus pushed again. It was doing it by itself. I can't stop it, can I, so what can I do? Is it time for me to start bearing down? It can't be time yet.

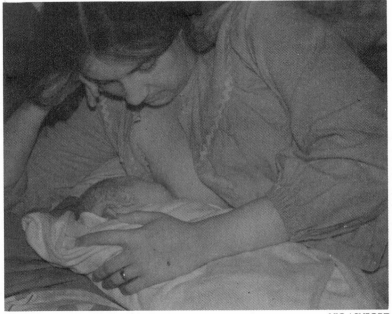

VIC ASHFORD

The contractions kept coming. Each one of them pushed. I started to feel that I would have to push too. I tried joining in, very carefully. I pushed with my stomach muscles, just a little. . .but, whoa, my uterus grabbed me and drove me along with itself. I couldn't push just a little. It had to be a lot. It did feel like pushing with a bowel movement, the books were right about that, only it's so huge! It was so powerful and uncontrollable. I might push myself inside out if I went too far. But who cares? I didn't try to hold back anymore. I pushed hard. I grabbed onto Vic, onto the folds of his clothes. I held my breath and pushed as hard as I could and it felt good. It felt better. The contractions didn't hurt so much any more. It was exciting. I'm pushing!

Pop! I heard a noise and fluid rushed out all over the bed.

"Oh, jeez!" cried Vic.

"Oh," I said, laughing, "the membranes broke!" I was startled back into speech and felt awake for a moment. The membranes. Vic grabbed a clean towel and mopped up the fluid. He put dry cloths under me.

"Something must be happening," he said, "You must be coming along." He looked at his watch. "It's three o'clock. The membranes broke at three o'clock."

I kept on pushing. I didn't care what happened. Little bits of feces came out during some of the contractions and I felt Vic wipe them away.

Now I was only pushing, still lying on my side. I had been pushing for a long time, it seemed, but I could keep doing it longer. Then, what's that? There was something in me, in my vagina. Something big and hard. What is it doing in there? How did it get in there? I reached down with my hand to feel what it was. Something was right there at the opening, only a few inches inside. It felt squishy and soft, covered with wet folds. Is it part of me? It's. . .I was starting to wake up. I pressed on it. Does it feel hard? It does! It's hard underneath the soft part. There is a hard bone under there. It's the head! The baby's head! I had forgotten. I have to push the baby out now. It's coming out. I have to tell Vic. Oh, I'm pushing again. I have to sit up. I'm supposed to be sitting up when I have the baby. But I don't want to move. I'm pushing again. No, I have to do something or it will just come out. No one will be here. No photographs. Where's Walt and the camera? Effort. Make an effort.

"Something. . ."

"What?" said Vic.

"Something there."

Vic looked. He didn't say anything. He backed out of the room and whispered, "It's time!"

Now everyone was coming in and there was talking. Rick S. helped me to sit up. He fixed the pillows behind me and lifted me up and up until I was sitting. Rick C. brought in a pan and arranged things on the table. Vic was in front of me, looking hard at my vagina, looking at the baby's head.

There were people all around me now. Rick S. was on my right side, holding on to my hand. When I pushed, he pushed too and squeezed my hand and concentrated so hard with me that I felt my mind drawn sharply to his side, as though I was leaning. Bill was on the left, grasping my leg, but then he left and Penny took his place and

Josephine. They were not as strong as Rick and couldn't counter-
balance the weight of his empathy. Bill adjusted a microphone on a
boom in front of me. I saw it for an instant, then it faded into oblivion.
I was pushing. In the far distance, I heard Walt's camera clicking. Rick
C. was standing by the table, bustling and moving things around. I
was pushing. Vic was right in front of me.

The contractions seemed farther apart now, with spaces of at least a
minute between them. When my uterus reared up to push, I bore
down with it as hard as I could, drawing several gasping breaths. Then
came a rest. I leaned back on my pillows and was completely quiet, inside myself. I could barely see. I felt dazed, but determined. Only
pushing was happening now. There was no more pain, but this hardly
mattered. I heard voices float toward me as through water. "Good!"
"Janet." "Look!" These were the voices of my friends and they sounded pleasant and encouraging but superfluous. I heard everything but
did not speak. Everyone kept out of my way. Penny reached forward
once to stroke my belly with her hand. "Ughh!" I groaned and looked
at her face for one focussed moment. What is she doing? She
withdrew her hand quickly, almost in fear, as though I was an animal.
Good. Don't touch me. I am pushing. That's all I am doing.

It seemed like a long time that I was sitting up and pushing, but then
Vic said, "Pant," and the time suddenly collapsed down into seconds.
What? Is it time already? I panted. The head was coming. "Now,
push," said Vic. The contraction was over and I pushed on my own, to
bring the head out smoothly. This was what we planned, yes. Is it happening already? I pushed as hard as I could. Yes, yes, yes, oh,
yes. . .oh, it's so huge. I have to get it out, out! It's so. . .oh! I felt a
burning. All around the opening it burned, just as it said in the books,
yes, just as it said. "More wetness!" I cried. Vic rubbed more lubricant
onto me, but by then I couldn't feel it; I had gone numb. Through the
watery air, the voices drifted toward me with soft phrases of excitement and praise. Another contraction came. I panted, sighing now in a
high voice with each breath. It ended, I pushed, holding my breath
and then grunting out at the end to grab a new breath.

"This has to stretch a little more," said Vic, concentrating hard. His
eyes and hands were focussed only on the place between my legs. The
next contraction came and I panted through it. "It's coming! It's coming!" said Vic, as the contraction faded. "A little push. A little push,"
he called softly to me, absorbed in his work, and I obliged and then he
cried out, in an intense whisper, "Ah, its face! Who's got the syringe?"

"It's out?" I asked. I hadn't felt it, only a burning numbness.

"Yes, it's out," said Vic, laughing with excitement. "A little push. A
little push now."

"Is it turned yet?" I asked, trying to picture what was happening.

"No, give it another little shove to get its head all the way out." I pushed again and then heard cries of "Oh, yes! Oh, great!" from all around me. The head was all the way out! I leaned back a little, incredulous. It's almost over now. The baby will be born?

"Doesn't seem to have any cord," said Vic, feeling around the baby's neck. Then, incredibly, I felt the baby's body moving, undulating inside me. "Here, its head is coming. Its head is turning," Vic whispered.

"Oh, I feel another contraction." I pushed again as hard as I could. This would be the last time, I knew it would. I could get it all out. Oh!!! I felt a succession of wet and knobby parts slither past me deliciously. So good, so good to get it out! I felt like speaking, at last—like speaking with my whole insides one great, warm and slippery, long-awaited word. The baby rushed outward all at once and seemed to splash against the air.

Now I was suddenly completely alert and clear-headed, as though a heavy fog had been torn away from my mind. I sat forward and looked at the baby. In one second I comprehended its wholeness, making an assessment of waving, glistening tubular limbs. Yes, perfect. All my peripheral vision was blank and there was only this baby in the center. It was shining in a clear, bright, and luminescent way, all covered with glowing white vernix and with pearly purplish-pink skin underneath. I looked at its face. It was perfect, a whole face. Walt cried out, "Boy!" and other voices echoed, "It's Rufus!" A stab of disappointment shot through me; not because it was a boy, but because I had wanted to see for myself. I was still busy looking at the face, carefully, carefully. Be quiet, everyone. The baby's eyes were closed but other things were happening. I saw a flush of pink pumping into the skin, spreading ever so steadily. There was no cry, no sound and the mouth was closed and calm. But the nose! The soft nostrils were flaring and I could see the breath passing. Expressions flashed like twitches across the muscles of the face, like cloud shadows chasing each other across a plain on a hard, blowy day. There was tension in the body; he held himself. The baby was alive.

"Hold him up with his head down," I said, suddenly remembering the prescribed procedure. Vic took Rufus by the ankles and shoulder and held him head down. His head was suspended and I reached for it to cup and support it. Rufus was very quiet and everyone was waiting for a sound. Vic pumped Rufus gently, bending him at the waist. I tapped the soles of his feet with my fingers. "Eeeeer?" said Rufus, letting out a single, small cry. High and clear, it sounded through a garble of mucus in his throat and created a momentary, absolute silence in the room. Then the air collapsed in sighs from everyone around me. "Four thirty-five," announced Walt. Everyone was moving and sighing and breathing. Suddenly, Vic was kissing me and my mouth felt caked and dry. Is it over now? Is this the end? The birth was over.

That first night the three of us slept deeply and I had no dreams. I awoke at six in the morning and thought at first that it was Christmas. It felt as though there was something wonderful in the house, some great present. Then I remembered the baby. I looked over and saw him sleeping in his little bed, lying beneath the great mound of baby blankets with which I'd covered him. He was fast asleep, but I picked him up anyway, just to have him with me, and he nursed sleepily. Then I put him back in his bed, without even changing his diaper, because I didn't know yet what the things are you are supposed to do with a baby, other than hold him close and nurse him.

The second night, when Rufus woke me with his crying to nurse, I was tired and angry and didn't act sweetly toward him. Before dawn I had a bad nightmare. I dreamed that a young kid, a teenage punk wearing a white T-shirt and with pale, close-cropped hair, broke into our house in the night, came into our room, and hacked off big clumps of my hair with a razor. The dream woke me in the dark, and I felt frantically over my head to see if my hair was still there. When I awoke later my breasts were swollen hard with milk, throbbing and painful. I grabbed for Rufus, hoping he wasn't angry with me. But he sucked and sucked until my breasts were soft again. He was unaffected by my dreams and strange thoughts. He needed me and my milk to live.

On the third morning I was sitting in bed, nursing Rufus, and looking down at his beautiful face. His eyes, nose and mouth were perfectly shaped and seemed to be set so very perfectly into his smooth face that I could barely comprehend such great beauty. It seemed an ideal, an archetype of beauty. This image of his face burned itself into my brain. Then suddenly I felt as though I had stepped off a roller coaster and landed, smack, on solid ground again. The labor and birth, the next two days, had been tumultuous. Birth doesn't end when the baby comes out. You've built up such speed by then that it takes a few days to slow down. I sat there, feeling like I'd finally come to a stop, and then I realized—Hey, I did it! I wanted to have the baby at home and I read the books to figure out how and then I really did it! It worked! I didn't have to go to the hospital at all; the doctors didn't touch me! Then I realized that if I could do that great thing, perhaps I could do other things as well.

A Death and Then a Life

BILL LONDON

1978, Idaho

It was going to be a white Christmas—the beautiful snowy holiday season that makes you want to relax by a warm fire. We had just moved to northern Idaho and bought ten acres of forest land. The plans for our future log cabin were jumbled in my head. We had settled in for the winter in the second floor of a huge old farmhouse. Our first baby was due any day.

We were apprehensive, of course, but Gina was in good health and everything seemed to be just fine, except that we had no midwife; there were none in that rural area. However, several friends who had attended births or had babies were going to be present. We had attended a Lamaze childbirth preparation class and had read everything we could find.

Labor began at 4:00 A.M. on December 21, 1975. It was hard work from the beginning and after twenty-four hours Gina was tiring noticeably. But the baby was starting to crown and would be born at any moment; we knew that for sure. Still, Gina pushed for hours. I massaged her with wheat germ oil and all of us offered our encouragement. Finally, his head pushed through, and seconds later his body was out.

Our son was born grey and lifeless at 10:00 A.M. on the 22nd. No attempts at suction, patting, or resuscitation were successful. We were shocked beyond tears, beyond words. Soon most of those present had gone, while we stayed upstairs trying to understand, or even realize what had happened, and waiting for the delivery of the placenta.

After several hours of massages and teas, the placenta still had not been delivered. Though there was no bleeding, I thought we were all too exhausted to really know what to do. So I drove the several miles to the nearest phone with the intention of calling a doctor. On the way I was stopped by the county sheriff and the county coroner, summoned by a neighbor's call that there had been a death—or a murder —at the farmhouse.

The coroner, a doctor, asked to see the baby immediately. The atmosphere relaxed as he explained that it was obvious the baby had died during birth and his long skinny body was evidence of inadequate oxygen and/or food during the pregnancy. He just wasn't strong enough to survive the long labor. The doctor suggested we come to the hospital to deliver the placenta. The sheriff agreed, mentioning that he had a "few questions" for me.

Looking back on it now, that afternoon was surprisingly easy. The recriminations and accusations were subdued. It was probably obvious to everyone how distraught we were. The interview with the sheriff was mercifully short. The doctor gave Gina a dose of Pitocin and a hard massage to deliver the placenta. I asked for the body of our son to bury him on our land. We were able to take his body home with us that night.

Gina's placenta had ripped at some time during her pregnancy, the doctor discovered. There was no cause that we could ever recall. In a hospital delivery, with continuous fetal monitoring, the stress on the baby might have been noticed and with an induced labor or a cesarean, he might have been born alive. A home birth with a trained midwife might also have resulted in a live birth. In our ignorance and naive faith, we just assumed everything would work out. When it didn't, we took months to put the pieces back together again. What saved me was the possibility that somehow the stillbirth was the best result. Perhaps he would have been retarded, an incomplete person because of the oxygen starvation. No one could say, and though it was a thin straw to grab onto, I clutched it tightly.

We busied ourselves with our day-to-day affairs: the enormous effort involved in building a log cabin and making a life in our new forestland home. I was deadened by our stillbirth experience, but it was obvious that Gina still wanted and needed a child. So I wasn't very surprised, as we sat in our new home in the early summer of 1977, to hear that she was pregnant again.

Again Gina was healthy and it seemed to be a normal pregnancy. I was uncertain about where to have the baby. My beliefs and principles had been pretty well shattered. Gina decided. She wanted a home birth, but was willing to have the baby at a friend's home in town, within minutes of the hospital. I was satisfied with that decision, because I knew that it was a long half-mile from our cabin to where we had to park the truck in winter and another ten icy miles to town from there.

We searched for a midwife. One woman, in a town sixty miles away, had attended a dozen births and was just beginning to call herself a midwife. She agreed to come to our birthing.

On February 27, 1978, Gina's labor began. We walked up the hill and rushed to town, only to see the pains subside. We stayed in town that night and by the early afternoon went back home again.

As soon as we got home, her labor began again. This time it seemed certain and the walk to the truck was slow. We stopped several times for contractions. Josephine, our neighbor and Gina's childhood friend, drove us to town. Gina's labor was strong and the interval between contractions short. I called the midwife, who promised to leave as soon as possible. In the urgency of things to do, I had little time to think, or luckily, to worry.

After a few hours, Gina was ready to push. My feeble response—"But we have to wait for the midwife"—was starting to sound ridiculous. Finally Josephine said, "Your baby wants to be born, and when a baby wants to be born, maybe you should let it." The logic was undeniable and for the next few minutes everything was automatic—the breathing, the panting, the pushing, the massaging, the crowning.

I remembered what I had learned: when the head is almost out, check for a wrapped cord. It was wrapped once and easily slipped over the baby's head as we settled back for what promised to be the last contraction.

It was. Suddenly, there was our baby, lying silently on my hand, caught at her hips half-way out. I saw a bubble at her mouth and knew everything was fine. As the baby lay on my hand, I suctioned her mouth and watched her breathe on her own. She never cried, but she opened her eyes, focused on me, and sighed. Then she closed her eyes and seemed to sleep.

As I watched, the deep red color of her own blood circulating moved outward from her heart, chasing away the bluish tint from her chest, then her face. It was like seeing the passage of a rainbow, or more like the rising of a sun, bringing warmth and indescribable joy. There were no dry eyes or unsmiling faces as she came alive in such a magical way.

But still we didn't know what sex the baby was and many long seconds later came the next contraction and delivery. A girl—alive, healthy, and happy, with ten toes, five on each foot.

In about fifteen minutes the placenta was delivered, whole and intact. I cut the umbilical cord and again held my daughter, already named Willow.

Then the midwife arrived, with explanations of icy roads. I didn't care. I was glad she had been late.

Stillbirth

BARBARA CROOKER

She said, "Your daughters
are so beautiful.
One's a copper penny,
the other's a chestnut colt."
But what about
my first daughter,
stillborn
at term,
cause
unknown?

Ten years later
and I sift the ground
for clues: what was
it I did?
Guilt is part
of my patchwork;
grief folds me up
like an envelope.

In the hospital,
the doctors turned
their eyes, told me
not to leave
my room.
But I heard them,
those babies in the night,
saw women from Lamaze
in the corridor.
They would be wheeled home
with blossoms & blankets,
while I bled the same,
tore the same,
and came home, alone.

Later,
women showered me
with stories
of babies lost:
to crib death,
    abortion,
    miscarriage;
    lost;
    the baby
    that my best friend
    gave up
    at fourteen.

They wouldn't let me hold her:
all I saw were fragments:
    a dark head,
    a doll's foot,
    skin like a bruise.
They wouldn't let me name her,
    or bury her,
    or mourn her.

Ten years later
and I do not have the distance:
I carry her death
like an egg
in my pocket.

A Lesbian Birth Story

CATHY CADE

1978, Northern California

As the oldest of five children, I've always wanted to raise children of my own, in addition to being economically independent and having other meaningful work. As I was growing up, my younger sister and brothers brought a lot of joy into my life. In my late teens and early twenties, when I was still in school, I could always imagine the children to come, but not a husband.

I came out as a lesbian at the age of twenty-nine, while I was working in the Women's Liberation Movement. Then it came to me in a flash one day: "Now, I can get pregnant!" Ironic as that sounds, it made sense because I'd always feared the servitude and dependency of being a wife and mother in a traditional heterosexual marriage. However, I discovered that I was still not ready to have a child; first I needed to learn what it meant to be a lesbian. I spent the next five years in a friendship circle of lesbian mothers, helping my lover Kate raise her young son.

At the age of thirty-four my life reached a cross-roads. Kate and I were separating amicably, and I was asking myself: "Is there something I'll regret not having done, when I come to the end of my life?" The answer came through loud and clear: "Giving birth and raising a child." I spent the next six months making a decision, going over the long-term emotional commitment, the financial commitment, the loss of time from my photography work. Looking deeply into myself, the message I got was: "You are strong enough." I've always been grateful for the "enough" and the awareness that I don't have to be perfect.

I made the decision to have a child alone, as a single woman. This was good for me. There was no possibility that I was making the decision because of someone else's needs or expectations.

I got pregnant through donor insemination, helped by a gay man who found a friend who would be an anonymous donor.[1] After inseminating during six of the next eight months, I was pregnant and ecstatically happy. It wasn't until my fifth month of pregnancy that I let myself think about how hard it had been to get pregnant. The insemination itself was simple. The emotional strain was another matter. Actually, it was not unlike what any woman goes through if she's been trying to get pregnant for a while. But there's the added pressure of knowing that most people, including many lesbians, might think that what I was doing was not right, or natural.

As I'd expected, I had a glowing, healthy pregnancy. I worked part-time delivering magazines to stores until I finished my sixth month. I received prenatal care from three feminist midwives and planned a home birth.

After my parents got over the initial shock, they eagerly awaited their first grandchild. I thought they might be nervous about my home birth plans, since all of my siblings were born in a hospital. But I found out that my parents had both been born at home and they thought it might be safer. My mother doesn't talk much about her births, but I've seen her sorrow about being discouraged from breastfeeding.

Shortly before I succeeded in getting pregnant, I started a relationship with Rae. After a few months, Rae and her fifteen-year-old daughter moved in with me. Rae had always wanted another child, but she had also been a struggling single mother for years and was just beginning to see the end of the heavy demands of mothering. The coming baby was clearly my project; it was unclear how she would participate. I had support from friends, and after fifteen years of wrestling with the question of how and when to have a child, I was thrilled to be pregnant.

1/5/78—It's two weeks before my due date. I had fun washing baby clothes at the laundromat today. I guess I look pretty big because a woman came up and started talking to me about her twins. People who would never talk to me before (because I look like a lesbian?) come up and start conversations. I don't like to think I'm accepted now because I'm "passing for straight," but I like the contact.

Elaine is pregnant, Karen's period is late, Lorraine is in her fourth month. I'm inviting Lorraine and Elaine to my birth because it meant so much to me that Judy invited me to hers. All these lesbians having babies!

1/17/78—I slept well last night and woke feeling a little weak, but in very good spirits. My mother called from Chicago around 8:00

A.M. We had a nice talk, then I drifted back to sleep. Around 9:00 I was half awake when I felt a trickle of water on my leg. I jumped out of bed. A great warm gush of water came pouring out as I yelled for Rae. I stood there with a huge grin, unashamedly getting the floor all wet. We were so excited. "The baby's coming!" We called the midwives and they were excited too. We called Andre in Sonoma County and Billie in Oregon. Billie called back to say she'd found a way to leave right away and hoped to make it before the birth.

Rae and I moved my bed and I happily put on new sheets, dusted, watered the plants, put baby clothes in the chest—still dripping water. At 11:00 I had my first small contraction. Rae suggested I take a walk. With my dog, Wicca, I ambled through the neighborhood, picking flowers and talking with an old man about his garden. All the time I was carrying the secret that I was in labor. The contractions got stronger. By 1:00 the contractions were still mild—five minutes apart and thirty seconds long—so I wasn't having to breathe with them. Everything felt like it was happening as it is supposed to. It was a beautiful morning.

In the afternoon I had lunch, rested, read a little, but felt too spaced-out to really read much. At 2:00 Andre and Lorraine arrived from Sonoma County. We talked about all the neat boy children we know. The conversation was wonderfully caring and supportive of me.

4:00—Kate and her son Guthrie came home (they live next door). I leaned out the window and yelled to them, "Guess what, I'm in labor!" Nancy, one of the midwives, came to check me and left.

6:00—I found this wonderful place—the toilet. It's secure, comfortable, and private. Kate was with me. I discovered that I liked to have her standing in front of me, her side to me. I held onto her leg and breathed into her side with each contraction. The solidity of her body and the warmth of my breath on her felt good. We timed contractions and Guthrie wrote the times down. Nancy called and we told her the contractions were still irregular, but were only two to three minutes apart and I was breathing deeply with most of them. She said she'd come right over.

7:00—I'm still on the toilet. Jean and Vinnie arrived, the women who first supported my idea of getting pregnant. Billie arrived from Oregon. I was so glad she'd made it, but didn't have much energy to show it. I took some contractions while leaning against Kate and the bedroom door jamb. People began to fuse with each other. I'm leaning on Kate; no, it's Vinnie, then Billie. Nancy returned and examined me; I'm five centimeters dilated. I lay on my side on the bed. I wanted someone putting pressure on my back. Someone else cupped my hands, loosely. Brenda came and took my feet, just as I'd always fantasized she would. People were taking shifts. I needed and wanted all the touching I was getting, about four women at a time, and I knew I wasn't asking too much of anyone.

10:00—Ruth arrived, my first woman lover and still a member of my family. I was in active labor and only partly aware of who was there. I felt my fanny being touched and was told it was Ruth. "Oh, yes, my fanny knows those hands." We all laughed. It's one of my favorite parts of the labor.

The telephone rang nearby. "Who is it?" I asked. Then I yelled: "GET THAT PHONE OUT OF HERE!!" I have to say that this was another high point in my labor—knowing what I wanted and putting my feelings out there.

Through my labor I learned that contractions start small, build up, and go down again like a wave or a statistically normal curve. The feelings come and go, but they do not go on harder and harder forever. I learned to have faith that the more I went up, the sooner I'd go down. I trusted and savoured the rests in between contractions.

Nancy talked with me and I was especially grateful for her skill in phrasing everything in a positive way, for I was so suggestible. After a while she sent most of the people out of the room, so I wouldn't get distracted. That was a good idea. She breathed with me, making a little noise. She said " 'Om' is nice sometimes. It helps let the energy flow." I tried my version of it—various "ahhs" and "ohhs." Billie joined me in the sounds and it really felt good. I got more and more involved with the vocal sounds we were making, feeling our differences and our similarities, and the different colors of our voices. I felt like an artist creating something. I played and played with it.

Thus I arrived at a place where there were no more spaces between contractions. I started feeling that I might not be able to go on. I just barely recalled reading that this was "transition." I couldn't believe I'd gotten there already and I made Nancy repeat twice that I really was at that stage. I remembered that transition stage usually isn't so long and I settled down to work hard. Ruth was at my head, the perfect coach. She kept reminding me to "let it go," and I did.

1/18/78, 2:00 A.M.—I was almost fully dilated, with an anterior lip. On the next contraction Nancy pushed it away.[2] I'd been wanting to push and now I finally could. I pushed, but it was clumsy and all wrong. I had to learn how to push, but I'd learned so much already I knew I'd be learning it soon. I pushed while on my hands and knees. I was noisy and reassured the others that it felt good. Yeshie and Sala, the other midwives, had arrived. Yeshie suggested a return to the toilet. I leaned into Yeshie as I had with Kate so much earlier—another lifetime? Then we returned to the bed and I lay on my side. Nancy had me put my finger in my vagina to feel the head move when I pushed. They saw dark hair. But was the head moving forward and slipping back or not really moving?

Yeshie asked me to squat next to the bed. She put her finger in me to measure the effect of my pushing. She told me to push harder, and with her encouragement I pushed as hard as I could. Then Yeshie and Nancy withdrew to confer. They decided to try a few more pushes and then we might need to go to the hospital. Although the baby's heartbeat was fine, I'd been pushing for three hours and was getting tired. I agreed. I felt the baby wasn't moving down.

Rae drove Nancy and me to the hospital and two cars full of friends followed. The only problem during the ride was what to do with the pushing urges? Nancy wanted me to conserve my energy. We hummed a little and I pushed a little, for it was hard not to.

At the hospital I insisted on, and took great pride in getting on the guerney myself. At this point I wanted a cesarean and I wanted it soon. The doctor wondered whether I might be able to push harder if they deadened the pain with drugs. I told him that it was not the pain which bothered me, that the pushing felt good; he believed me. Another doctor came to confer. I was asked to push again while he felt, but I was flat on my back and unable to do a decent push. This was when I lost control. "Nancy, I can't do a good push like this; I can't do it any more." I felt ashamed.

They prepared for the cesarean. I was still taking contractions, feeling tired and less than ever on top of them, but still trying. Nancy told me, "That's one of the last." I sat up for the spinal anesthesia and soon all was numb. Nancy was at my head telling me what was happening. It scared me that I couldn't feel my legs anymore. The anesthesiologist standing by my head got mad when he learned that I had eaten a popsicle recently. He said, "She'll throw up, choke on it, and die." I started to get scared, thinking, "I'm going to die." Then a calm voice inside me took over and said, "I don't think I'll go down that path." I turned my thoughts elsewhere.

6:00 A.M.—Nancy was cooing about the baby, cooing and cooing, unending words, my only link with reality. A drape was in front of my face. I couldn't see anything but Nancy, whom I wouldn't have recognized behind her mask if she hadn't said her name. She said, "It's a boy." I asked, "Are you sure?" I had so much wanted a girl. Nancy cooed about his wonderful color and told me they were suctioning him. I was fighting to stay awake and trembling from severe cold. I'd never been that cold; the insides of my bones were cold. Finally the baby arrived on my chest; warm, huge and wrinkled, with a pointed head and a face like a baby gorilla. The best part was his smell. I tried to touch him as much as I could. I tried to slip my hand under the covers, but it was so cold and he was wrapped.

He's out! He's alive! He's a baby, of mine! They took him away. They were sewing and sewing, and sewing me. I drifted in and out of consciousness. My legs and lower trunk were "not there." I couldn't feel them and couldn't move them. My legs felt like a huge redwood tuning fork with four feet between them. I was wheeled away.

I was tucked into a ward bed, feeling dopey and barely conscious. I was glad later that my friends left me notes to read. I was getting warmer. Nice nurses kept taking my blood pressure. I was glad for the I.V. I dozed. The next great thing to happen was that I got a little feeling in my toes. It was going to be all right. I awoke feeling euphoric.

I kept trying to tell different nurses and doctors that it had been a great labor, but the baby just didn't come out. And it was a great labor. I got a clarity and sense of my own power, unfettered by self-doubt or guilt, that serves me to this day. When I have hard times I often find that the pain comes in the form of contractions and I know how to handle it.

But there were some difficult things to deal with because of the cesarean. Carly didn't feel like the baby who was inside me. I had Nancy describe over and over what the birth looked like. I wish I could have seen him come out. What was the real cause of the cesarean? The medical records say "cephalopelvic disproportion."[3] Was it a missed posterior?[4] Could it be that I "chose" the hospital out of fear of asking too much of my friends during the first days after the birth?

Carly was born at 6:00 A.M. By 4:00 P.M. I was finally awake enough to demand to see my baby. The separation had been too long for us. He'd been in an incubator—all nine pounds of him—because of a respiration difficulty. The doctors thought he might have swallowed meconium.[5] I now suspect that the drugs for my anesthesia affected him. I finally saw Carly and he looked so beautiful it blew me away—though he looked nothing like the baby I'd seen in the operating room.

In all, I liked the non-pretentious, down-to-earth small county hospital. I liked the fact that people were getting paid to take care of me. The nurses were in favor of breastfeeding and helped me and Carly get started.

1/20/78—It was good for me to be with other new mothers, sharing the joys, nervousness, ignorance. My friends came to see me one at a time and that's all I had energy for.

LISA KANEMOTO

1/21/78—Rae came to take me home. After firm and persistent struggle, I'd gotten Carly released early. Rae and I drove to the hills with Carly and as the sun set, we celebrated our first anniversary, exchanging presents and eating cookies.

My welcome home was warm and wonderful. Billie was staying another week to help out. Betsy arrived with Judy's expressed and frozen breast milk, in case I wanted to go out for a bit, plus a beautifully typed copy of the article we'd been writing on donor insemination.

Then I was faced with my first night alone with this tiny—well, not so tiny—baby. I'd never heard him cry, never changed his diapers, and didn't know what to dress him in. I was nervous, but we made it through. Morning found Carly, Rae and me—a newborn and two lesbians—sitting on my bed, with Rae reading Dr. Spock aloud to me on the importance of not overdressing babies.

Carly had his sixth birthday last week and I am now the mother of a kid who has lost his first tooth. I love Carly so much I don't know what to do with it sometimes. The years have been good to us. I do live more deeply and my photographs are sometimes stronger as a result.

Rae moved down the street when Carly was three months old. We broke up a few months later. Elaine moved in and she, Becky and I lived together with our babies. For the last three and a half years Carly has had two mothers, Mama Cathy and Mama Sleazy.

I've been trying to get pregnant again for the last year. It's been hard, but I feel it will happen. This new baby will be born into a family of two mothers and a brother. Again I plan for a home birth. But in case I need a cesarean, I would like to see what can be done about the cold operating room and get an agreement to drop the drape so I can see the baby being born. I hope to arrange for Sleazy or a friend to stay with the baby if I can't. I would like the baby's whole family— Carly, Sleazy, and friends—to be recognized and treated well by the hospital staff.

Unexpected Forceps

LOUISE HENKIN WEJKSNORA

1979, New York City

I became interested in childbirth before becoming pregnant, so by the time I conceived I was aware of issues and choices. My reading had made me comfortable with natural childbirth and had helped me distinguish between my feelings about labor (that it would probably hurt but I could manage it) and my feelings about hospitals (summarized in the word "terror"). I would have liked a home birth, but I did not want an unattended birth and I couldn't find anyone to attend me at home. Also, my parents, living in the same city, were highly uncomfortable with home birthing. My husband, who was doing postdoctoral research in biology, understood that birth is basically safe, but was nonetheless concerned that what is true for populations does not necessarily follow for every individual. On the positive side, we had full health insurance coverage at the big teaching hospital across the street from our student apartment, and the physician I first saw there, while passionately against home birth, was really very dedicated to making the hospital humane. I also liked his common sense attitude towards pregnancy and birth, and the way he dealt with patients as fellow humans.

This doctor encouraged me to gain plenty of weight (I was visibly skinny), but was vague on what I should eat. Jacqueline Gazella, however, was the nurse who assisted him in diagnosing the pregnancy and as she was then publishing a book on prenatal nutrition,[1] she made it her business to give me some dietary counseling that first day. Towards the end of my third month, I attended a morning-long early pregnancy class sponsored by the hospital's clinic, which filled in the outline Jacqueline had given me and also made me aware that I could tour the hospital. I did so shortly thereafter and generated a list of leading questions to raise with my doctor.

I wanted to avoid several things, like the IV and liberal use of Demerol, which appeared to be standard. He reassured me that his own common practices were in line with what I wanted and then suggested that I might feel more comfortable with midwives. I was interested indeed and he introduced me to two certified nurse-midwives who practiced in the same clinic. I decided to switch to them that very morning, but I also saw this doctor a few more times and arranged for him, rather than a stranger from the staff, to be my back-up physician.

In the third trimester of my pregnancy I took a childbirth education course which refreshed what I already knew and helped involve my husband. The course was the teacher's own mix of Lamaze, Bradley and ICEA philosophies, along with her special emphasis on nutrition.[2] I came to labor after a beautiful healthy pregnancy, having gained thirty-five pounds and feeling pretty comfortable with my arrangements.

I had a lot of Braxton-Hicks contractions in the last weeks, and an exam at full term found me to be three centimeters dilated and ninety percent effaced, with the baby well engaged. So when my waters broke at 8:24 A.M. the next morning, the midwife told me to meet her at the hospital. There she and my doctor agreed that I would probably have the baby that day, but that I wasn't in labor yet and could go home if I wished until it started. Waiting for the elevator though, I had several strong cramps which really required my concentration while they lasted. I decided that I didn't really want to go home if it meant trekking back when I felt even worse. I felt pretty silly, as a "hospital-phobe," muttering that I'd rather stay.

My husband and I were escorted to a labor room and introduced to a nurse, and when the midwife saw me settling in and not complaining of pains, she went off for a bit of breakfast. It was nearly 10:00 A.M. There was no comfy chair, so I sat on the bed. Unfortunately, the bed was too high for me to easily maneuver my pregnant, laboring bulk on and off; so once on, I was stuck. My nurse checked the baby's heartbeat with a fetoscope, as I had requested, instead of with an electronic fetal heart monitor. I became chilled and I remember how cold the fetoscope was, even though she and my husband tried to warm it. Soon I was in very hard labor and the nurse stayed with us between checks. The contractions hurt, but I could recognize with confidence what was happening and the pain didn't upset me. About 11:00 A.M. the midwife stuck her head in to see if I was in labor yet and found me doing transition breathing. She also stayed and found me to be seven centimeters dilated. A little before noon I started pushing.

Everything was going well. About 12:40, with the head becoming visible during contractions, the midwife asked if I was still comforta-

ble about giving birth in the labor room as discussed. I was. But with
the next contraction the nurse heard a problem with the heartbeat.
After the midwife listened during the following contraction, she had a
fetal heart monitor brought in. With the external monitoring we could
hear nothing at all, perhaps because I was semi-sitting. The midwife,
who knew I considered the internal heart monitor attachment barbaric, then wanted to use it. I had to believe that she knew my feelings
and wouldn't be suggesting it without a reason, so I said OK. We did
hear a heartbeat with the internal monitor and we all heard it drop to
nothing during the height of the contraction, then recover as the contraction passed. Even one second of no heartbeat is quite enough to
make one think about stillbirth and I started sending the baby mental
messages to hang in and be OK. The midwife sent the nurse running
for the doctor, who was in his office. He arrived, was briefed, and did
a quick exam, which confirmed the midwife's analysis that the baby's
head was unexpectedly unevenly calcified. They called this condition
"craniotabes." The doctor then came to my side and somehow managed to explain to me, in one sentence, in the middle of labor, what I
needed months of subsequent reading to confirm for myself: that they
couldn't tell whether the kind of heart rate deceleration we heard
meant danger or not, but that if we did nothing there would be no
way to know if we'd guessed right until it was too late to change our
minds. He advised a forceps delivery, feeling that the fifteen or twenty minutes it would save could make a real difference if there was
trouble. Although I had an intuition that the baby was all right, and I
really wanted to deliver it myself after nine months of pregnancy and
several hours of labor, I found it impossible to decide to take a chance.

In the delivery room my doctor told me he was giving me a pudendal block—the only medication I had. All the years of reading paid off
then, just in knowing what a pudendal block was and why he was doing it (it is a local anesthesia given for the early episiotomy necessary
for using forceps). I felt the forceps go in, then he told me to push with
the next contraction, which I did while he pulled. He then saw that
birth was imminent and got rid of the oxygen mask they had put on
me at the first signs of fetal distress. He got my glasses back on and got
the overhead mirror adjusted so that I could see the birth, all before
the next contraction. The head was born with the second push-and-
pull, the doctor suctioned the mouth, and I finished delivering my
baby. It was 1:23 P.M., about 35 minutes since he'd been sent for, five
hours since my waters had broken.

I asked and was glad to be told I had a girl. I then demanded to
know why she wasn't crying and was told she was grimacing, a good
sign. A moment later, seven and a half pounds of pink, breathing baby

landed on my chest. She was making a tiny rusty whimper instead of a yell, but was in perfect condition, without even a bruise on her face.

Ruth stayed on my chest during the whole twenty or twenty-five minutes it seemed to take to repair the episiotomy, plus third-degree lacerations caused by the forceps. During that time I delivered the placenta, my husband cut the cord, and Ruth was given a quick checkup at my side, dried, weighed, wrapped, and given back to me. It was definitely not the halcyon "bonding" time I'd imagined, but this time with Ruth did serve the purpose of "recognizing-and-claiming" her. While I had really expected a bright, healthy child, somehow the fact that she was gorgeous was an amazing bonus.

By the time the stitches were finished I was shaking with cold, and Ruth was chilled too, so I was discouraged from trying to nurse then and she went to a warmer in the nursery. I was helped to walk to the recovery room, where I felt wiped out and sorry for myself. I didn't have a sense of personal failure, since it was the baby's problem and not mine that prevented a natural birth, but I was badly disappointed, and really upset over the episiotomy. I had a certain mourning to do to resolve my feelings about the not-so-little cut. Meanwhile, I felt really unconnected with having given birth. I was brought some lunch, but my appetite had disappeared when labor began.

During the later afternoon I got clean and warm, eventually used the toilet, and received visitors. I waddled to the nursery but couldn't do much for my crying baby. I was too inexperienced to realize that once I was warm myself I might have asked to have her in bed with me. After my lukewarm, lousy hospital supper, Ruth was finally considered to have her body temperature stabilized, and I got her in my room, where she remained for the rest of my stay except for one hour each morning.

I finally had my baby, but I didn't know quite what to do with her. I'd never had a rapport with a baby before and it didn't come automatically. I knew she must be hungry, since when she reached the age of four hours old a nurse had asked if I wanted them to give her a bottle and I'd said no, I was going to nurse. My request had obviously been honored: no fed baby would be fretting like that. Despite my inexperience I managed to get my breast and her head in proximity to each other and touched her cheek with my nipple. She immediately did all the rest and nursed with satisfaction. I was glad there was something I could do. She was exclusively breastfed for five months and extensively to a year, and we didn't finally wean until she was almost two.

Once born, Ruth's skull calcified properly and her fontanelles closed normally.[3] The problem became insignificant once she was out.

I went home after forty-eight hours, recovering my appetite when I walked in my own door. My mother came almost every day for several weeks, until I was more secure with my baby and my ability to care for her. And I did (to my great relief) fall thoroughly in love with her as time passed.

My birthing of Ruth was disappointing to me, but not devastating. I had been anxious throughout pregnancy to assure myself that my birth attendants' attitudes and practices were in tune with my own preferences. I put a lot of nervous energy into that quest and I feel that it paid off when I was not able to make decisions for myself. My care-providers, on their own, made decisions I could approve and were careful to keep me informed and included. The doctor gets many points from me because he did not high-handedly diagnose "fetal distress." Rather, he came to my side and tried to explain. He suggested a forceps delivery "just in case." The forceps delivery was not, it turned out, necessary—but in the circumstances it was not unwarranted. Although I really am mildly phobic about hospitals, which I'm sure didn't help, there were enough other factors to make me believe that the "distress' might have happened even in a home birth: the ruptured membranes, plus craniotabes, plus "stage-fright" were all involved. I later realized that I was subconsciously worried about whether I would be a good mother and when it became apparent that birth was becoming imminent, I experienced anxiety as well as relief. The "fetal distress" started just at that point and I no longer consider this coincidental.

But despite my basic satisfaction with the care I received, I no longer see the point of planning to give birth in a hospital again. It was a trained ear with a fetoscope that detected Ruth's apparent fetal distress; the fetal heart monitor only confirmed it. And since I would never accept medication for pain, who needs hospital-based technology for either monitoring or comfort? Being just across the hall from the emergency back-up meant, in fact, being half an hour away. For all the frantic efficiency, when I thought about it later I realized that there were at least nine contractions between the time the nurse heard something awry and the time we entered delivery—and there are three to five minutes between second-stage contractions. I could, if need be, have gone from home to hospital in that much time. In fact, I speculate that even with the craniotabes problem, if I had begun the birth at home and then had to transfer, I might have delivered naturally, without the forceps. My midwife thought that the baby's heartbeat recovered somewhat during the transfer from labor to delivery. If we'd been at home I imagine we'd have started moving to the hospital when the fetoscope first revealed a problem, instead of waiting to use an electronic monitor (not available at home anyway) to confirm the diagnosis. I would probably have reached the delivery room at about the same time, but the decision about what to do would have been deferred by some ten or fifteen minutes and if some heart rate recovery did take place I might have squeaked through with a normal birth. Maybe. At any rate, partly due to my need to understand what happened at Ruth's birth, I've continued to read, learn, and be part of the alternative birth movement. I know now how to find a birth attendant for the place of birth I choose. What I want now is to have another baby and do it differently—at home.

Angry and Happy
At the Same Time

GAYLE SMITH

1979, Boston

I never wanted to have a hospital birth, but I didn't know where to find a lay midwife to do a home birth and I didn't actually have the courage (or the support, except from my husband) to give birth at home alone. In my first pregnancy I didn't have as much knowledge about the birthing process as I do now. So I gave myself over to the medical establishment at one of the major teaching hospitals in my area. This hospital boasted of having a birthing room and nurse-midwives, and they allowed fathers to stay throughout the birth. I wanted to have a birth attendant who was knowledgeable, caring and sympathetic and this hospital sounded like the right place. First mistake!

I signed on with one of the nures-midwives, who followed me for prenatal care. But I never quite felt comfortable with her as she was always very detached and made offhand remarks which tended to be racist—such as insisting on calling my husband "boyfriend," even after I corrected her. I am a black woman and had been married for a year when I became pregnant. There were other slights to my intelligence, especially when I asked questions about my pregnancy or made specific requests concerning how my birth would be managed. Looking back, I realize I didn't really say much about my care. I didn't think I had much choice. Also, I had to deal with the physician who worked with the midwives. He was typically condescending and oblivious to my needs. He dismissed my questions with curt requests to "leave things up to me." I wanted to talk about the possibility of avoiding an episiotomy. The doctor claimed in advance that I would probably need one and he would not promise to try to avoid this procedure. I let it pass because I didn't think he was going to deliver my baby anyway. Fortunately, I guess, he didn't.

My labor started on Saturday, August 18, at 5:50 A.M. I was awakened by a contraction. I thought it was just another Braxton-Hicks contraction. I had to go to the bathroom but I didn't feel like getting up. At 6:00 A.M. I had another contraction and decided to get up to go to the toilet, still thinking "Braxton-Hicks." I was four days overdue and quite impatient, but I didn't think this was really labor and I didn't want to get my hopes up. But as I got up I happened ·to look back at the bed and there was my bloody show. So this was it. My feelings ran from elation to disbelief. At 6:10 another contraction came, so I woke my husband. I showered while he changed the bed, then we tried to relax while we timed the contractions. We were too excited to eat or rest. Second mistake!

At 10:00 we were joined by my grandmother who came, I suspect, to make sure we were really going to the hospital and not planning to do anything foolish like trying to have her great-grandchild at home. My contractions were about seven minutes apart by now and not terribly uncomfortable. At noon the contractions were between five and seven minutes apart, so Nana called a friend who had previously agreed to take us to the hospital. I called the hospital and was told to wait until the contractions were two minutes apart. Finally, about 4:00, the contractions got to be between two and four minutes apart. I called the hospital and was told to keep waiting. I should have listened to them. But my grandma was getting nervous and quite impatient and insisted I go, so at 4:30 P.M., off we went.

I figured that with contractions coming every two minutes, I should be about six or seven centimeters dilated. But after I had been admitted and checked, the nurse cheerfully told me that I was two centimeters dilated. I was shocked! Only two centimeters after almost eleven hours and contractions every two minutes! Up to that point I had been dealing quite well with the labor, but after I heard the nurse's pronouncement it was all downhill.

I asked to labor in the birthing room but was told I had to be at least four centimeters dilated before I could get in. So I spent the next two or three hours trying to get comfortable. I tried walking, lying down, and sitting in a rocking chair with pillows, but my discomfort was increasing and so was my anxiety. I was doing the fast shallow breathing I'd learned in my childbirth class and a nurse and doctor came in to tell me that I should go back to the slow deep breathing or I'd tire myself too early. So I tried breathing more slowly and lost control of all contractions from then on. I never could get back on top of the contractions.

At 8:00, three hours after being admitted, I was examined and found to be four centimeters. Again I asked about the birthing room and was told that I would need a nurse in attendance at all times there and that it was too busy just then for them to be able to spare a nurse to be with me. In the meantime I was offered a painkiller, which I refused at first, but upon the staff's insistence I accepted a combination of Nisentil and Vistaril.[1] This did take the edge off the pain I was feeling, but I couldn't really tell if I hurt more from the contractions or from my disappointment at not being able to get into the birthing room. I'd also asked not to have electronic fetal monitoring, but the staff insisted I have this before I could use the birthing room.

At about 10:00 P.M., just as the medication was wearing off, I was checked again and was found to be still four centimeters. By this time I was ready to give up on the birthing room altogether. The contractions were still two minutes apart and painful and I wanted more analgesic, but they told me I couldn't have more because it had apparently slowed down my labor. I was nearing the end of my rope. I couldn't get comfortable. I was in bed, strapped to that damned monitor, and lying almost completely flat on my back. Every time I tried to put the bed up someone would come in to check the monitor and crank it down again. I was becoming very vocal about my discomfort and I was told to "shut up" quite a few times.

At 11:30 P.M. I was checked again and had progressed to five and a half centimeters. I was offered an epidural block, to which I consented. But by the time the anesthesiologist finally arrived, set up and administered the epidural, it was about 1:00 A.M. The contractions were still two minutes apart. I was given a test dose which lasted about one hour, during which time the staff tried to determine how effective the spinal was by sticking me with pins, all of which I could feel quite well. When the test dose wore off completely, they gave me some more and I felt great relief. I wasn't numbed at all but the contractions felt as though they were far away. I felt more relaxed. It was now 2:00 A.M.

During this time another patient was brought into my labor room and she was just about to deliver, so everyone's attention was taken up with her and I was left all alone. They had made my husband leave during the administration of the epidural and he fell asleep outside my room. When I asked to have him come back I was told he was sleeping and to let him sleep. Well, I was tired too and if I couldn't sleep, I didn't think he should either. But nobody went to get him, so he slept on. In the meantime, the other patient (who I heard had gone into labor at 10:30 that evening) was being moved across the hall to a vacant labor room for her delivery and with all the moving around I thought my bed would be pushed right out the window. The nurses insisted on keeping the window open because they were hot, even though I was freezing. After the woman delivered at about 2:30, the excitement died down and my husband was finally awakened.

I was checked again at 3:15 and finally I had gotten to ten centimeters—complete dilation. My amniotic sac had been artificially ruptured when they administered the epidural and an internal electronic monitor had been inserted, so I was still laid out flat on my back. The epidural was steadily wearing away. I was told I could start pushing, which I did in earnest. After a few pushes every bit of sensation returned. I had already asked for more anesthesia when I felt it was wearing off, but I was told the anesthesiologist was very busy with someone else and I'd have to wait. So I pushed on and the feelings were incredibly strong. I was shouting and screaming and at one point the doctor told me to shut up because I was disturbing all the other patients. She said that if I didn't shut up they would not take me into the delivery room. I told her I didn't care what they did—I was dying and nobody was helping, or even cared. All the while I continued to push. I felt an incredible burning-tearing sensation, reached down, and felt a smooth wet thing. It was the baby's head. Then the nurse told me to put my legs down—*closed, together*! I couldn't believe she asked me to do that, not with the baby's head right there and ready to come out. I didn't think I even could put my legs down, but she evidently thought otherwise because she slapped my legs down on the bed so they could move me to the delivery room. All the while I was yelling and screaming and they were yelling back at me to shut up.

When we got to the delivery room, who should be there but the recalcitrant anesthesiologist. Who needed him now? But he did his little bit and injected me with something. It must have been water, because I swear I felt everything they did to me. I felt the episiotomy (even though I begged and pleaded not to have one) and then not more than five minutes after I got to the delivery room my daughter was born, at 3:45 A.M. First her head was born and then after two more contractions, her little body. I really don't know what all I felt. I was very angry and happy at the same time. At first they laid her on my stomach, but I didn't even want to hold her. My first comment on seeing her was, "Oh, she's ugly!" Well, she was. Her cord had been wrapped around her neck; it had to be clamped and cut before her body was born. She was all blue and had lots of molding of her head and her nose was smashed flat. My husband almost missed the birth because he had to change clothes and I never even got a chance to get onto the delivery table. I had her right on the same bed I had labored in. I often wonder why they bothered moving me at all. But move me again they did, onto the delivery table for the ultimate torture. The placenta delivered within five minutes of the baby and was "apparently intact," as they say. Then they placed my legs in stirrups and one of the doctors proceeded to place her whole gloved hand inside of my uterus, god only knows why.[2] I practically bit my tongue off to stifle a scream. At that point I didn't feel I had the right to yell, since I wasn't in labor anymore. After the doctor finished her manipulations came the episiotomy repair. The doctor claimed to have given me practically an entire bottle of xylocaine, but I felt each and every prick of the needle as she placed the stitches. When she finally finished I was so grateful to be getting out of there that I actually apologized for having made such a scene earlier.

Looking back, I feel rather foolish for apologizing to those people for my reactions to their unsympathetic, barbaric attitudes and behavior. At the time though, I just felt embarrassed for having behaved so badly. Such is the nature of the conditioning we women get: we turn ourselves over to the medical establishment and feel grateful for the poor treatment we get, as if someone were doing us a great big favor.

I can't help but feel that the somewhat negative nature of my daughter's birth colored my relationship with her. It was as if we got off on the wrong foot, because I was so deeply disappointed that the birth didn't go as well as I'd planned. I also felt guilty about not totally accepting her immediately after she was born. Most of all, I'm still very angry at almost everyone involved in my "care and treatment" that evening. One of the most disappointing facts is that, aside from the anesthesiologist and my husband, I didn't see any men all night. Every doctor and nurse was a woman. The fact that these women were so totally without feeling for the emotional and physical needs of their patients is just another pitifully sad commentary on the American medical establishment; it so totally dehumanizes the very ones we hope and expect would care the most about other women's pain and sufferings.

All I can say about my second birth is that by comparison—well, there is no comparison. It was just totally different. Even though my son's birth also occurred in a hospital (not the same one, I assure you), I endured none of the same horrors. I had a very kind and sympathetic male obstetrician and supportive nurses. This really made a world of difference. I was much more loving and accepting of my son at his birth than I was of my daughter. We have a much closer relationship even now. My daughter is more independent and also closer to her father, who got to spend more time with her in those first few minutes after her birth than I did. He spent nearly a full hour with her until she was taken to the nursery. He even accompanied her down to the nursery, whereas I only had a few minutes with her in the recovery room.

My faith in my body was eventually restored, and along with it my faith in the tendency for nature to take its logical course most of the time. But I am firmly resolved that during any future pregnancies and births, I will take a more active role in the prenatal management and I'm definitely not going to give birth in a hospital again, except under the most extreme circumstances. That may sound radical, but I have lost the ability to place blind faith and trust in the medical establishment. Since the births of my children, I've become involved in a local community-based organization which seeks to teach the women of our community about the alternatives available to them during their childbearing experiences. My involvement with this group, which also deals with home birth, came about as a result of my dissatisfaction with my two hospital births. I will continue this work and I'm prepared to accept totally the consequences for future actions based on my firm beliefs.

Toxemia and
An Induced Labor

JENNIFER CRISSEY FISHER

1980, Southern California

After my third child was born, I fulfilled a long-cherished dream and became a childbirth educator. By the time I became pregnant with my fourth child, I had been teaching for almost two years. During that time I had encountered some real horror stories about what goes on in hospital maternity wards. I could hardly believe some of the things that happened to my students. My own experiences with hospital birth were not terrible; I encountered just the usual annoying problems such as long separation from the baby after initial contact in the delivery room, and one baby being given milk formula in the nursery despite continual reminders not to do so because of a family history of allergies. These problems were bad enough, but nothing compared to what happened to some of my childbirth students. The longer I was in contact with hospital birth through my students, the more wary I became of hospitals. I also began working as a volunteer labor coach at a local hospital and what I saw there didn't encourage me either, though the hospital was excellent in many ways.

During this time I had the opportunity to observe a home birth. I noticed that the woman having the home birth had nothing difficult to handle except her labor itself: no IV, or shave, or forced move from one room to another. The beauty and spiritual quality of the birth impressed me. After much discussion and prayer, my husband Leif and I decided to have our fourth baby at home. We didn't mention our decision to our families. They wouldn't have understood (my father is a physician) and I didn't want the stress of arguments. But most of our friends were informed of the decision.

We chose a lay midwife and began prenatal care. I followed her instructions, including eating a superb diet. I didn't have what I'd call an easy pregnancy—I never do, though I love being pregnant—but I was very healthy. I visited my doctor and discussed my plans for a home birth. Although he doesn't do home births, he was willing to check me occasionally and serve as back-up.

My due date was February 1. During the first week of December there was a very slight rise in my blood pressure (it was still well within the usual "normal" range) and I had a trace of protein in my urine. My midwife counseled me to take garlic capsules to help lower my blood pressure and to increase my protein intake to 125 grams a day instead of 100. I had some swelling, as I always do during pregnancy, but it was not excessive. I followed the midwife's recommendations.

A few days later I had a feeling that something was wrong. I had no particular symptoms—no headache or visual disturbances, for example—but just a feeling something was not right. I called my obstetrician's office and asked to be seen. This was Tuesday, December 9, the day John Lennon died. The receptionist said the doctor was out doing a delivery and there would be a long wait when he did come back. Did I want to wait until Friday instead? I told her I didn't think it could wait and she said to come in.

At 5:30 the doctor checked me. I had a plus-3 reading of protein in my urine, pitting edema in my legs, and a blood pressure of 173/124 (normal is about 120/80, and for pregnant women usually even less). Those symptoms added up to a diagnosis of toxemia of pregnancy. I could hardly believe it and neither could my doctor. In the childbirth circles in which I move, Dr. Tom Brewer's publications on a high-protein, normal-salt diet for prevention of toxemia are regarded as second only to the Bible.[1] My doctor also advises this diet for his patients and almost never sees more than the mildest cases of toxemia in his practice. I knew I had followed the diet perfectly, yet here I was with toxemia. I thought, "Well, that's the end of the home birth."

The doctor explained that I needed to be in the hospital—I knew that, of course—and that it might be necessary to "interrupt the pregnancy." I thought, "Oh, he means cesarean." But a few minutes later, when he actually said "the cesarean," the words hit me in the pit of the stomach. At this point I was seven weeks before my due date.

The doctor told me I could sleep at home that night if I would stay in bed and watch for danger signals and go to the hospital in the morning. Since it was already 6 P.M. they wouldn't start tests until the morning anyway. I entered the hospital the next day and was placed on bed rest, put on a high-protein, normal-salt diet, and given phenobarbital to help me stay sleepy and resting.[2] Tests were done on me and the baby. My blood pressure stayed at about 160/120. After a few days the baby began to show signs of trouble and the doctor suggested I transfer to a high-risk perinatal center. I had a choice of the county hospital, a local hospital with a children's hospital next door, and Memorial Hospital in a nearby city. I chose Memorial because it has a nation-wide reputation in dealing with high risk pregnancy. My doctor supported me in the decision and told me that he would send his wife there if she needed a high-risk center.

I transferred to the new hospital in the evening, and apparently going to the car and sitting through a forty-minute drive were too much for me, for I arrived at the hospital shaking and needing blood pressure reducers and magnesium sulfate, a drug used to prevent convulsions.[3] This drug burns when it is injected; they gave me a loading dose, which caused severe pain in my arm and severe anxiety. When morning came and my husband returned (he didn't know I would have such a miserable night or he wouldn't have left), an ultrasound and amniocentesis were done to determine the baby's maturity. Her size agreed with my dates and her lungs were found to be mature, indicating she would probably not have breathing problems even if she had to be delivered immediately. This news was a relief.

Memorial Hospital has primary care nursing, which means that you are assigned a registered nurse who cares for you every day, even changing sheets and doing other tasks normally left to nurses' aides. My nurse was superb. She had an understanding of and interest in home birth and treated me as an equal. She played a big part in making a difficult experience as positive as possible.

The doctors I saw were a high risk team consisting of an intern, a resident, a fellow, and others right up through the head of the high risk obstetrics department. I had seen a documentary film on this doctor's work on a public television show and it had influenced my decision to go to Memorial. I was surprisingly pleased with the team, even though I had never met them before. They were a little upset with me at first. They weren't used to patients who questioned their decisions, I think. But once they realized that I was not attacking their competence as doctors, but simply taking part as an informed consumer in decisions regarding my medical care, I think I grew on them!

The first little run-in we had was over the thiazide diuretics they wanted me to take. I had read of the dangers of these in Brewer's book, *What Every Pregnant Woman Should Know*.[4] I hoped that with my situation and my diet, my symptoms would improve. However, they did not. While I still feel that probably most toxemia is preventable by good nutrition, I know from my own experience that it is not entirely preventable. My diagnosis was chronic hypertension with superimposed severe toxemia. The Memorial doctors were puzzled too; they said it was not a "textbook case" of toxemia.

When I told my doctors I didn't want to take thiazide diuretics, they were surprised and concerned. The next day the head of the department came in and told me that he agreed with me, in any case, that the proper thing to do was not so much to try to treat the toxemia, as to get the baby born. Birth always "cures" toxemia.

They wanted to do a "serial" induction. Because I had given birth before, they were reasonably sure that by giving me Pitocin every day to cause contractions, they could ripen my cervix and induce labor even though I was still six and a half weeks from my due date.

The induction started on a Monday. I wasn't given breakfast, just in case I went into labor right away. I was transferred to the labor and delivery area, put on a fetal monitor, and given magnesium sulfate and Pitocin.[5] All day I had strong contractions. I had no lunch. At 6 P.M. I was checked. I hadn't really made any progress and was sent back to my room for dinner and a night's sleep. This pattern was repeated Tuesday and Wednesday. As they prepared to send me back to my room Wednesday night, I told the doctor, "Look, I'm willing to go on with this induction every day, but I'm not going to be starved anymore. I want breakfast and lunch every day." The doctor agreed and said I could have the next day off. They would try again Friday. Thursday I had strong false labor all day. By Friday morning I was one centimeter dilated. I ate a big breakfast, the induction was started, and I went into labor.

The labor was absolute hell. My cervix just wasn't ready to go and forcing it open with drugs six weeks before my due date caused an abnormally painful labor. By the time I reached three centimeters the contractions were as strong as transition contractions. Not only was I in terrible pain, but with each contraction my already high blood pressure went up. Leif and I had previously discussed with the staff the possibility of medication. I knew that a labor induced that early was likely to be very difficult and I asked the staff whether the fact that my baby was premature meant I did not have the option of medication. The doctor told me, "You always have that option." The only medication I'd had in my other three labors was one dose of a tranquilizer in each of the first two.

So at three centimeters dilation, with strong contractions and rising blood pressure, we asked to confer with the anesthesiologist. We all talked it over and decided that under the circumstances it was worth taking the risk of an epidural, even though I was only three centimeters dilated. At that hospital epidurals aren't usually given before five centimeters, for fear of slowing the labor. The anesthesiologist told me that if my blood pressure dropped too much, a common side effect of epidurals, I would need an immediate cesarean. (All through that long induction I was sure I would end up with a cesarean anyway, which made me feel I might be going through all that pain for nothing. It wasn't until I was actually on my way to the delivery room that it dawned on me that I wasn't having a cesarean.)

The epidural was administered. It worked perfectly on the right side—I could feel nothing—but the left side wasn't numb. I pointed this out to the anesthesiologist. He checked me and confirmed it; the epidural was placed just slightly wrong. He told me he felt a bigger dose of the medication would take care of the problem, but he didn't want to give it to me yet. Later, when my body had had a chance to adjust to the medication, he would come back and try the bigger dose. If that didn't work, we could start over and re-do the epidural. I said okay and went back to doing my labor breathing.

A little later my membranes ruptured with considerable force. There was a huge amount of amniotic fluid and the bed was soaked. The nurse tipped the bed so my legs were higher than my head. I think she was afraid the cord would prolapse. She refused to change my sheets because she didn't want me to move around too much. Even later, when they were permitting me to turn from side to side, they wouldn't change the sheets. I see no reason they couldn't have pushed a fresh bed next to mine and simply had me roll onto it, but they wouldn't. I spent the rest of my labor in a completely soaked bed.

Time went on. Suddenly my contractions became unbearably strong and I had the most intense rectal pressure I had ever experienced. I told the nurse to get the anesthesiologist quickly, to give me the stronger dose he'd talked about. She said she was sorry, but he was taking care of a woman who was in the middle of a cesarean and couldn't come.

Then the baby's heart beat dropped to 48 beats a minute (normal is 120 to 160). Immediately the room was full of people hanging over the fetal monitor. I was given oxygen, but no one really paid any attention to me except Leif, who couldn't get very close to the bed because of all the people in the room. They checked me. I think I was about six centimeters dilated. The baby's heart beat was coming back up between contractions, so they felt they could safely hold off a little longer. All this time I had a terrible urge to push because of the rectal pressure and I was trying hard not to. After half an hour of this, I repeated forcefully that I had to push, and they examined me again. I was fully dilated. The doctor said to me, "Mrs. Fisher, do you remember, in your other labors, the pushing part, how long it took?" I replied briskly, "Two minutes with the last one." He said, "Take her in."

Another contraction began, with that terrible pressure, and I cried out, "Can I push?" The doctor said very calmly, "Why don't you wait? If you push now you're going to have the baby here." I said frantically, "Can't you just deliver the baby here?" He replied, "We'll have you in the delivery room in two minutes."

At this point the anesthesiologist came rushing in. I said, "Do something about this rectal pressure!" He said, "You're a childbirth teacher. Don't you know what's causing that pressure?" I said, "Yes, of course I know. Do something about it!"[6] He said, "I'm giving you your test dose right now." (Later I asked him why he was talking like that, and he said, "To take your mind off what was happening.")

We got to the delivery room. I was panting and blowing like mad to keep from pushing. They told me to sit up on the delivery table so they could give my "bottom dose"—a bigger dose of the epidural medication to numb the birth area as well as just the abdomen. I refused—I was beyond being reasonable at that point and sitting up was the last thing I felt like doing. I saw the anesthesiologist and the nurse shake their heads at each other and the anesthesiologist went ahead and put the medication into the tube anyway.[7] It didn't numb the birth area until after the baby was out, but it did take away that terrible urge to push. So maybe it was worth having, because it's important not to deliver a delicate premature baby too forcefully. As soon as the urge to push disappeared, I said, "I'm not pushing, honest!" The doctor said he knew I wasn't—my uterus was delivering the baby. I could feel the momentary burning sensation just before the head was born and then felt the head coming out. I'm so grateful the epidural didn't numb me for the birth sensations. I'd have hated to miss that.

I kept looking at the wall for a mirror but there wasn't one. I said, "Oh, I wish I could see." The doctor said, "Sit up, you can see." I propped myself up on my elbow and watched the baby being born. I said, "Oh, look at the baby!" The baby was so cute. The doctor handed it to the pediatric team who had been summoned by a frantic call of "Pediatric team to delivery room, stat! Pediatric team to delivery room, stat!" The doctor said, "It's a little girl type." I hadn't even thought to ask about the sex and said, "A *girl*?" then "Oh, Leif, it's a girl!" We had three boys already and were fully expecting another one. Leif was taking pictures all this time.

"When will she start to breathe?" I asked. "Oh, she's breathing," said the obstetrician. She began to cry when the pediatric team suctioned her out. Despite being six weeks early, her Apgar score was a good 8/9. They wrapped her up in a blanket and gave her to me. Leif came over and we touched and kissed her. She was in such good shape that they wrote special orders for her to be in the regular nursery instead of the "growing nursery." I feel very sure that the reason for her good condition was my excellent nutrition during the pregnancy. She weighed four pounds, eight ounces and was seventeen inches long. She was born at 6:49 P.M. Friday, December 14, and we were both released from the hospital Sunday morning, a day and a half later. We named her Megan Laurel.

Looking back, I don't know why I had such a traumatic pregnancy and delivery, except that perhaps God wanted me to experience these things to improve my abilities as a childbirth educator. My midwife told me, "It always happens to midwives and childbirth educators." Maybe it does. If it ever happens again, though, I won't agree to a serial induction. A cesarean couldn't be as bad as what I went through with that labor; and I wouldn't be worrying about what the stress of labor might have done to Megan's brain. She is clearly extremely bright (she started talking at eight months) but I know I won't feel completely at ease until she is in school and showing no learning disabilities.

I don't know whether it's because we went through so much to get her, but Megan is special to us. She has attracted more attention all her life than any other baby I ever saw. Everyone is enchanted with her. And I still, three years later, thank God for her every day.

The Birth of Willow

MARTIN PAULE

1981, Maryland

It is mid-March and we awake to our daily routines: showers, bed-making, breakfast and all the rest. Rose says that this is the day. I'm dubious. After all, there have been no clarion cries from the heavens, no storks seen fleeting against the still wintery sky. It's much too or-dinary a day for such a remarkable event as the birth of our baby. We go about our work.

At lunch Rose is insistent: our baby will come today. Subtly, her conviction creeps through me. I must admit there's a special air of an-ticipation after all. Rose says that she's feeling contractions. Not the trial-run variety but the real thing. Now I'm convinced.

The batteries in the camera are dead, and there's no film. A calami-ty! The events of this day must be caught on film. We decide to go to the town nearby to get the photo stuff. As soon as we hit the road the contractions start coming closer. By the time we pull up at the drug store it's evident that the drive has been a powerful stimulus to labor.

While I see about the film and batteries, Rose goes to the bathroom in the back of the drugstore. The elderly, rouged clerk knows. She beams in anticipation as she directs Rose to the potty.

The drive back home has the effect of plunging us deep into active first stage labor. I fill the bathtub, all the while mentally scanning the inventory of birthing supplies we will need. While Rose bathes she keeps me posted on the contractions. They're becoming more insis-tent and more tightly spaced. I'm working quickly now. The bed is remade using two sets of sheets interspersed with a layer of plastic sheeting. The theory is that after the baby has come we'll merely pluck off the soiled sheets and—voila!—a clean bed ready for snug-gling. (Bad theory, it turns out.)

After getting all the birthing supplies laid out, I call our midwife Brenda. She says she'll be out in a couple of hours; she has to come

from Baltimore, a good haul. I call Patricia, who will be our birth assistant. She's birthed most of her kids at home and Rose and I take great comfort in knowing she'll be here to help.

The sun is already low, casting long shadows in our bedroom. I've lit some of our favorite incense and an Indian raga pulses softly. Lying on the bed with Rose, I give her steady counterpressure in the small of her back. She says that helps. We seem to be working outside of time now. Though I glance at my watch every now and then, timing the contractions, it's as though we are standing in a great void awaiting the challenge of the next few hours; not afraid, not anticipating, just doing what seems right for the moment.

Downstairs our neighbor John (we live in a two-family home) is preparing dinner. The aroma of food drifts up to us. Normally the smell would be delectable but for now we have no appetite. John has promised a birthday cake in honor of the day. His wife, Nancy, has joined us along with Patricia. Rose says that she's hot and Nance cools her brow with a wet cloth while I continue working to alleviate the pressure at the base of her spine. Patricia delicately performs effleurage on Rose's swollen belly.[1] The baby has clearly dropped and entered the birth canal.

Nance and Patricia's voices join mine as we gently encourage Rose in her work. Without pre-arrangement the three of us lock into Rose's breathing rhythm. I realize that we are subtly influencing the way in which Rose breathes. When her rhythm starts to speed up or becomes scattered we three are able to stabilize it through the regulation of our own breathing.

Brenda arrives and her quiet assurance reinforces the powerful yet peaceful feeling at hand. She does a quick exam and says that the baby is doing well and Rose is dilated almost to ten centimeters. Brenda's contribution is perfect throughout. Respectful of our wish for a gentle, non-interventive birth, she retires to the sideline, only occasionally checking on our progress.

Transition comes and it's classic. Rose gets downright snappy. She wants to be massaged, then she doesn't; she's hot, then she's cold; she's thirsty, then she's not. "Turn off the music," she demands. The tape is quickly stopped. "Stop talking," Rose insists. There is silence. She can't seem to find a comfortable position. Sitting, standing, squatting—nothing brings comfort. We stand by beaming our love to Rose in her travail, knowing that this can't last long. And it doesn't. As quickly as transition came on, it fades. The contractions have slackened a bit. Then after a time (what time?—the planet is surely stilled in its revolutions awaiting our birth) Rose says that she wants to push.

First she tries squatting but finds the position ineffective. Then she tries kneeling, chin on the window sill, but still says that she's having trouble bringing herself to bear down on her sweet burden. We try everything. Pillows, an inverted chair, a bean bag chair—but nothing seems to work.

At last we find a way that works. It's unorthodox, but who cares? Patricia and I stand on either side of Rose, each supporting her under her arms and thighs. Rose is in a semi-standing position as though she is seated in a swing, her legs stretched out as though building the momentum needed to begin the first arc that starts the swinging process. She pushes with each contraction and says that though it burns and hurts she feels that she's making headway.[2]

Brenda takes up a position on her hands and knees to try to see what progress we're making. She's a good sport; our futon bed sits right on the floor and in order to get any kind of view Brenda must assume an ungainly position. In time she says that the baby is crowning. Between contractions I manage a peek. "The baby's head is right there!" I tell Rose, "You're nearly there!"

The pushing is really hurting Rose and I know that she wants to yell with the pain. But instead, she starts singing! At least you would call it that if you were generous. It comes out a little like Tarzan singing scales, punctuated with a gripping "oooeeeaah" for a grace note. When we talk about it afterwards Rose 'fesses up and says it was the most socially acceptable way she could scream without actually screaming.

Rose is getting tired. She's been pushing for a couple of hours now and though the baby's crown is in plain view, it seems that we are at an impasse. The baby's not coming down anymore. With each urge to her uterus, Rose seems to be losing the effectiveness in her pushing.

For the first time, a small knife of worry cuts through the room. Rose rests for a time and then tries pushing some more. But it's no good. She can't seem to bring any force to bear. It's as though she's run her last mile and her muscles no longer will obey.

Patricia is the one who solves the dilemma. Her many years spent doctoring her family with homeopathic medicines produces an intuitive flash within her. She asks if we have any Gelsemium in the house. John checks and it turns out that we do. Rose is promptly given a dose.[3] The Gelsemium works almost immediately. Rose seems suddenly restored and full of resolve. It's a good thing too for Patricia and I are about at our strengths' end after having supported Rose bodily for the past three hours. My muscles are beginning to spasm in exhaustion. I don't know how Patricia has managed to keep up her support.

Rose now gives a mighty push and the baby's head comes into view. Without catching a breath, Rose bears down, focusing every fiber of her being into the push and the baby is born—head, shoulders and everything! Later on Brenda quietly comments that it's a good thing Rose wasn't lying down or the baby would have shot out the window.

We ease Rose into a sitting position on the bed while Brenda quickly clears the baby's nose and mouth with a syringe. "We have a girl," I hear myself telling Rose, "She's a beauty." The baby cries for just a moment and then is quiet. Brenda does a quick exam and says that the baby is whole and healthy. The ball of pinkness which is our baby is wrapped in a receiving blanket and given to Rose to nurse. With no fumbling, the baby finds Rose's breast and begins to suckle. I can't disconnect my eyes from our baby. I am stunned by this act of magic—for that is all that birth can be called—this act which has brought our daughter to us.

The placenta comes after a bit and Brenda says all is well, though as a result of that last mighty push she has some needle and thread work to do. While the stitching is being done I support Rose from the back, all the while watching over her shoulder as the baby nurses. I am entranced. The baby's purity and sweetness are indescribable.

After the sewing's done, John brings up bowls of rice and steaming vegetables which quickly vanish. This baby-bearing business produces powerful appetites. This is followed by a luscious birthday cake and fruit juice. Rose says she's feeling stronger now and wants to take a bath. We draw a lukewarm bath and she and the baby get in. Our daughter is a true Pisces—she's delighted with the water. Quickly she relaxes in the soft warmth, letting her limbs explore this watery place. While Rose and the baby linger in the tub, I put fresh sheets on the bed. During the night's course the bed and surrounding room have become a shambles. But getting fresh bedclothes on the futon seems to be the only important business for the moment. One by one, our friends and helpers take their leave.

Rose and the baby towel dry and we all snuggle together in our bed, delightfully exhausted. With one dim lamp burning we share a special time together. It is long past midnight when sleep at last overtakes the three of us. Sometime around dawn, when the windows are tinged with the scarlet of sunrise, I awaken. The previous night's work seems as though it has been a dream. Yet the proof of its reality lies on the pillow between Rose and me. Our baby sleeps quietly and thoroughly, relishing the peace that follows a long, hard journey.

We name our baby girl Willow some two weeks later. Rose and I love the sound of this name. It's only later that we realize that our baby was conceived at a time when we planted a willow sapling alongside the little stream that runs through our garden.

Sixteen and Determined

CHANDRA ROWE

1982, Sacramento, California

I think my labor started on Thursday, the day before my baby was born. I started getting a lot of uncomfortable contractions in my lower abdomen and I could not sleep much Thursday night. I tried all kinds of different positions, but none of them felt comfortable to me. The next morning came and I was still having the contractions. I tried not to think about them. I got ready for school and work. I walked around a lot more than usual because walking felt better than sitting or lying down. While at work I tried to do the things I usually do, but I ended up walking around with every contraction.

I work in the office of the high school I attend. After I finished work I went to class as usual. This class was a program for pregnant teenagers and it was supposed to get us ready for pregnancy and birth. I was sixteen at this time. I told my teacher I was having some kind of uncomfortable feeling down in my lower abdomen, but that I didn't know what it was. I thought maybe it was just the pressure of the baby because the head was very low and just starting to engage in my pelvis. I tried to watch a birth movie in class but the contractions seemed to be coming more often. I really didn't believe they were contractions because the baby wasn't due for another two weeks. Also, I figured that contractions were supposed to hurt more and that I would feel them all around my belly, not just in my lower abdomen.[1]

In the pregnancy class we had been learning all about how the baby grows. One of the ways we did this was by having prenatal checks in class. During these checks we kept track of the baby's growth. We listened to its heartbeat and we tried to figure out its position. We also learned about our own health status. On this day David, one of my childbirth teachers, palpated my uterus to see how low the baby was and if the head was engaged. He said the baby was engaged but he thought I would not have the baby for another week.

After this check, I really didn't think I could be in labor. When school was over I went shopping for about an hour. I kept feeling cramping and the pressure, but still I didn't think these were contractions so I didn't think about timing them. After shopping I was very tired since I hadn't gotten any sleep the night before. I took a short nap. I could still feel the sensations but I could sleep through them. When I got up, they were still there. They really didn't hurt that much but they were uncomfortable.

My mom called from work and I told her I was still having the uncomfortable feelings in my lower abdomen. She was getting very nervous and worried about me. She had told me that morning that she thought I would be having my baby very soon. Well, I still needed my papers signed by the pediatrician if I wanted the home-style birthing room at the hospital. It was Friday and it happened to be my brother's birthday. Mom and I needed to get his cake and some things for the party he was having that night. After my mom got off work about 4:30 P.M., she picked me up at home so we could run the errands together. We went to the pediatrician's office to get the papers signed. At that point my mom wanted to start timing my contractions. I didn't want her to because I really didn't think they were the real thing. She was getting very nervous because the contractions seemed to be coming closer together. My mom started timing them and found they were about five minutes apart. I kept telling her not to worry because this wasn't labor.

After we left the doctor's office we went shopping for a gift for my brother. My mother was still timing. We went to the bank and then we went to another store. In the stores I didn't feel like walking too fast and I had a hard time keeping up with my mother. Once in a while I would stop and do a little Lamaze breathing. The contractions started coming about two to three minutes apart. I really wanted to pretend that it wasn't happening, but they were coming closer together and I found myself breathing through them. Mom really looked worried. I kept telling her not to be concerned, but she wanted to hurry home. We got back home and she told me to call the doctor. I didn't want to, but I did. The nurse told me to come to the hospital and get checked. I didn't have my suitcase packed yet, so I started to pack, but I did it very slowly because I still didn't think it was real labor. We had to leave about ten minutes before my brother's birthday party was supposed to start. We left a note on the door telling the guests that the party was postponed to a later date.

I got to the hospital about 7:00 P.M., I had already pre-registered so all they had to do was take me upstairs to check me. They found I was already dilated to six centimeters! I was shocked! I hadn't wanted to go to the hospital because I thought I would be sent back home and that would have embarrassed me. They took me to the home-style room and the doctor came in soon after. Actually, when I had called the doctor's office earlier, I had learned that my own doctor wouldn't be on call that night. I really didn't like that news at all because I had talked to my doctor about the way I wanted to have my birth. He knew and had agreed that I was to have it as naturally as possible. I didn't know the other doctor or feel sure what to expect from him. When the new doctor came in he checked me and said I was only five centimeters and he said he wanted to break my water bag and give me an IV. He also wanted to put a fetal heart monitor on me. I looked at my mom and said, "No way." I told the doctor "No!" I felt disappointed and very mad at this type of intervention. He wanted to do all that to me, even though I had no problems and had prepared so carefully. I asked him why and he said that an IV was necessary "just in case something happens." Then he asked me if I didn't want my labor to go faster. He said, "It will go faster if I break the water bag." Again I refused. I believe he then tried to make me feel guilty by telling me that he had to go do a "C-section" on a teenage girl who had only been in labor for an hour and the baby was already in trouble. He thought that since I was also a teenager I would have problems. I knew I wouldn't since I was really prepared. Then he told me that he would tell the nurses to go ahead with these procedures but I could refuse if I wanted. Before he left, he reminded me that if anything bad happened it would not be his fault.[2]

After the doctor left my labor slowed down for a while. The contractions were not coming as often as they had when I first got to the hospital. I think this was because the doctor really upset me. I called my boyfriend's sister and asked her to tell Juan that I was in the hospital. I called David, my teacher and labor coach, but he was at a baseball game. I left a message. Juan's sister and two of her friends came around 9:00 P.M. to see how I was doing.

While I was waiting for Juan and David, I walked up and down the halls and looked in the nurseries and relaxed with each contraction. Juan got there a little while later and he was really worried about me. Most of what he had heard about having babies was negative. He had had no childbirth training. David called me and asked how I was doing. I told him about the new doctor and about how he seemed to be trying to take over. David told me that this particular doctor had a reputation for doing a lot of intervention and that he did many cesarean sections. This information made me realize what I was really up against and I knew I wouldn't let the doctor do anything unless I really thought it was necessary. David got to the hospital soon after our conversation.

I started feeling better after Juan and David were there. I still hadn't dilated any since the doctor had upset me. I was still having contractions, but they weren't lasting as long as they had before. The nurses were really nice but they told me that the contractions needed to be harder. I was standing against the wall massaging my stomach through each contraction. Now they were coming closer and harder. The nurse came back in about 10:15 and asked me to lie down so she could check me. The only time I would lie down was during these checks. As I was lying there I started feeling that I couldn't do it anymore because the pressure of the baby seemed so hard against my rectum. David was sitting on one side of me and he asked Juan to come over and sit behind me and rub my back. David kept telling me to do my breathing, because I kept saying I couldn't do it anymore. I didn't know at the time, but I was in transition. David started blowing in my face so I would keep doing the blowing with him. It felt like I needed to push. The nurse told me I was dilated all the way but that I couldn't push until the doctor got there. Juan was rubbing my back and David kept telling me to blow rather than push. David asked the nurses three times if I could push, but they kept telling me to wait for the doctor. He asked one last time if I could push and they finally said yes. So, I looked at David and he looked at me and we knew that we had to get the baby out before the doctor got there. I didn't want that doctor there because of the way he treated me earlier. I was afraid he would break my water bag and give me an episiotomy. David looked at me and I felt that he must have been thinking the same thing. I started pushing and a resident doctor came in. She also knew I wanted to deliver before the other doctor came. I told her I didn't want an episiotomy, so she started massaging my perineum. This young doctor must have thought I was going to need a cut anyway though, because I saw the nurse hand her the needle for the local anesthetic. I knew that she was going to cut me regardless of what I wanted. I had to think fast. I asked her if she could give me the injection while I was pushing. She said no. My next contraction came and I pushed and held it so she couldn't give me a shot or a cut. During this contraction my water bag broke by itself and I pushed the baby out. The other doctor came in just as I was delivering. I felt so relieved and I was so proud that I had done it without any interference! The resident laid my son on the bed. The doctor told her to stimulate the baby because he wasn't moving. She picked him up and he began to move. It was 11:49 P.M. when my son was born. The resident cut the cord and wrapped the baby up and handed him to me. The doctor looked very surprised and then he congratulated me. I guess he was surprised that I did it without him and without any trouble. I was in the home-style room so I got to stay there about two hours or more after I delivered. Then I went to my room, where I stayed about a day and a half.

My birth experience was really exciting and if I could have changed anything I would have probably waited longer before going to the hospital. Also I would have been more aware of the fact that my doctor had some doctors backing him up who did not agree with my ideas.

I gave birth to my son, Steven Vincent Trillas, on June 25, 1982. He weighed six pounds, seven ounces and he was eighteen and a half inches long. He was fine and very healthy.

Home Birth After Two Cesareans

DEBORAH REGAL

1982, Ann Arbor, Michigan

I will always remember my feelings when I found out I was pregnant with my first child. Never mind that in July 1977 I had only been married four months, that my husband and I had no money and were both college students, or that the pregnancy was not exactly planned —I was ecstatic! My husband, Randy, was less enthused than I. However, when miscarriage threatened a month later, it became apparent to me that he truly wanted that child.

Following the miscarriage scare, I quit my job and left school to protect my baby from exposure to toxic chemicals in the chemistry lab. Since my identity had to that point been entirely wrapped up in my education, I felt at loose ends. After a period of depression, I pulled myself together and commenced preparing for the arrival of the new life within me. I immersed myself in the pregnancy and reveled in every new facet. I was conscious of my nutrition, avoided alcohol and all drugs, chose the "best" doctors, and took childbirth classes. Childbirth books were my constant companions.

Despite all of this preparation, I felt uneasy about the birth. My fear of the pain and memory of the horror stories that I had heard from relatives while growing up certainly did not help. Also, the childbirth classes and books seemed to dwell on procedures that repulsed me. I did not want an enema, shave, episiotomy, etc., but nobody even implied that I had the right to question or refuse these procedures.

As a result of this uneasiness within me, I became increasingly sure that something was going to go wrong. Ten days after my baby's theoretical due date, my water broke when I sat up in bed. I dutifully called the teaching hospital where I was to deliver and was told to come in. Off Randy and I went to the hospital. I was admitted, my clothes were taken, and Randy and I were left to make ourselves at home in the stark labor room. My contractions had not yet begun. About 11:30 A.M. I asked for some food. The staff refused at first, then finally gave in and ordered me a tray of jello and boullion. Yuk!

Following "lunch" I was hooked up to a pitocin drip to help my body get those contractions started, even though my membranes had only been ruptured for four hours.[1] Next, an external fetal monitor was connected to my bulging belly and I was told to lie down and remain still. The contractions were very painful and I desperately wanted to be massaged and to change positions. These comfort measures were prohibited because of the monitor. In addition, I was allowed nothing by mouth. I was hungry and thirsty. I needed to move, eat, and drink.

To make a long story short, after thirty hours of internal and external monitors, continuous pitocin, unrelenting back labor, muscle relaxants, a paracervical block, frequent internal exams, X-raw pelvimetry, and every breathing technique in the book, I gave up. I was exhausted and my loving, supportive husband was at his wit's end. At seven centimeters dilation, I pulled out the pit drip and asked for a cesarean.

My request was granted, and because of my fear of spinal needles, I had general anesthesia. As a consequence, poor Randy was shooed out to the deserted waiting room to pace and worry. Tiny Jeremy Randolph was born healthy but groggy that cold March afternoon without either of his parents there to greet him. My heart ached for his loneliness.

My physical recovery from the ordeal was rapid, but I was in terrible shape emotionally. I felt as though I had failed at giving birth, was inadequate as a woman; and I was jealous of all my friends' vaginal births. I grew depressed and considered sterilization and suicide. I never wanted to go through childbirth again. I was experiencing grief for the loss of my baby's ideal birth.

My saving graces were Randy's undying love for me, that dependent little baby of mine, and time. Since I was breastfeeding successfully and Jeremy was growing into a responsive, happy person, I started to regain some of my lost self-esteem. I was on the long road to emotional recovery.

Time did heal most of the wounds left by my first childbirth experience, or at least I thought it had. The true test came when, nine months after Jeremy's birth, I became pregnant again. I was overwhelmed by conflicting emotions triggered by this second pregnancy.

Outwardly I accepted the "necessity" of a repeat cesarean, but a rebellion was raging internally. I desired to labor, to give birth, and to greet my baby. Instead of asserting myself and searching for supportive information on vaginal birth after cesarean (VBAC), I was silenced by my new doctor's warnings that a vaginal birth was too dangerous. His arguments against VBAC included a projected increase in the risk of uterine rupture because of my babies' births being so close together, and also the suggestion that my pelvis was probably "inadequate." Even though this opposition silenced me externally, that little voice within me still cried out for a vaginal birth.

Filled with that secret dream, I turned my energy toward producing a healthy baby. I ate an abundance of nutritious food and exercised sufficiently, playing with little Jeremy and his friends. My husband was busy with school and work but spent as much time as possible at home. I felt us growing closer as a family.

Since the doctor had agreed to wait for the natural onset of labor to perform the repeat cesarean, I secretly planned to wait at home until labor was so advanced that only a vaginal birth would be possible. However, as the due date neared, I had second thoughts about this covert plan. "What if my uterus *did* rupture?" I wondered. My fears began to mount.[2]

These fears surfaced in the form of mysterious pains in the area of my previous incision. These sharp pains awakened me one morning and sent me into a panic. I went to my doctor, and even though he could find nothing in particular wrong with me, he suggested that I have an elective cesarean the following morning, just in case my incision was separating. I agreed. My dreams of a vaginal birth were shattered.

After a tearful goodbye to Jeremy, Randy and I entered the hospital that afternoon. I was a wreck. I hated the staff, the routine, myself, and even my unborn baby. Even though Randy was allowed to stay with me all night, it was the longest night of my life. I felt like a caged animal waiting for slaughter.

Early the next morning, October 18, 1979, I was taken to the delivery area and prepped. Randy and I were separated for the administration of epidural anesthesia. There was a rare complication and the epidural turned into a total spinal. I was sedated and lost consciousness at that point.[3]

Fortunately, Randy was allowed to be present anyway to greet Justin Curtis. Since Justin was born at 37 weeks gestation (about three weeks before his due date), there was some concern about his lung maturity, so he was whisked away to the nursery. Thankfully, his lungs were fine. My uterus was also fine; there were no signs of scar separation.

As soon as I was able to breathe on my own again I was moved to the recovery room. Randy was with me and Justin joined us soon after. He was a little dark-haired angel and I fell in love with him instantly.

Apart from a persistent spinal headache and sore nipples from breastfeeding, my physical recovery was uneventful. On the other hand, once again I was an emotional disaster. The anesthesiologist's nonchalant remark, "So what if you didn't see your baby born? You have him for the next eighteen years anyway," infuriated me. It did matter! I grieved again for another lost birth.

My struggle to put my birth traumas to rest led me to Boston to C/SEC, Inc.'s Cesarean Update Conference in October 1981.[4] What a relief it was to finally be able to unload my feelings and share them with other women who had experienced cesarean grief. As an added bonus, Nancy Wainer Cohen spoke about vaginal birth after cesarean. Her refreshing new approach changed my attitude and my life. VBAC was possible for me![5]

I returned home from that conference bubbling with enthusiasm. A few days later, my third child was intentionally and lovingly conceived. Not only was there excitement about his impending arrival, but also about the wonderful possibilities for his birth. The work was now underway.

Surprisingly, my doctor was supportive of my hope for a VBAC. Since attending my second birth he had become more aware of the importance of the emotional needs of birthing women. Not so surprisingly, however, the hospital nurses, anesthesiologists, and my doctor's associates had more reservations. The consensus was that I could attempt a VBAC but would have to be monitored closely. Oh, no! I was determined not to get on that merry-go-round of labor intervention again. Consequently, I began to think about alternatives to hospital birth.

After an exhaustive search of the literature and local birth resources, Randy and I chose home birth. Pat and Jan, experienced lay midwives, planned to attend the birth and my doctor agreed to provide hospital back-up. In addition, the newly selected pediatrician consented to come over after the birth to examine the baby. An elaborate protocol was drawn up so that all parties involved were clearly informed about what conditions would lead to transport to the hospital and so on. At last, all my desires were out in the open. The burden of my secret birth fantasy had been lifted.

I did encounter some resistance from family members. They were concerned about my safety. I offered to provide them with reading material on VBAC and home birth, but they still were not convinced. Despite my desire to allay their fears, I had to go through with my plans. I knew in my heart I was right.

Preparing for the birth was all-consuming. I exercised daily, both yoga and vigorous walking; kept a daily nutrition record, especially noting my protein intake; and rested every afternoon. Perineal massage and daily doses of red raspberry leaf and comfrey tea were also on the agenda.[6] Randy practiced techniques learned in Bradley method classes with me, which helped to better define his support role.

Jeremy, four, and Justin, two-and-a-half, were also involved in preparing for the birth. I provided them with books, pictures, and slides about birth. Randy and I talked with them often about the baby and answered their questions. I decided to wait until the actual birth day to see if the boys could be present for the birth.

As the mercury soared near my mid-July due date, I became impatient. I was big, hot, and tired. Two active little boys on the outside, and one filling my insides, soaked up my energy reserves. Not surprisingly, my spirits took a nosedive. Due to my exhaustion, doubts about my ability to give birth crept back into my mind. As a result, I feel, my body refused to initiate genuine labor.

Because I was beginning to talk about scheduling a cesarean and surrendering again, Randy took charge. He called the midwives and told them about my depression. Coincidentally, Pat happened to run into a friend of hers, Brody, who knew how to induce labor using accupressure massage.[7] It seemed the momentum behind my birth plan was still going strong. Arrangements were made for Brody to come over that same evening.

I packed up the boys and sent them off to my parents' home nearby. It was hard to say goodbye, but I needed a tranquil house at that time to rest and focus on the birthing energy. I explained this to them, and they were eager to be with Grandma and Grandpa.

Brody and Jan came over at 8:00 P.M. Brody massaged points on my hands, feet, and legs. These massages ached slightly and lasted only a few minutes each. Brody left an hour later and I was on my own. By 10:00 P.M. my contractions were seven minutes apart and intense. My body was working! At that point I knew I was going to actively participate in that baby's birth. I called Randy at work and asked him to come home to share the labor with me.

I went up to the baby's room, curled up in the rocker and became involved in my birthing work. Randy soon joined me and then the midwives, and I shared with them all what seemed like a proud secret, laboring while the rest of the city slept. The contractions were strong and painful yet filled me with a glowing energy. I had not slept in eighteen hours but I was not tired at all. I breathed, rocked, relaxed, and worked all night.

The dawn of the new day brought with it the urge to push. After trying several positions, I ended up on the floor on my side with Randy's shoulder supporting my top leg. Pushing hurt like crazy. I never dreamed it would be such hard work. My vagina burned and stretched and slowly, slowly my baby descended. I turned myself over into a modified squat and reached into my vagina to touch my baby's head. Presto! I was renewed.

An hour or so later I pushed that last big push and my baby's head emerged. I closed my eyes, pushed gently again, and out slid his vernix-covered body. His lusty, welcome cry filled the air. It was 8:00 A.M., July 30, 1982, and the birds outside the window were singing a lullaby to my baby. Joshua Aaron had arrived!

Joshua was beautiful. His head was perfectly shaped and he was more alert than either of his brothers had been at birth. He was busy looking at Randy and me and only nursed a little. After I held and stroked my new son, his intact placenta was expelled with one push. I was filled with appreciation for that large, shiny red organ that had helped me nourish my baby. I saved it to show my boys.

The midwives tended to a small perineal tear. Then Joshua and I were treated to a soothing herbal bath. I was filled with spiritual peace. I was tired but content.

Joshua was examined by the pediatrician when he was five hours old. All systems were fine. He was a big baby, weighing nine pounds, four ounces, which put to rest all my fears about the adequacy of my pelvis. Randy and I reiterated our desire for our baby to remain intact, and no circumcision was done.

Jeremy and Justin were thrilled, after some initial fuss about having a new brother instead of a sister. They smothered him with kisses and took turns holding him. He was "their" baby.

I look back now on my children's births and see how they led me through a process of tremendous personal growth. The first two births showed me areas to work on and exposed painful wounds, but the third experience let me tap inner resources that I never knew existed. My home birth was a peaceful, healing experience. My inner self was enriched by the process of growth and I am better able to give of myself to Randy and all my precious sons.

Katy Jane: Anencephaly

PEGGY CANNON

1982, Ontario, Canada

It had been a strange pregnancy. I had difficulty making contact with the baby. For an awfully long time I couldn't even feel her. Then around 20 weeks my tummy bulged, and the baby moved. It was a few weeks more before I began to feel the telepathy. Tentatively at first, then strengthening gradually, I felt that this was a sweet baby that might be different from our other two children. I wasn't really worried, but I hoped she might not be too different.

Blooming with good health, I went to my prenatal appointment at six and a half months. Midwife Natalie asked if I wanted an ultrasound. A doctor I had seen early in the pregnancy had suggested the possibility of anencephaly.[1] Natalie's face told me she didn't believe it, but my chest seemed to go all solid and heavy. I stayed cheery and smiling and said, "Well, why not ultrasound?" But I knew. I didn't need ultrasound to tell me. I knew. My baby was anencephalic.

The next few days passed in bleak depression. I thought back to the pictures of anencephalic babies in the textbook for midwives I had read a few years earlier—bulgy eyes, long monkey arms, no skull, exposed undeveloped brain. The baby would be unable to live outside the womb. I felt sick, revolted. The once active baby became very quiet and barely moved. As I calmed, I began to feel that the baby was frightened too. Time and again I would hear that anencephalic babies lack that part of the brain which makes us human, but I have never been able to doubt that when I pulled away from my baby, she reacted with a very real fear of her own. When I could still my fears and love her, she resumed her activity and loved me back.

The obstetrician who did the ultrasound recommended a "mini-C-section." I was 28 weeks pregnant; too late for an abortion, too early (he said) for an induction. I resisted. I knew Natalie well enough to know that she would never approve of a C-section, but she never said so. She and her husband Terry, our family doctor, sat with us, let us talk and talk, and waited while we changed our minds again and again. They let us know they would support us in whatever we needed to do. They helped us explore all our options: the cesarean, induction now, induction later, or carry the pregnancy to term for delivery at home or in the hospital. Because I had suddenly begun taking on excessive amniotic fluid (polyhydramnios), we might reasonably expect an early labor.[2] Then again, anencephalic babies can be very postmature because they lack a pituitary gland which may play some part in stimulating labor.

Unable to decide, my husband Roger and I closeted ourselves at home with obstetrical texts. For three days we read and talked, and yes, we cried. But I determined to put aside grief for a bit. I wanted so much to do this "right," to make a clear-headed decision. We needed to regain control of our lives, and I wanted to be the best mother I could be for this baby.

Because our fear of the baby's deformity was so strong, we rejected a home birth. Roger pointed out that a neutral setting might be less difficult emotionally, and he did not want the pain of memory imprinted on our home. For some of the same reasons we did not want to "let it happen." I feared delivering in the supermarket or on a roadside. I fantasized about the unsuspecting birth attendant's reaction. The environment surrounding the birth would be very important and we felt we needed to be certain of our arrangements.

Natalie and Terry continued to listen when we needed them. Natalie helped me to investigate hospitals and methods of induction. Finally she referred us to a doctor at a large medical center, an hour and a half away. This doctor thought they could provide the kind of environment we needed and he was willing to experiment gently with prostaglandins, a hormone widely used in Europe to stimulate labor but still very new and untried in Canada. We hoped the prostaglandins would ripen the cervix and prepare it for Syntocinon.[3] In some cases prostaglandins have actually started the labor and allowed it to progress somewhat naturally.

We had three weeks to wait for the scheduled induction, time enough to accept the deformity and to grieve over the inevitable death. I would be 32 weeks pregnant. The polyhydramnios was increasingly uncomfortable. I couldn't sleep. I was glad it would soon be over. I fretted about the baby, about the pain an induction might cause it to suffer. It seemed the baby and I had attained a kind of peace, as though we had accepted each other's fear as well as love. All that was left was to mother her as an anencephalic baby might need to be mothered.

I searched the books for clues about what senses she might have and what I might do to keep her comfortable for the short time that she might live. Anencephaly is relatively common as a birth defect, occurring at a rate of about one to two per thousand births. Yet there seemed to be no information, as though anencephalic babies had been ignored or forgotten. At first I was angry and frustrated. Later I realized the books had nothing to say because anencephalic babies virtually have no senses or perceptual processes. They cannot swallow or nurse. The best I would be able to do was to hold my baby, love her, and hope that she would know we cared.

Then, as I looked forward to the birth with something like anticipation, the baby died. Movement stopped, but just as obvious was a feeling of "nobody's home." It was as though she had literally packed up and gone. I was disappointed, but for a baby who could never live outside the womb, who was so very "wrong," perhaps death inside was finally something "right."

Roger and I checked into the hospital together. Roger had a roll-away bed in our private room and he never left my side. Emotionally he was as much involved and as much a patient as I and the nurses gave him that consideration. Those few days of preparing the cervix and inducing labor slowly were good for us. Roger and I had a chance to focus on each other and our feelings about what we were experiencing.

When the labor finally began, we were ready and welcomed it. But the contractions slowed, stopped, and began again in short, annoying high-pitched bursts. After a long off-and-on night, I was exhausted, depressed, and crying. A woman doctor whom I had not met before came in and simply sat close to me and waited. When I could talk, I explained that I preferred to deliver in the labor room and that I was not keen on pain relievers or an epidural. I wanted to experience the birth fully and to go home as soon as possible afterward. The doctor gave me her understanding and approval.

I had never before faced death directly. Natalie had prepared us for what we might see, but as the labor gathered strength, my fears nearly paralyzed me. My mind sought frantically for a way out of this. But the machine kept pumping Syntocinon and the contractions wouldn't let me quit. They kept coming and building. This baby, in whatever condition, was going to come out.

Roger held me, breathed with me, and looked so confident that at times I almost forgot and thought we were having a "real" baby.

Natalie came, rubbed my back, and helped us change our breathing to accommodate a powerful premature urge to push. The nurse moved around us, caring and supportive, urging me away from my fears back to a more accepting, birthing frame of mind.

At five centimeters dilation the pressure became too much and the doctor ruptured the membranes. The brown tinted water poured out of me, soaked the bed, and ran onto the floor. We felt the baby was small enough that I would not have to dilate fully in order to push. When it was clear that my uterus would push in spite of my panting and blowing and making strange noises, the doctor sat on the edge of the bed and told me to go ahead. There were drapes stacked nearby, but no one suggested we use them.

One push and a tiny foot emerged. I pushed again, and there was a round purple bum. I put my hands around it and just held her. A final push, and she was lying on the bed. I sat up straight and wondered why I had been afraid. Katy was so little . . . she was mine . . . and I loved her.

The doctor put some scissors in my hand and asked me to cut the cord. The nurse rummaged in our Lamaze bag and found the blankets I had brought. I wrapped Katy completely in a soft flowered receiving blanket and then again in a white lace one. The choice of blankets had been very important. Not only were they a final attempt at being Katy's mother, but I felt that to anyone she encountered between us and the crematorium it would be a signal, our way of saying she had been loved and cared for and not just abandoned. Roger and Natalie cuddled her, then I passed her to the nurse who held her sweetly in her arms and took her away.

I had a warm shower and we walked back to the ward. Roger and I cuddled in my bed and slept until evening, when friends came to take us home.

I have some sadness left and a little pain. It was a sad birth, though intensely powerful and fulfilling too. But there are no empty arms around our house. Sometimes I look at my family and feel that someone is missing. But it isn't Katy. We accepted Katy. We loved her as she was, an anencephalic baby never meant to come home.

A Grandmother Welcomes and Remembers

SONIA MARGULIS

1982, Oakland, California

The shrill ringing of the phone woke me at five o'clock that morning. "It must be the wrong number," I thought, half asleep. But Willie, who had been awake for some time, said "It's probably news of Judy. I'll bet she's in labor."

As I picked up the phone I heard a cheerful voice. "Sonia, congratulations. You have a granddaughter." Confused, I muttered, "What do you mean? Judy had her baby?"

"Yes. She just gave birth to a beautiful little girl."

"How is she, and how is the baby?"

"Everything is fine. Judy had a very easy birth and the baby is healthy."

"Why didn't they call me? I was supposed to welcome the baby into the world."

"It was too late. The baby came so fast that there was no time."

I was disappointed that I hadn't been there to witness the birth, and yet the relief that I felt was overwhelming. Mothers always worry about their daughters giving birth and I was no different. In this case we were all particularly concerned because the birth was at home.

I remembered the anxiety that Adele, Judy's mother-in-law, expressed. "Doesn't it bother you that she will not have the baby in the hospital? What if something goes wrong?" And when Adele met Judy's doctor, Karen, at the baby shower, she was even more worried. "This little girl is going to deliver my grandchild?"

"Stop worrying, Adele. Karen is a wonderful doctor and she specializes in delivering beautiful, healthy babies. Didn't she do a great job when Jacob was born? And a second child is usually easier. Besides, the hospital is only five minutes away, so there will be no problem to get her there if anything should go wrong."

Actually, I was reassuring myself as well as Adele when I said this. I am not a nervous mother, but in the back of my mind there were doubts. Home births are still not the accepted procedure. Why must my daughter be a pioneer?

I was still dressing when a picture flashed through my mind of the birth of my brother some seventy years before. I was five years old, loved and cherished by my parents, grandparents and uncles. Then one day all the attention seemed to end. I remember that day very clearly.

I was awakened by a great deal of activity in our small Bronx apartment. It was still dark and Mama and Papa were up. I could hear Mama's voice. Something was happening but I didn't know what. Papa looked worried and Mama seemed to be complaining.

When Mama got out of bed, she washed and dried her beautiful long hair, braided it and let it hang down her back. It almost reached her hips. She looked like Rapunzel from the fairy tale. When she dressed in a gray sweater and skirt, I was disappointed. Rapunzel would have worn a long flowing gown. Mama would have been even more beautiful than the maiden in the story.

But Mama was not smiling. She paced up and down the living room all day long, moaning and groaning, while Papa stood by helplessly. If only I knew what was going on! No one paid any attention to me. I felt guilty. Was it something that I did? I always felt guilty when Mama wasn't feeling well. As the hours dragged on, the pacing increased and the moans became louder.

In the late afternoon Papa went out to make a telephone call. When he returned, he told me that Miss Katcher was coming. I loved Miss Katcher. She was an old friend of the family, a grandmotherly woman who was short, bosomy, dumpy, with white hair which she wore in a severe bun. She always dressed in the same black skirt and white blouse. She spoke only Russian. Fortunately, I could communicate with her since I was still in my Russian-speaking years. My parents had emigrated from Russia just before I was born. Papa called Miss Katcher the "Acushurka," and explained that she was something like a doctor without a diploma.[1] I was happy that she was coming. She was kind and friendly and usually played with me. Sometimes she would even bring me a story book and read to me. Perhaps she would tell me what was wrong with Mama.

But when Miss Katcher arrived in the early evening I was disappointed. She hardly looked at me. She carried a little black bag, just like a doctor. She put on a white uniform and ushered Mama to bed. That was the last I saw of them.

Papa put me to bed at the usual hour but I could not sleep. The activity in Mama's bedroom increased. The moans and groans became screams and came faster and faster. What were they doing to my Mama? Suddenly there was a blood-curdling scream that seemed to cut through every fiber of my body, and then I heard an infant's cry.

I cried myself to sleep and when I awoke the next morning it was quiet and peaceful in the household. Papa gave me my breakfast and then told me that he had a surprise for me. He took me into Mama's bedroom. She was lying with an infant at her breast, all smiles, looking very heroic and proud. She had fought her battle and conquered the world. That was how I learned that I now had a brother.

Life after that was not the same. No longer was I the wonderful cherished child with whom Mama and Papa spent time, singing to me, playing with me, or telling me stories. No longer was there peace and quiet in the household. The baby cried a great deal and both Mama and Papa were nervous, not knowing what to do. I felt completely ignored except when Mama needed my help. Mama would be very impatient with me if I asked for something. I rocked the baby when he cried and sometimes I played with him so that Mama could attend to her household chores. I felt unloved. At times I even felt guilty, as if I had done something wrong. If I could only go back to those happy days when I had all of Mama's attention.

My thoughts ended abruptly when Willie called to me, "Aren't you dressed yet? Come, let's go."

"I'm coming, I'm coming," I answered and ran down the stairs.

Judy and Jeff live just a few blocks away from us, so we got to their house about fifteen minutes after the actual birth. A celebration was going on. Four smiling young women, each holding a glass of champagne, were surrounding the king-size bed in which Judy, with a beautiful baby at her breast, was holding court. Jeff, the proud father, stood by snapping picture after picture. We got into the swing of it, sipping champagne and hugging and kissing everybody.

We looked with amazement at the women, at their sparkling eyes and their joyous expressions. Each one looked as though she had performed a miracle. Each one had shared the pain and now was claiming her just deserts. They had helped to bring this baby into the world and felt so much love for her. What a wonderful way to be born!

"Oh, Mom," cried Judy, as she saw the tears of joy in my eyes. "I'm so sorry that you weren't here to see Hannah's birth. I asked them to call you, but Karen said it was too late. And sure enough, with the next push Hannah appeared."

"Don't worry about it. I'm so happy that you were able to deliver so quickly and everything went so smoothly. You are a lucky woman."

While I held the baby in my arms for the first time, Judy filled me in on all the details of the birth. Karen, her doctor, had come the night before, fully equipped with medical supplies, instruments, and an oxygen tank. She had spent the night there. They had called our son Michael, who had promised to care for Jacob, their two-year-old, during labor. They woke Jacob and explained, "Jacob, do you remember how we told you that when Hannah was about to be born, you would go to sleep at Jesse's?" (They had the name already prepared since the amniocentesis report told them they would have a girl.) Jacob, half asleep, nodded. "Well, when you come home from the Little School tomorrow, Hannah will be here." Jacob was well prepared and went with his uncle Michael very willingly. He loved his aunt Laurie and he and his cousin Jesse were good friends. He enjoyed sleeping at their house.

When the labor pains increased, Jeffrey telephoned their aides, all friends who had been expecting their call. Rubi had a ten-month-old boy at whose birth Judy had assisted. Judy D. had a girl just a few days older than Jacob. Judy C. was the midwife who had given Judy her prenatal care and was anxious to be present at the home birth. They were all there by 2:00 A.M., taking turns together with Jeffrey in holding Judy's hands, lifting her whenever she had a contraction, looking into her eyes, and making the same "ohming" sounds that she made. They comforted her, loved her, and shared in the pain. Jeff and Judy had taken a Bradley refresher course in preparation for the birth. Karen was with them throughout the labor, but decided to take a nap. She had just fallen asleep when she heard Judy's loud cry, "What's that coming out of me?" Karen came running. She found that the water had broken. Judy was fully dilated, and was ready to deliver. Judy said, "Call my mother." But it was too late. It took just a few minutes and two strong pushes for the baby to come out.

While Judy was relating this, I looked at the baby. She was wide awake, watching everybody and observing her new surroundings. I wondered why she wasn't crying. Karen explained that today babies are not slapped when they are first born. A baby needs the bonding with its mother, not the slapping hand of a strange doctor.

I felt that I had missed something. I should have been there, helping with the birth. I should have watched Hannah entering the world. I was envious of the women around me. I was merely an observer.

Despite the fact that the women had been awake most of the night, no one wanted to leave. We talked about births in general and I, being a veteran, told of my experiences: the hours of laboring alone in a hospital room, my fears, the drugs that were given to me, the feeling that no one cared, and the screaming that I did with each contraction. Judy C., the midwife, told us that many women scream to ease the pain.

Judy decided to take a shower. As soon as she left the bed the three women, like a well-trained team, without saying a word stripped the bed and put on fresh linen.

Rubi was the first to leave. She had to get back to Joey, her ten-month-old son. Judy thanked her and said, "I'll never forget how you looked into my eyes, how you helped me, and how you told me that I was doing great."

I wanted to help too. I could at least cook for them. We went home and cooked chicken and soup with matzo balls, stewed vegetables, a tossed salad, and a fresh fruit compote—enough food for two days.

My concern now was for Jacob. How would he greet Hannah's arrival? He had had plenty of preparation. They had talked about the baby from the moment they knew Judy was pregnant. Jacob was aware of Judy's changing body and would occasionally try to feel the baby's kicking. He knew that he would be the big brother. Every available book on the subject had been read to him. Yes, he was well prepared. But how would he react?

At first he was wonderful. He loved the baby; he petted and kissed her. The first morning after the birth, Judy sat with Jacob while he was eating breakfast. He insisted that Judy bring Hannah so that she could watch him eat. Usually he would dig into the cereal with his hands, but that morning he used a spoon, careful not to get his fingers dirty. "See, Hannah, this is how you eat your cereal." He boasted about his baby sister to his classmates in the Little School. He was the only one in his group to have a baby.

But gradually, he began to realize that even though he loved his sister, he hated being the big brother. It meant giving up too much, and the hardest part was when Hannah was nursing. He couldn't have his mother then. He once asked if it was possible to put Hannah back in Mommy's tummy. Another time he said to Judy, "Mommy, do you remember when there were just the three of us?"

Jeff and Judy were well aware of Jacob's conflicts. They devoted extra time to him. Jeff would sometimes take a few hours off from his job so that he could devote himself completely to Jacob. Judy would occasionally get baby-sitting help so that she could be alone with him. Such lucky children to have such understanding parents!

Hannah is now ten months old and a beautiful, healthy, bright, active child. She is a joy to all who encounter her, always smiling and happy, crying only when something bothers her, truly a magical child. She and Jacob are now friends. They love each other. Hannah loves Jacob's toys but he is not ready to share them. He will sometimes punch her when she grabs his things, but Hannah only laughs. She loves it.

I drop in to see them once in a while. At times Jacob will wave me away with "No Son-ee-ya," his name for me. But other times he welcomes me. The other day when I rang the bell, I waited several minutes until Judy opened the door. Jacob had told Judy to hide and pretend that no one was at home. Instead, Jacob was hiding. "You know," I said as I walked into their house, "I came to see Jacob. I missed his birthday party because I was ill. The last time I saw Jacob he was only two years old. I want to see what a three-year-old boy looks like." He came out of hiding, laughing.

"We just sent Jeffrey and Hannah off for a walk," said Judy. "We wanted to be alone."

"O.K. I'll leave now that I saw my three-year-old grandson."

"No, don't go," said Jacob. I stayed a while, read a story to him, and upon leaving invited him to have dinner with us. He wasn't quite ready to say "Yes," but promised one day soon to let me know.

Two generations away from him, I understand Jacob's feelings, remembering so clearly my own experiences with a new baby.

Miscarriage: The Silent Wail

MARIAN McDONALD

1983, Northern California

On a steamy Sunday afternoon, I dashed around Oakland from one political meeting to another, then home for a brief meal and a chance to wash up. Once home, I made the familiar beeline to the bathroom and struggled out of the ever-tightening jeans.

Then I saw the blood—frightening and ominous, just like that, suddenly and irrevocably. I grabbed my childbirth book "bible" and searched the index for "miscarriage."

"I'm just reading this because I should know what might happen in case of a miscarriage," I said to myself, "not because I am, because I'm not, I can't be, not me! This is just a coincidental bit of blood, not great rivers of blood that a miscarriage would be." I tried to control the panic inside me.

At my evening meeting I tried to pay attention to the discussion. But I had to keep checking, keep going to the bathroom to see if—oh, no! It was just a drop of dark brown blood, but it was still coming. The combination of the heat and my panic made me ill; I had to leave.

At home I found my old friend Karen, talking with Ramón. What should I do? I had to share with Ramón the fear that was engulfing me. I checked to see if, by some great chance, the bleeding had stopped. But no. "Ramón, I'm bleeding!" I spilled out, and went for the phone. Within moments I was talking to an "advice nurse" who told me not to worry, to lie down and drink wine, and call back if the bleeding increased. By this time I was in a daze and perfunctorily drank some wine and lay down.

I didn't really sleep that night, nor did Ramón. I tossed and turned with fitful dreams.

"Did you check?" Ramón asked, as I got out of bed in the morning.

"No," I said, feeling somewhat guilty. In all those sleepless hours of fear, I had not checked once to see if the blood was still there. I did not really want to know.

I went to the bathroom. "Ramón, it's—I'm going to call the hospital."[1]

"Well," whined the advice nurse I finally reached, "You can wait until nine o'clock for an appointment—after all, you waited all night."

I waited all night because that's what the nurse last night told me to do! But I swallowed that indignity and took the nine o'clock appointment. I called my job to say that I had a "medical problem" and then we were off.

Never have I felt such a restrained and detached manner as I did that morning with the nurse who examined me. She said my cervix was closed, that there was a 50/50 chance things were all right, and that I should take it easy and not have sex. All I wanted to have was a baby, to know that things would be all right. She also admonished me for my busy schedule, my running, and for not eating enough.[2]

"Call me if the bleeding gets heavier," she said, "or becomes bright red." Heavier or bright red. Heavier or bright red. I memorized her instructions.

By the time we got home the twinge of pelvic pain was becoming a cramp. Besides being a very bad sign, this was uncomfortable, especially in the wretched heat. We resigned ourselves to waiting it out at home. Ramón had the day off and could stay home with me. I don't remember what we did for the next few hours, but by early afternoon Ramón was off for a walk and maybe the movies. We agreed that he would check in periodically to see how I was doing.

Alone, I felt a deep emptiness and a cold, cold fear. Like a robot, I called person after person, to let them know I couldn't make my various appointments that day. It seemed as though I were someone else, making all those calls, while my real self was counting the last precious moments of my pregnancy.

By four o'clock it was bad. I had lots of pain and cramping, and the dark brown blood was interspersed with bright red blood. Oh, no, no, no!

The heat was awful too. I got dressed to go out and get some ice cream, the only thing I could think of to eat. As I walked to the corner store, I relished being a pregnant woman seeking ice cream in her barrio on a sweltering day.

When I returned, things were worse. A big red clot of blood came out. I called the hospital and waited a long time for the emotionless nurse. "Take two Tylenol and see if the pain goes away," she said. "If not, then come in to the emergency room."

Ramón called, after I had passed some more red blood. The cramps were now labor pains, but I was not yet trained for labor and I fought the pain. The heat was ganging up on me too and by the time Ramón got home I was about to crack.

Then it all peaked, in the space of an hour. First the diarrhea, slowly, then accelerating. And the heat, the cold sweats, which combined to keep me sliding all over the toilet seat. I used a chair to hold myself up on the seat. I was losing lots of fluids, all at once. I felt dizzy. Ramón was frantically fanning me with pieces of cardboard. Then, suddenly, a strange feeling, a feeling of water gushing. The sac had burst! I gasped and said to Ramón in a wail, "Our baby's dying, Ramón! The sac burst! We lost the baby!"

The fierce diarrhea and cramping were echoed now by vomiting. My body was leaving me, betraying me in all ways. I felt I would faint, but the pains and the gagging and the effort of holding onto the chair kept me conscious.

Ramón was beside himself. He had never, in eight years, seen me in this much physical distress. He didn't know what to do. "What is the emergency room number, Marian? Where can I find it? What should I do?"

Then the nurse was trying to speak to him in her lousy Spanish, and he was eager to say in plain English what was happening. Finally, my vomiting subsided enough so he could give the phone to me. The nurse asked, "Do you speak English? Come in to the emergency room at once!"

There was a long wait at the emergency room and many dull, plodding questions. The cold and efficient doctor jammed the speculum against my cervix as I writhed in pain.

"Yes, you are miscarrying," was her cold pronouncement. "We'll have to do a curettage."[3]

I blurted a bunch of questions: "Are you sure?" and "Why?" and "What will you do?" I could not keep back my tears. "Can you run some tests?" I asked, remembering the business about "collecting the fetus."

"No, we only run tests when a woman has had three miscarriages."

Three miscarriages! I couldn't believe it. You mean someone has to go through this three times before it's taken seriously?

But before I could become too outraged, or feel my impending grief very much, they started anesthesia.

The curettage was nothing compared to the pain and agony of the whole day. I was in a slippery consciousness, a wet fog of nowhereness, and only in the very back of my mind did I know or grapple with the fact that we had lost the baby.

Arriving home at 11:30 that night, we both felt I should call my folks to let them know I was all right. My mother had happened to call earlier in the day, and knew I might be miscarrying. And so I made the call that woke them in the middle of the Ohio night, to say that they would not have a grandchild in March.

Then to sleep, to sleep, at the end of such a long and difficult day, a day that was only the beginning.

"You have reached the advice nurse for ob-gyn. Your call will be taken in the order received."

The wait for the advice nurse never seemed as long as on that day, two days after the miscarriage, when all of a sudden the inevitable grief of losing our much-wanted baby hit me. I felt so deeply grieved, so pained, I did not know if I would survive. I had lost something, someone, so very close, so very intimate, that I felt I had lost a part of myself.

"I have just had a miscarriage and I would like to talk with someone about how I'm feeling, about my grief," I said to the nurse.

"What?" she asked, "You want to have an abortion?"

"No, I had a miscarriage, and I want to talk with someone."

"Well, how far along are you? When do you want to have the abortion?"

"NURSE, I HAD A MISCARRIAGE, I LOST MY BABY!!!"

I was dumbfounded at the insensitivity. Didn't she realize it was hard enough for me to say those words once, let alone three times?

Finally she got it and said, "I'll switch you to psychiatry."

But I didn't want someone in psychiatry! I didn't need a shrink! I just needed someone who knew what I was going through, who could walk through some of it with me, who could tell me I wasn't going to feel like this forever.

No matter. I was desperate, but I found that I couldn't see anyone in psychiatry for several days. I didn't have a gun to my head or someone else's, so I wasn't an emergency. By this time I was falling apart. I had taken the initiative to get some help and it was turning into a major battle. What was I going to do?

Then I remembered a birth resource book I'd just bought, which had sections on miscarriage and infant death.[4] I turned to the right pages, read the reviews of the books listed, and began to call local libraries to find them. Someone, somewhere, sometime must have dealt with this right and I hoped they had written about it.

I remembered that the hospital had a library and to my surprise and relief they had just the books I was looking for. I felt both relieved and anxious. For now that I could "talk to someone" who had been through all this, I was going to have to get a lot closer to my pain, feel it more fully, before I could resolve it. That scared me.

Once I got home, I curled up with my newfound book-friends. The phone rang. It was my friend Attieno, who was deeply saddened by my news. Just a week before we had walked in the park, amid the stunning trees and the deep peacefulness, and shared the wonderful news of my pregnancy. She had been so delighted that it had been a great pleasure sharing the experience with her. It was something that would always bind us. The same for the miscarriage. Her compassionate words, her sharing of my grief, meant a great deal to me and sealed our developing friendship. With other friends, their support, or lack of it, would be an important sign for me. It either brought them closer or removed them from me, whether I wished it or not.

Talking with Attieno and with other friends helped a lot. My parents also were incredibly helpful and supportive. They were very saddened by the loss. "I didn't realize how much I was looking forward to the baby," my mother said. She and my father, who is a family doctor, searched for information for me and the things they sent were very helpful. One of the articles they sent pointed out that the depth of grieving for a fetal loss is irrespective of gestational age. That fact stuck in my mind and was a great weapon against the many future comments that diminished what I was going through—"It's all for the best," "You can try again," "This is nature's way of saving you from having a deformed baby." I began to see that an important part of resolving my grief was fighting to have it acknowledged. This is something you don't have to do if your brother or parent or spouse dies, or if an older child dies. Not that grieving is ever easy in our society, or ever painless anywhere. But no one expects you to "jump back in" right away after that kind of death; no one expects you to be "back to normal" quickly.

So with my library books, and some good conversations with friends, I began the grieving process, which at first seemed like an endless and dimly-lit tunnel. It was an experience I could never have gone through were it not for Ramón.

Sometimes couples going through the grief of miscarriage suffer estrangement from one another as one impact of the grief. But for us, just the opposite has been true. Our relationship has been strengthened and tempered and broadened by going through this together. During the first several days we were both very depressed, but we kept talking to each other. Ramón had to go to work, but we would have time together when he got home and we would hold each other, sit quietly together, or talk. That time was essential for both of us and helped me to keep my bearings. Ramón had lost an infant years ago, and a toddler, and for him the grief of losing a child was not new. But he had never really had a chance to deal with all that grief. Any loss triggers remembrance of all the old ones; so all Ramón's sad memories reappeared and his old pain echoed our current agony. Ramón also knew that part of my sadness was the feeling that I did not have forever to have a child. I would soon be thirty-five and quite possibly I had endometriosis, which can lead to infertility.[5] He understood all of this, helped me to see how those fears were affecting me, and consoled and assured me constantly.

But one's partner and friends are not always enough. I still needed that help I initially sought out. I decided to take the option of seeing a psychologist on a short-term basis, to grapple with my grief with a trained person. I also decided to look for a support group for women who have had a loss in pregnancy.

Finding a group wasn't easy. But eventually I learned of a childbirth group which provides referrals for birth options. I was very impressed by the sensitive and supportive response I got. They gave me the names of women to call and our new Pregnancy Loss Support Group came together for the first time within a week or so.

At our first meeting it was as if someone had physically removed a great heavy burden that was bearing down on my shoulders. We all shared our feelings about our losses, about the wonderful, anticipated, beloved babies we had lost at the end of our first trimester, at sixteen weeks of pregnancy, at five months, at birth, on the day after birth. We all knew we had lost our babies—either babies we knew well, whose fingers and toes we had seen and touched and whose faces would be forever imprinted on our minds, or babies whose future birth we could only dimly imagine. For each of us there was a deep and irrevocable loss that had changed our lives. Through the group we discovered a collective sense of loss and grief that we could slowly transform, through sharing. On that first night we experienced great waves of feeling, interspersed with long moments of quiet, unrestrained weeping. But in time we moved to a place where we could be more in control of our feelings, without denying them, without being afraid of them. From this kind of sharing comes a sense of hope, fragile and sometimes elusive, but hope nonetheless.

It has been eight weeks since I first saw the drop of dark brown blood on that sweltering day. Since then the leaves have changed and the days have become cooler and darker. Halloween, which was my thirty-fifth birthday, has come and gone. I have had my first period, at long last, and now have just two more to go through before trying again to get pregnant. Ramón and I have decided to get married after the holidays, before settling in to making another baby.

I closed out with my "grief shrink," who was very helpful and sensitive. I am planning to leave the support group sometime in the future. Ramón and I plan to write a letter to the hospital about the insensitive treatment I received. My grief is becoming part of my daily life, but in an ever diminishing way, as I plan for the future.

For now, I am closing the chapter of intense grieving with these thoughts: I have struggled to acknowledge my grief, deal with it, and cope with it. And I have. Now I hope to share what I've learned about the silent wail which is miscarriage.

The Lost Children

BARBARA CROOKER

the ones we never speak of—
miscarried, unborn,
removed by decree,
taken too soon, crossed over.
They slip red mittens in our hands,
smell of warm wet wool,
are always out of sight.
We glimpse them on escalators,
over the shoulders of dark-haired women;
they return to us in dreams.
We hold them as they evanesce;
we never speak their names.
How many children do you have?
Two, we answer, thinking three,
or three, we answer, thinking four;
they are always with us.

The lost children
come to us
at night
and whisper
in the shells
of our ears.
They are waving goodbye
on school buses,
they are separated from us
in stadiums,
they are lost in shopping malls
with unspeakable pools,
they disappear on beaches,
they shine at night in the stars . . .

A Native American Birth Story

MARCIE RENDON

1983, Minnesota and South Dakota

A Native American birth story. Is it any different than any woman's birth story? Any mother, the world over, could come upon a woman in labor anyplace and recognize what was happening. And feel at one with, be supportive of, the woman in labor.

Ever since I can remember, I knew I wanted to have my babies at home. There was never a question in my mind whether I would have children or not. I just knew I would and that I wanted them born at home. I figured, women have given birth since time began, our bodies know what to do and how to do it.

There isn't a birth story. There are birth stories. Mine began with my asking, "Grandpa, tell me again, how were you born?"

"In the snow, girl, just dropped in the snow. My ma didn't know nothin. Raised in mission schools. Didn't know nothin. Just dropped in the snow. Till my grandma heard her cryin and came out and found us. Thought she had to go to the bathroom; went out and dropped me right in the snow. Raised in mission schools. Didn't know nothin.

"Now your ma, she was born the old way. In the fall, during wild rice season. Right there in ricing camp. Your grandma and me were ricing when your ma started to be born. Three old ladies helped her. They stuck sticks in the ground like crutches. Your grandma squatted, hanging on them under her arms. They had medicines for her. Right there. Knew what to do to help your ma be born. Yep, right there in ricing camp, your ma was born. The old way, no trouble. Me, I was dropped in the snow. Thought she had to go to the bathroom. Didn't know nothing. Raised in mission schools."

My birth. Born to an alcoholic mother. Suffering withdrawal along with her during the hospital stay. Nursing, etched in my being as a wordless memory. Remembering her story, laughing. "When I was

nursing I had so much milk. My breasts were so big I'd take bets in the
bar. I'd take bets that I could set a glass of beer on my tits and drink
the foam off. Got a lot of free drinks that way." Laughter. Laughter
that filled the whole room. Caught everyone up in it. My mother,
dead in my eighteenth year, from alcohol.

Birth stories. My daughters, children of my grandfathers' and
grandmothers' dreams. You were a reality long before my passion and
your father's seeds conceived you on those winter and spring nights.
Visions preceded flesh from my womb. And my generations shall be
as one. Spirits healing my mother's madness, my father's sadness. As
the daughters of my grandfathers' and grandmothers' dreams touch
hands with wind and water, light and love.

"Tell me Mom, how was I born?" asks my seven-year-old.

Conception. Christmas Eve. Warm glow as the spark of your being
ignites. I remember standing at the window that night watching the
lights glitter on the snow, knowing that night that you were started in
me.

"Your daddy told me I was crazy because I wanted to have you at
home. I asked all over, trying to find a midwife. Everyone told me
there weren't any, that midwives were a hundred years ago. So I
decided I'd have you at home alone. I kept saying, 'Women have
given birth since time began; my body knows what to do.' And your
daddy just kept telling me I was crazy. As it was, I didn't get any support to have you at home and we ended up in the hospital. They
strapped me down and I had to physically fight the nurses, doctor and
anesthesiologist not to be gassed or drugged. Your daddy just kept
telling me to be good and cooperate. I had back labor and I just kept
seeing the fear in his eyes and wishing it would go away. I just wanted
to have you my way, with no interference. And you ended up being
born by forceps because I wouldn't cooperate. All my energy went into fighting the nurses and doctors until my body just gave up and they
pulled you out. But you were a beautiful little girl. When I first got to
hold you and nurse you, you just smiled right at me. They didn't want
me to nurse you. They kept giving me sugar water to give to you.
They told me you'd dehydrate and have brain damage if I didn't give
it to you. So I'd drink it myself or pour it down the toilet to keep them
off my back. When we went home I was black and blue from where
the straps had been, from fighting them so hard to have you the way
I'd wanted to have you." My first daughter. Rachel Rainbeaux. My
"One of Many Dreams." Rainbeaux. The one who fights for life with
every ounce of muscle and energy in her little body.

"And me, Mommy, how was I born?" asks my five-year-old.

"You, my girl, were born in a midwife unit. Again, I wanted to have you at home, but couldn't find a midwife to come. So the midwife unit was a compromise to your dad, who was still too scared to do it alone at home.

"You were conceived in Denver. I remember standing outside after work, waiting for your daddy to pick me up. It was April and it started to rain snow. Huge, soaking wet snowflakes. At the same time I could feel my body ovulating. That night we made love and right afterwards my whole body started to shake. I told your daddy, 'I'm pregnant. You have to get me something to eat.' He thought I was being really silly. I said, 'No, for real, get me something to eat.' So he brought me a big bowl of cornflakes. That's the night you were started.

"You were born in a hospital midwife unit. The whole birth was beautiful. Calm. Peaceful. Except I had back labor again, even though I'd made one of the nurse-midwives promise I wouldn't have back labor twice in a row. Only during transition did I lose it; the back labor got so bad I said, 'That's it. I quit. Give me a cigarette. I'm done.' Everyone just laughed at me and ten minutes later you were born. Another beautiful girl who smiled right at me. I got to hold you right away. Hold you. Love you. Nurse you."

"And my foot, Mom. Tell me about my foot."

"You were born with a crooked foot. So they put a tiny little cast on it the day after you were born and then you had surgery on it when you were four months old."

Simone. My Starfire, with the warmth of a soft summer night, the flicker of eternity in her eyes. Rainy Day Woman—life giver—love flows out of your being and waters the souls of those you touch.

The next four years. Mothering. A divorce. Single parenting. Welfare. Apprenticing. Midwifing. Mothering.

"And the baby, Mom," the seven and five-year-old say. "Where was she born? You finally got to have one of us at home, didn't you?"

My baby, four months old and growing. My home birth. What will I tell her when she's old enough to ask?

"You, my baby girl, were born at home. On the living room floor. Twenty-four hours of the hardest work I ever hope to do. Twenty-four hours of excruciating back labor. You were conceived November 2, 1982. It was right after the full moon, but it was a really cold, dark, hard night. Your dad and I had been seeing each other off and on. That just happened to be one of the 'on' nights. But the thing I remember most was that for about a month before that, every night when I'd go to bed, I'd hear three knocks on the window. I'd say, 'Bendigan, come in,' like I was taught to say when spirits are heard. Well, November 2nd was the last night I heard the three knocks. Again I knew I was pregnant right away. It was so free this time, because I knew I could do whatever I wanted with the pregnancy and birth. I could have women around me to be supportive of me. I spotted a little blood in the third month, so in the seventh month we went up north to be doctored by a medicine man for a low placenta.[1] The very first time he saw me, he said, 'Another girl, huh? Well, we'll keep prayin for a boy.' He also told me my delivery would be dangerous, to not have anyone around who would be afraid. Well babe, you were born in the heat of the hottest summer I remember. We spent all our money all summer going where it was cool—swimming, air-conditioned shopping malls, swimming, to friends' houses that had air-conditioning, and swimming again. Your birth. Like I said, long and hard. Twenty-four hours of excruciating back labor. I walked and squatted the whole time. Trying to dance you down into a more straight up and down position. We had a grandmother, a midwife and an apprentice here to help us. Three of the most beautiful women I've ever seen. At one point I got a contraction band around my uterus, looked like a rubber band being tightened around my belly.[2] I got scared for you. I said, "I want to go in." I started praying the Serenity Prayer—God grant me the serenity to accept the things I cannot change (the band, the back labor, the pain), and the courage to change the things I can (my position). I walked from the dining room to the living room and squatted down by a chair. The band disappeared and I started pushing. Hard work. Three hours of pushing during which time I visualized the Viet Nam war. Telling myself, if my brother could live through that, I could live through pushing one baby out. Just before you were born I told them I was bleeding. They said no, there wasn't any blood. Your head was born, your shoulders stuck. As soon as you were completely born the blood gushed out. Your cord was too short to nurse you or even pick you up enough to tell if you were a girl or boy. But you were lying on my belly. The first thing you did was lift your head up, look at me and smile. Another beautiful girl. They had to call another midwife to help stop the bleeding and fix the tear. And you baby, you never missed a beat. Like a turtle, your little heart never even flickered a sign of distress. Born at home. I held you, nursed you, loved you. Another beautiful, beautiful girl."

Awanewquay. Quiet, calm, peaceful little woman. Awan. Fog Woman. Three knocks announcing your intention. Birth and death inseparable. Birth—the coming of the spirit to this world. Death—the going of the spirit to that world. Fog Woman. The cloud of mystery. With your two sisters I felt strong, powerful. After they were born I felt, if I can do that, I can move mountains. Well, honey, with you I moved the mountain. With all humbleness, I moved the mountain.

A Native American birth story. It is the story of the generations. I gave birth because I was born a woman. The seeds of the future generations were carried in my womb. I remember conception because the female side of life is always fertile first. I gave birth three times as naturally as possible, given the situation, because as a woman my body and heart knew what to do. I nursed because my breasts filled with milk. I remember their names because that is how they will be recognized by their grandfathers and grandmothers who have gone on before. I am a mother because I was given three daughters to love. I am a midwife because women will continue to give birth. That is my story. Megwitch. I am Marcie Rendon, Awanewquay, of the Eagle Clan, Ojibwe.

For Alva Benson, and for Those Who Have Learned to Speak

JOY HARJO

And the ground spoke when she was born.
Her mother heard it. In Navajo she answered
as she squatted down against the earth
to give birth. It was now when it happened,
now giving birth to itself again and again
between the legs of women.

Or maybe it was the Indian Hospital
in Gallup. The ground still spoke beneath
mortar and concrete. She strained against the
metal stirrups, and they tied her hands down
because she still spoke with them when they
muffled her screams. But her body went on
talking and the child was born into their
hands, and the children learned to speak
both voices.

She grew up talking in Navajo, in English
and watched the earth around her shift and change
with the people in the towns and in the cities
learning not to hear the ground as it spun around
beneath them. She learned to speak for the ground,
the voice coming through her like roots that
have long hungered for water. Her own daughter
was born, like she had been, in either place
or all places, so she could leave, leap
into the sound she had always heard,
a voice like water, like the gods weaving
against sundown in a scarlet light.

The child now hears names in her sleep.
They change into other names, and into others.
It is the ground murmuring, and Mt. St. Helens
erupts as the harmonic motion of a child turning
inside her mother's belly waiting to be born
to begin another time.

And we go on, keep giving birth and watch
ourselves die, over and over.
And the ground spinning beneath us
goes on talking.

At the Birth Center

SARAH FRANKLIN

1983, Northern California

I had almost resigned myself to a fate of permanent pregnancy when, eight days after my due date, very light contractions began while my husband Lynn and I were out at a movie. I knew I didn't have enough energy to have a baby that night, so I asked the contractions to stop so I could rest, and they obliged me. They resumed very infrequently and lightly the next day and continued during the night, making sleep almost impossible. At 4:30 A.M. I gave up on sleep and crawled into the bathtub with a copy of *Spiritual Midwifery*.[1] The contractions were ten to fifteen minutes apart, the bathroom was freezing, and I couldn't understand why Lynn didn't want to get up! By 5:45 A.M. (I had the clock on the side of the tub) I felt that the contractions should be picking up and tried to figure out why they weren't. In *Spiritual Midwifery* it is mentioned several times that fear can hold up the progress of labor. I asked myself what I could be afraid of, and what came to mind was the only fear that I had not resolved during the pregnancy—the deep lurking fear that something might not be normal about my baby. I decided at that point simply to have complete faith that the baby would be perfect. The fear dissolved and ten minutes later the contractions stabilized at five minutes apart. I convinced Lynn it was time to get up. We spent some time at home and then I decided I didn't want to be in the car later on when the contractions would be harder to deal with. So we drove to the birth center.

I chose to give birth in a free-standing birth center in my community for several reasons: a friend of mine had had a good experience there two years before; I'm deeply suspicious of some hospital practices and ill at ease in a sterile, metallic environment; and, I didn't feel comfortable enough in my own home for a home birth. I've always been an inept housekeeper and the thought of looking at the dust in the corners of my house while in labor didn't appeal to me. The birth center offered a homey atmosphere, gentle professional care, and a choice of birth attendants. I chose a very good obstetrician, Dr. B., instead of one of the several nurse-midwives with admitting privileges, because he has a wonderful combination of expertise, common sense, and sensitivity which is very rare among professionals I've met. Also, it felt right to me to have a male care-provider present for the birth.

I was admitted to the birth center at 9:00 A.M. Dr. B. had been notified and he stayed in phone contact with the nurses during the day. Around 10:30 I spoke to him on the phone and he said he felt I would do beautifully. Of course, I was determined right down to my bones that everything would be fine, so I thought he was just observing the obvious. But it helped to know that he had faith in me.

When I was admitted, the nurse checked and found that I was three centimeters dilated. Since it was still early in the labor, Lynn went home to pick up some forgotten item and as soon as he returned at about 11:00, the contractions sped up to three minutes apart. The nurse, who was also a midwife, said that of course I couldn't have the baby without Lynn there. From this I learned even more about how my emotional state affected my ability to birth.

Next, Lynn and I went for a brief walk outside, with me stopping every few paces to breathe my way through mounting sensation. It was a misty Sunday morning, and though I felt very vulnerable in labor, I also felt glad to be a woman and glad to be alive doing this wonderful work.

During the walk "back labor" began in earnest. The pain relented only slightly between contractions, so that by 1:00 P.M. I was very demoralized because I felt I didn't have the inner resources to deal with constant pain. I had also begun to feel very alone because Lynn didn't really understand how to help me. The nurse had been urging me to walk more and I had no energy or will left to walk with. The birth center requires that every laboring woman have a "doula" to assist her, in addition to family, friends, and birth center staff.[2] A doula is available to do anything the family needs, such as fix food, run errands, or provide back-up labor support. My doula, Orit, arrived at 1:30 and found me sitting on the floor with a heating pad stuffed down the back of my drawstring pants, looking very forlorn. She knew immediately how low I felt and rushed over, flowers in hand, to hug and comfort me. I cried and cried and began to feel at last that there was hope and help.

I rested on the bed and Orit gave me some extract of blue and black cohosh teas—which tasted vile—plus lots of frozen yogurt and more tea laced with an intense amount of honey, to speed up labor and give me strength.[3] Up until the last few minutes before the birth, Orit followed me around with tea and "laborade" to keep me from becoming dehydrated.[4] We then decided upon a bath to help relax my back and the major pelvic floor muscles, so off I went with my entourage of people and food. The nurse who had been with me was needed to help another woman who had just given birth in the other room and a new nurse arrived who knew intuitively just what kind of attention I needed. With her in place, something inside me finally relaxed and the labor really picked up.

Orit handed me two small black combs and explained that if I held them tightly in both hands during contractions, the sharp teeth would press acupressure points on the palms of my hands that are associated with lessening the intensity of labor pains.[5] They did help and I refused to let go of them for five more hours. Between combs and careful light back pressure, we finally conquered the back labor.

At 4:00 P.M. I was checked again and had progressed to seven centimeters. My progress was slow but steady. Shortly I began walking again. I walked around the birth center house, hanging myself around the neck of the nearest person who could supply pressure on my back. Without that pressure I could not bear the sheer pain in my back, which hurt more than my belly. I knew then that without support I could not have tolerated the labor on my own. I understood why women want drugs in labor and I had complete compassion for those who request them. It took everything I had to deal with each contraction, and I am a strong person. It never entered my mind, though, to ask for a pain killer. The birth center does not stock them anyway, so it wasn't a possibility. I was willing to stand almost any pain to give my baby the healthiest start in life. My Bradley teacher had said that personal labor support takes the place of drugs and I was filled with overwhelming gratitude for the people who were giving and giving to me during that long day.

No matter how fiercely painful my experience was, I was determined not to give in to anger or irritability and I let my support people know how much I appreciated their efforts. In fact, I became more polite the more pain I was in, saying "thank you" constantly until I couldn't talk at all. It was amusing to see how ingrained politeness is in me.

Next, combs in hand, I headed for the shower. I am always happier in water. I stayed there until the hot water was gone, then put on my nightshirt and got back on the bed. The contractions were slowing to five minutes apart and were so intense that I lost almost all my ability to go along with the energy in them. Transition! A bit earlier, while walking, I was thinking about my grandmother, who had nine children in thirteen years. I'd said, "I can't believe anyone would voluntarily do this again!" The nurse had answered, "You get amnesia." During each transition contraction Lynn would push my head towards my chest so that I couldn't arch my neck and back in panic and complete tension. This maneuver saved me from drowning in a tidal wave of sensation.

The nurse checked my dilation and found that I was "complete." I had given up on the idea of labor ever ending, so this was wonderful news. I hadn't yet had to stifle an urge to push, which I'd heard was unpleasant and common, and I was relieved about that. The nurse told me I could do whatever my body told me to do, so I just lay there in amazement, wondering how I could translate all these various urges into pushing! I was lying on my side at first, which made me feel miserably out of control; so I moved into the adjacent bathroom and began to push while sitting on the toilet. I thought the pushing of labor would be no different than having a bowel movement and I was right, except that with the effort I was putting into each push I was quite afraid that I would burst something vital in my head somewhere. I began to feel there was no way I could push that baby out! Absolutely no way. And yet I was the only one who could do it. I quickly reviewed the options in what was left of my mind: cesarean section or forceps. Those didn't sound like options at all. So, faced with this complete contradiction—that I was the only person who could do something which I felt couldn't be done—I asked Orit, mother of two, who was sitting on the floor outside the bathroom door, "Tell me I can do this!" She looked at me as if I were joking and said, "Of course you can do it!" I thought, "Well, if she says so, maybe it's possible." So I kept on.

By this time, Dr. B. had arrived and was sitting in the corner of the bedroom in the rocking chair, reading medical abstracts, an oasis of calm on the periphery of a hurricane. I moved from the toilet to a birthing stool, still in the darkened bathroom. I refused to move out of there, feeling like a mother bear in her cave. The nurse checked me again and thought she might be feeling a lip of cervix, so Dr. B. came over to check, forced to lie on the floor with a flashlight to get access. But the "lip" was just a fold in the baby's scalp.

At last I made my final move over to the bed, where I lay propped up on pillows, holding my legs open. I finally felt that I could give everything I had to pushing; it felt right, and I pushed my heart out. The baby descended rapidly. All of my life I have been one to hold back from giving my full measure to anything, so it was a healing experience for me to finally give completely.

When the baby's head started to show, Dr. B. put his book aside and started to prepare for the birth. Lynn leaned over to me and said, "You can tell something's really happening—B.'s out of his chair!" The only thought I could muster was, "Maybe there really is a baby in there." When the head finally crowned, I reached down to touch it and was utterly amazed to feel this new being for the first time.

The baby was a bit too blue, as the head was born with both the right hand by the left ear and the cord all presenting at the same time. I pushed the body out quickly and Dr. B. told me to reach down and lift the baby up onto my chest. A baby! A real baby! I was thrilled though I have to admit that, after all the wonderful stories I had heard about instantaneous cosmic "bonding," my first thought after he was born was, "Thank God, no more contractions." The baby took a few seconds to breathe, but after Dr. B. suctioned out the mucus he cried loud and long. I had felt he would be all right and had never been really worried for his safety. I feel all my positive attitudes paid off. Benjamin was indeed perfect.

Lynn cut the cord and the placenta was delivered with no problem. Benjamin and I made our first uncoordinated attempt at nursing and I was glad we had a few days to get it right. Dr. B. quickly sewed up a small tear without using an anesthetic.

While Benjamin was being checked and weighed, I hit the showers once more, feeling both tired and triumphant. Lynn took a shower with me and by the look of him he was more tired than I was. Later, with the whole family cleaned up and in fresh clothes, our pediatrician came and checked Benjamin. He said, "Oh, what a handsome baby." I didn't care if he said that to everyone; I was thrilled and convinced that this was the best baby ever born. (I still am, though I admit there are some other really fine ones!) Two hours after the birth, we drove home in the quiet night.

I waited until I was twenty-nine to have a baby because I had always been overwhelmed at the prospect of pregnancy and motherhood. And yet it was always something I hoped I could achieve. I worked hard to make informed decisions, to eat well, to train myself to focus on attitudes and habits that would serve me and my baby best. Each stage of pregnancy and birth was a challenge and helped me to grow into a better person than I was before. Because I was able to give birth the way I wanted, which took courage for me, I have felt much better about myself ever since in all areas of my life.

Lushness, Magic, Mystery and Work

JONATHAN LONDON

1983, Northern California

She's three days overdue. But it's OK. It's her first, our first. It's to be expected. It's her second day of "false labor." The contractions started Tuesday night at fifteen minute intervals, over egg rolls and tea. We were so excited. We were sure it was coming, maybe in the morning. We lifted our small cups and toasted, "To Aaron, or Erin!" and sipped the tea from China.

But it didn't come in the morning; her contractions were erratic. I spent that day and the next re-reading the instructions for natural childbirth. I'm the "coach." I'm not scared; perhaps I'm dazed. But I never doubt Maureen's ability to handle what's to come.

Jan, our midwife, checked Maureen's cervix in the afternoon, but it was still at zero dilation. We were frustrated, but Jan said the head had dropped to minus-1 station,[1] and estimated Maureen would "kick in" to real labor very early tomorrow morning. Jan is very calm, authoritative, and reassuring.

But by half-way through our favorite TV show, at 10:30 P.M., Maureen is in much discomfort. I've got the watch in one hand, her hand in the other. The contractions are coming regularly every five minutes, have been for four hours.

By midnight the contractions are causing enough pain that she decides to take them in a hot shower. Until now, she's been able to relax through the contractions by visualizing pleasant memories from childhood or the feeling of sitting naked in Crater Lake bathing in the sun. I still don't feel nervous, but as if I'm riding a reined-in horse. It is a tense calm. I am a warrior, in Castaneda's sense of the word. A tender warrior. Together, we will walk the path of the heart on a tightrope.[2]

At one in the morning we call our neighbors and ask if we can use their bathtub. Maureen can no longer keep standing in the shower and we don't have a tub. They say sure, come on over.

Maureen sinks down in the hot water. "Ah," she sighs, "this feels good." I stuff towels behind her in the tub to cushion her back. But the contractions are four minutes apart now and coming strong. I run around. There is so much to do, so much to remember to do. My leg is bothering me from a sciatic pain caused by a back injury, but I'm on the run, I'm running now. Tea? I make her tea. She's thirsty, I run for water. She's too hot in the tub. I put a cool washcloth on her forehead. I kneel beside her on the tile floor and hold her hand, her back. We breathe like the books said to breathe, in and out, in and out.

By 1:30 the warm water is no longer helping; she's hurting, I can see it. I help her up and I dry her. We walk around the house, my arm around her waist. She's bent over. She feels nauseous. She's almost hysterical when she asks me for a pot. I run for a cook pot from the kitchen and she fills it with vomit just as I reach her. She retches over and over.

I call Jan at 2:00 A.M. We agree to meet at the hospital in 45 minutes. We've already decided against a home birth because it's our first, and we live out in the country. We want to play it safe. We hope to use the labor room only, with no doctors, and give natural birth.

At the hospital I roll Maureen to the elevator in a wheelchair and up to the labor room. I go back and load the chair high with supplies for the night: pillows, a robe for Maureen, a change of clothes for both of us, an ice chest full of orange juice, iced tea, food (we want to avoid hospital food), and a bag with clothes and diapers for the one who is coming, the one we are waiting for, the one we've been rehearsing for all these months.

Jan joins us at 3:00 A.M. and checks Maureen's cervix. It has dilated to just two centimeters! "Oh no!" cries Maureen. "My God!" I say. Only two? But her cervix has effaced, Jan informs us. There are still eight centimeters to go, but the word is: Go.

We know we're in for a long hard night. Her contractions have plateaued at every three to four minutes, but they're coming on stronger. I hold Maureen's hand and remind her to breathe deep, not to tense up, to blow the breath all out. I try to make her comfortable in the narrow, sagging bed; I stuff pillows here and there, under arms and legs and back and head, and constantly rearrange them. She's doing fine, I tell her, but she's intent on what is happening to her. She's concentrating, struggling to remain on top of it. I wipe her sweating face, feed her ice chips, offer sips of juice. I try to encourage her but we don't talk otherwise, unless she requests something, for her thirst, her back. It's the middle of the night and we are fighting exhaustion, but there is no hysteria. We are almost grimly calm. Not truly calm.

We are on the thin membrane of an enormous sack of water.

It's 4:30 A.M. Jan checks Maureen's cervix. It has dilated to just four centimeters! We're crushed. We've worked this hard, this long, and there are still six centimeters to go. We are at the bottom of our spirits; the whole night weighs on us. We almost lose sight of the goal, caught in this now of pain and endurance. I help Maureen out of bed and we walk the corridors. It feels as if we're an old couple, inching painfully along, Maureen bent over at my side, in my holding. I look in at the intensive care nursery and I see the tiny, premature babies with tubes taped to their noses. Worry about the outcome jabs me in the gut. I cry and try to keep Maureen from noticing it. I'm crying over her pain and over the trauma of the new born, who comes into this world out of the warm womb. Just then her water breaks! It trickles down her legs.

Back in the labor room the contractions intensify and I dart around trying to be of help. I dip the washcloths in cool water, ring them, fold them, and place them on Maureen's hot brow, beaded with sweat. Her lips are parched. I dash over and hand her chips of ice to suck. I climb into bed with her and try to coach her through the hard ones. We try some Lamaze techniques; we try some Bradley. My sciatic leg is torturing me. Maureen forces a brave smile at me, even says, "Poor boy, poor boy." I am so moved that she can see me through her own pain. We are fiercely together, in a powerful connection based on love. I am so proud of her.

But the contractions get worse and the long hours of labor and no sleep pile up and now when one comes she cries, "No, not again! No! I can't do it." "But you are doing it!" Jan assures her. "No," she moans and I say, "Yes!" "Yes?" she says, so sweet, so weak, I almost break. I begin to wonder if natural childbirth is worth it, for someone undergoing such a long, hard labor. Maureen is asking for something to ease the pain now. "I'm sorry," she says, between contractions, "I thought I could do it but I can't." Jan has been firm yet compassionate and finally decides to give her a small injection of Nisentil so Maureen can catch an hour's sleep and be better prepared for transition and pushing.[3] Jan feels that there's enough time left so that the drug will have no effect on the baby at birth, or on Maureen. It works. Maureen slips off into a fitful sleep and I'm able to lie down for the first time all night and rest my back. I dose for half an hour on the labor room floor.

It's 6:30 A.M. and Maureen is stirring and moaning. The drug has worn off and the contractions have awakened her. They are coming on with more power than ever. I am at her side again, coaching her to breathe. Inhale through the nose, slow and deep, and blow it out, slow, steady, like blowing on a candle flame without blowing it out.

The flame, it is burning in us, it is burning bright.

At 8:30 Jan again checks Maureen's cervix. I prepare myself for the worst. "It's nine centimeters!" she tells us. It's the best thing we've ever heard! We are charged with new hope. We're elated and the adrenalin is pumping through us and we are fully awake and working.

Labor is work, but there is nothing to compare with the intensity of attaining this final centimeter! We are on the verge of full dilation, on the verge of pushing the baby out. The contractions are coming in monster waves now, giant forces of nature. Her stomach turns to hard rock with each one. I tell her: "Open your eyes! Look at me! Focus on your breathing! Breathe!"

Jan says it's time to walk her, to escalate the dilation. Maureen hobbles at my side and an overwhelming desire to push comes over her. She cries, "I have to push!" Jan says, "Yes, push! Do what your body tells you to do; it's time!" Maureen almost collapses. I hold her beneath her arms and she pushes, squatting on the floor. Jan gets on her other arm and between us Maureen presses all her energy down. Push! And again. Her legs are trembling and growing weak, so we get her back into bed and crank the bed up and prop her with pillows for pushing. The doctor comes in, our family doctor; he's required by the staff to be here at birth.[4] The duty nurse comes in; we haven't asked for one but she's a friend of Maureen's. She wheels in a small cart of delivery instruments. Jan climbs up on the bed and positions herself between Maureen's legs, at her feet, at the ready. She pulls on rubber gloves and reaches in to feel if the baby is in position. It is. Maureen pushes and we all push with her. "My back! Jonathan, my back!" I press my hand into the small of her back and wedge my forearm and elbow between it and the bed for support. I'm all twisted and bent over and my leg's killing me and it isn't—it's beyond that and I'm beyond it. "Keep pressing my back!" she demands, and I press and she pushes, air screaming out between compressed lips under immense pressure, her cheeks puffing out, her face in an agony of effort, beyond pain, in a realm unto itself. "Breathe it out!" I tell her. "Breathe the baby out!" But Phyllis, the nurse, is of a different school, and is urging, "Hold your breath! Hold it! Hold it! Hold it! And push! Push! Push! Push! Push!" Maureen is arching her back and holding her breath but it's tearing out of her mouth pressed by great cries of absolute effort rising with the waves crashing through her.[5]

"You can see the head!" Jan says, and I twist around and look and see the peach pit of crumpled scalp and damp hair for an instant, coming forth with each push, receding with each pause. "Oh! I can see the head! Maureen, the head!" I shout. I'm overwhelmed. Joy is pounding in me like a great drum. I try to hold a mirror there for her to see, but she's in the harness of her tremendous effort. "Oh God! Here it comes!" she cries. "Push! Push! Push! Push!" cheers the nurse, "Breathe it out! Breathe it out!" I coach. She pushes with all her being and out pops the head! "The head! Maureen! The head is out!" It's face down and I can only see the back of the head, with its sworls of blond matted hair wet with mucus. I'm crying and laughing. Jan tells Maureen to catch her breath now and rest and wait for the next contraction. She checks to see if the cord is wrapped around the neck and makes sure the shoulders are in position. Maureen has a moment to gather her will and her last ounce of energy. "Here it comes!" Maureen cries. She grunts and pants and the chorus rises around her and out squirts a wet, wiggly body! It slithers through Jan's arms and onto the bed. She gathers it up with, "It's a boy!" "It's a boy, Maureen, a boy!" I sing. Jan gently places him down on Maureen's breasts. Maureen offers him her nipple and he soon latches on and begins to suck. Maureen is a new person; she is bathed in joy and shines with a light that might be holy. And I'm a new person. I am pressed out beyond my skin and embraced in a moment larger than me, older than me, eternal.

When the umbilical cord stops pulsing, I cut through it with a pair of scissors. We are three.

In a short while the placenta is born and Jan wraps it in a plastic bag for us to take home and bury beneath a tree we hope to plant.

Later, Jan sews Maureen where she tore when the shoulders were born and Phyllis brings us breakfast, which we gobble, though the food we'd brought remains uneaten. The doctor, who had chimed in at the birth with his calls of encouragement, has checked out our newborn and declared him healthy, with an Apgar rating of 9 and 9. I'd expected a blue, wrinkled baby with a pointed head. But he's pink, clear skinned, and his head is almost round! I thought newborns are supposed to be born ugly, but he's gorgeous! And big: eight pounds, six ounces.

I thought fathers had to learn to love their newborn, but I love mine with a love beyond words, now.

We leave after four hours—after hugging and laughing and thanking Jan and Phyllis—and drive home: a family. The baby car seat—empty going—now cradles life.

Throughout the birthing, we were totally involved with the work and mystery. It was a mindless experience during much of it—magical and miraculous. Out of the lush confusion of birth comes one clear fact:

Here, meet Aaron—he's a real beauty.

MAUREEN WEISENBERGER

Bibliography

NON-FICTION BIRTH ACCOUNTS

Bean, Constance. *Labor and Delivery: An Observer's Diary.* New York: Doubleday, 1977 (out of print).

Childbirth educator and activist Constance Bean observed births in the hospital and at home and describes what she saw. Experiences include a premature baby, the administration of epidural anesthesia, cesarean section, "natural childbirth," circumcision, fetal distress, and hemorrhage. Even without commentary, the description of these births stands as a strong criticism of hospital maternity care.

Chesler, Phyllis. *With Child: A Diary of Motherhood.* New York: T.Y. Crowell, 1979.

Feminist psychologist Phyllis Chesler (*Women and Madness*) provides a diary account of the pregnancy and birth of her first child at age 37.

Davies, Margaret Llewelyn. *Maternity: Letters from Working Women.* New York: W.W. Norton, 1978.

First published in 1915, this is a collection of accounts by 160 British working-class women who describe their experiences in childbearing and mothering. The women were all members of the Women's Co-operative Guild and their birth accounts were intended to help let the government and society know what kind of support and services women need to make childbearing happier and safer. Many of these stories are characterized by poverty, poor nutrition, lack of medical care, birth injuries, high mortality rates, lack of family planning, and sexual abuse, all of which contribute to very poor maternity experiences.

Friedland, Ronnie and Carol Kort, editors. *The Mothers' Book: Shared Experiences.* Boston: Houghton Mifflin, 1981.

This book is an anthology of seventy-two stories and poems by mothers, who discuss a wide range of birthing and mothering experiences, including normal pregnancy, postpartum adjustment, breastfeeding, adoption, being a birth mother, teenage motherhood, cesarean section, birth defects, illness, miscarriage, and death of a child.

Gaskin, Ina May. *Spiritual Midwifery* (2nd Edition). Summertown, TN: The Book Publishing Company, 1978.

Almost half of this 473-page book is devoted to a collection of sixty-seven "amazing birthing tales," home births which took place on

The Farm, a spiritually-oriented farming commune in Tennessee, and were attended by a team of "empirical" or self-taught midwives. The stories suffer somewhat from a uniformity of language and description because of the writers' strong communal sense of a shared reality, but the management of the births is exemplary, The Farm's birth statistics are excellent, and the stories provide a firm grounding in the "normalcy" of childbearing.

Lang, Raven. *Birth Book.* Felton, CA: Genesis Press, 1972 (distributed by Science and Behavior Books, Palo Alto, CA).

This book documents the home birth movement which began in the Santa Cruz mountains in California in the late 1960s. Included are beautiful photographs and personal accounts of about twenty-three births, mostly attended by self-trained lay midwives. The parents are predominantly "counter-culture" couples who place emphasis on spirituality, self-sufficiency, and community involvement in birth.

Michelle, Karen. *We Gave Birth Together.* New York: William Morrow, 1983.

Photographer Karen Michelle provides excellent color photographs and parents' commentary by four couples who gave birth at the Maternity Center of New York City, a free-standing, out-of-hospital birth center.

Moffat, Mary Jane and Charlotte Painter, editors. *Revelations: Diaries of Women.* New York: Random House, 1974 and Vintage Books, 1975.

This collection of diary excerpts by famous and lesser known women covers love, work, and power and includes fascinating accounts of birth and mothering by Evelyn Scott, Frances Karlen Santamaria, Kathe Kollwitz, and Martha Martin.

Moran, Marilyn. *Birth and the Dialogue of Love.* Leawood, KS: New Nativity Press, 1981.

Marilyn Moran is an advocate of medically-unattended, do-it-yourself home birth which allows husband and wife to intimately and privately experience labor and birth as a "love encounter." Her book includes nine detailed personal birth accounts from couples who share her philosophy along with a Christian religious orientation.

Santamaria, Frances Karlen. *Joshua, Firstborn.* New York: The Dial Press, 1970 (out of print).

An American woman has written this diary account of natural childbirth and mothering while living in Greece.

Ward, Charlotte and Fred. *The Home Birth Book.* Washington, D.C.: Inscape Publishers, 1976 (out of print).

The personal, medical, psychological, sociological, and practical dimensions of home birth are discussed in this excellent introductory book, which is unfortunately out of print. Included are profiles of eleven home birth families, which include descriptions of their births and many photographs.

BIRTH IN FICTION AND POETRY

The following works include accounts and discussions of birth in fiction, poetry, essays and commentary, and myth and folk tales.

Anthologies and Commentary:

Cahill, Susan, editor. *Motherhood: A Reader for Men and Women.* New York: Avon Books, 1982.

Melzter, David. *Birth: An Anthology of Ancient Texts, Songs, Prayers, and Stories.* San Francisco: North Point Press, 1981.

Rich, Adrienne. *Of Woman Born: Motherhood as Experience and Institution.* New York: W.W. Norton, 1976.

Riley, Madeleine. *Brought to Bed.* Cranbury, NJ: A.A. Barnes, 1968. (Commentary and excerpts from birth accounts in English literature since the 18th century; out of print.)

Sorrel, Nancy Caldwell. *Ever Since Eve: Personal Reflections on Childbirth.* New York: Oxford University Press, 1984.

Fiction:

Bagnold, Enid. *The Door of Life.* New York: William Morrow, 1938 (out of print).

Bryant, Dorothy. *The Garden of Eros.* Ata Books, 1979.

Courter, Gay. *The Midwife.* New York: New American Library/Signet, 1979.

Jong, Erica. *Fanny: Being the True History of the Adventures of Fanny Hackabout-Jones.* New York: New American Library/Signet, 1980, 1981.

Lessing, Doris. *A Proper Marriage.* New York: New American Library, 1970.

Piercy, Marge. *Small Changes.* New York: Doubleday and Co., 1972.

Williams, William Carlos, *White Mule.* New York: New Directions, 1937.

Poetry:

Bolinger, Judith and Jane English. *Waterchild.* Claremont, CA: Hunter House, 1980. (Includes "From a Pregnant Year," poems by Judith Bolinger and "Spirit Entering Form," photographs by Jane English.)

Derricotte, Toi. *Natural Birth.* Trumansburg, NY: The Crossing Press, 1983.

Ehrlich, Karen Hope. *Birth Song.* Karen Hope Ehrlich, publisher (P.O. Box 956, Ben Lomond, CA 95005), 1979.

Mattison, Alice. *Animals.* Cambridge, MA: Alice James Books, 1979.

McMahan, Peggy, et al., editors. *Mother Poet.* Albuquerque: Mothering Publications, 1983.

Merriam, Eve. *The Double Bed.* New York: Marzani & Munsell, 1958.

Plath, Sylvia. "Three Women: A Poem for Three Voices," in *Winter Trees.* New York: Harper and Row, 1972.

USEFUL BOOKS ON PREGNANCY AND CHILDBIRTH

Ashford, Janet Isaacs. *The Whole Birth Catalog: A Sourcebook for Choices in Childbirth.* Trumansburg, NY: The Crossing Press, 1983.

Edwards, Margot and Mary Waldorf. *Reclaiming Birth: History and Heroines of American Childbirth Reform.* Trumansburg, NY: The Crossing Press, 1984.

Kitzinger, Sheila. *The Complete Book of Pregnancy and Childbirth.* New York: Alfred Knopf, 1981.

Korte, Diana and Roberta Scaer. *A Good Birth, A Safe Birth.* New York: Bantam, 1984.

Rothman, Barbara Katz. *Giving Birth: Alternatives in Childbirth.* New York: Penguin Books, 1984.

Wertz, Richard W. and Dorothy C. Wertz. *Lying In: A History of Childbirth in America.* New York: Schocken, 1979.

Glossary of Common Childbirth Terms

Apgar score — A test developed by neonatologist Virginia Apgar to evaluate the newborn baby, usually at one and five minutes after birth. It measures five factors: heart rate (pulse), respiration, muscle tone, reflex irritability, and color.

Back labor — Labor in which the pain of the contractions is felt in the lower back as well as in the cervix or lower front abdomen.

Bloody show — A discharge of blood-tinged mucus from the cervix as it begins to dilate in early labor.

Bonding — The process by which the parents and child become emotionally attached; there may be a critical period for optimum bonding during the first minutes after birth.

Bradley method — A method of childbirth preparation based on the teaching of Robert Bradley, an American obstetrician. It uses deep relaxation rather than distraction techniques to cope with labor pain and emphasizes the goal of a totally drug-free birth.

Braxton-Hicks contractions — Mild, painless contractions of the uterus which occur intermittently during pregnancy before the onset of true labor.

CNM — Certified Nurse-Midwife.

Cervix — The narrow lower end or "neck" of the uterus, which extends from the body of the uterus into the vagina. The cervix is closed during pregnancy and dilates to a diameter of about ten centimeters during labor to permit passage of the baby.

Contraction — The rhythmic shortening (contraction) and thickening (retraction) of the uterus during labor, which works to efface and dilate the cervix and push out the baby.

Crowning — That stage of delivery when the largest diameter of the baby's head is encircled by the vaginal opening.

D & C — Dilation and curettage; a procedure in which the cervix is opened just enough to admit an instrument which scrapes the endometrial lining of the uterus; often used after a miscarriage to empty the uterus.

Demerol — The trade name for meperidine, a narcotic analgesic commonly used to alleviate pain in first stage labor.

Dilation — Enlargement of the opening of the cervix caused by the contractions of the uterus during labor; often measured in centimeters of diameter.

Effacement — Thinning of the cervix as it is drawn up into the body of the uterus during labor.

Electronic fetal monitor — A device for continuous measurement and recording of the fetal heart rate during labor.
> **External monitor** — An ultrasound transducer, attached to the abdomen with a belt, monitors fetal heart rate, while a "tocotransducer," attached by another belt, measures the frequency of uterine contractions.
> **Internal monitor** — An electrode, attached directly to the fetal scalp through the vaginal opening, monitors fetal heart rate.

Engagement — Descent of the fetal head or other "presenting part" (could be the buttocks or feet in a breech presentation) down into the pelvis, past the pelvic inlet. This usually occurs just prior to labor (in a primapara) or just after the beginning of labor (in a multipara).

Epidural block — A form of regional anesthesia in which an anesthetic drug is injected into the epidural space between the lumbar spines of the lower back, below the level of the spinal cord; used for pain relief in first and second stage labor.

Episiotomy — A surgical incision of the perineum to enlarge the vaginal opening for birth.

"Exam" — Usually a vaginal examination done by inserting two fingers into the vagina to measure the cervical opening and determine the extent of dilation.

Fetoscope — A modified stethoscope used to listen to fetal heart tones during pregnancy and labor.

First stage — See Labor.

Forceps — An instrument made of two spoon-like, curved blades which are inserted into the vagina and used to pull out the baby during delivery.

Full term — A pregnancy of at least thirty-eight weeks gestation from the date of conception or forty weeks from the date of last menstrual period.

IV — Abbreviation for "intravenous"; a continuous "drip" of drugs and/or fluids into a vein.

Induced labor — Labor started artificially by prematurely rupturing the amniotic membranes or by giving an oxytocic drug (Pitocin) or both.

Labor — The process of uterine contractions which dilate the cervix and expel the fetus and placenta. Usually divided into three stages:
> **First Stage:** The period of effacement and dilation of the cervix; begins with the onset of regular contractions and ends with complete dilation of the cervix.
> **Second Stage:** The period of expulsion of the baby through the birth canal; begins with complete dilation and ends with the birth of the baby.
> **Third Stage:** The period of expulsion of the afterbirth or placenta; begins with the birth of the baby and ends with the delivery of the placenta.
> (Also see Transition.)

Lamaze method — A method of childbirth preparation developed by Fernand Lamaze, a French obstetrician; also called the "psychoprophylactic" method; uses a variety of patterned breathing techniques to distract the mother from the pain of labor.

Midwife — A person, usually a woman, who attends women in childbirth.
> **Nurse-midwife** — A registered nurse with special training in midwifery; legally recognized in most states.
> **Lay Midwife** — A non-nurse midwife, often self-taught or trained by apprenticeship; legally recognized in only a few states.

Paracervical block — A form of regional anesthesia in which an anesthetic drug is injected on either side of the cervix; used for pain relief in first stage labor.

Pelvic floor — The muscular structures stretching across the bottom of the pelvis which support the pelvic organs; the urethra, vagina, and rectum pass through the pelvic floor.

Perineum — The triangular area of tissue between the anus and the back of the vaginal opening; the site of the episiotomy incision or sometimes of perineal lacerations or tears resulting from birth.

Pitocin — the trade name of a form of the hormone oxytocin; used to induce labor or augment labor contractions.

Placenta — The blood-rich organ which makes possible the exchange of nutrients and waste materials between the fetus and the mother; it is attached to the fetus by the umbilical cord.

Placenta previa — A condition in which the placenta develops low in the uterus and partially or completely covers the cervical opening.

Prolapsed cord — A condition in which the umbilical cord falls below or in front of the presenting part of the fetus; can cut off oxygen supply to the fetus if the cord is compressed.

Pudendal block — A form of regional anesthesia in which an anesthetic drug is injected through the vagina into the pudendal nerves on either side; used for pain relief during actual delivery of the baby and subsequent episiotomy repair.

"Pushing" — The mother's voluntary abdominal bearing-down efforts during second stage labor; these are in addition to the involuntary, expulsive contractions of the uterus.

Rh incompatibility — A condition in which a woman with Rh-negative blood conceives a child with Rh-positive blood; if their blood mixes at delivery the woman can develop antibodies which may harm any subsequent Rh-positive baby she bears.

Second stage — See Labor.

Spinal anesthesia — A form of regional anesthesia in which an anesthetic drug is injected into the spine, usually between the lumbar spines 3-4 or 4-5; used during late first stage and second stage; eliminates pain from the waist down and removes the urge to push.

Stages of labor — See Labor.

Toxemia — A metabolic disorder of pregnancy also known as:
    Pre-eclampsia — a toxemia of pregnancy characterized by increasing blood pressure, edema, and protein in the urine.
    Eclampsia — A severe form of toxemia characterized by convulsions and coma in addition to the symptoms of pre-eclampsia; can result in death.

Transition — The last phase of first stage labor in which the cervix opens to complete dilation of ten centimeters.

Trimester — A period of three months, used to divide pregnancy into three parts.

Ultrasound — In obstetrics, a diagnostic procedure for visualizing the fetus in the womb through the use of high-frequency sound waves which bounce off the fetus and other soft body parts, creating a "picture" which can be seen on a television screen; used to determine fetal size and position, dimensions of the head, probable length of gestation, location of the placenta, etc. Use of ultrasound in pregnancy is assumed to be safe, but it is unknown whether there are adverse, long-term effects to the baby.

"Waters" — Colloquial term for the amniotic fluid contained within the amniotic sac.

About the Contributors

Janet Isaacs Ashford was born in 1949 in Los Angeles, where she attended the University of Southern California (major in violin and composition) and the University of California at Los Angeles (B.A./psychology, 1974). Janet became interested in writing about childbirth as a result of the home birth of her first child in 1976. Her work as a birth advocate led to the publication of *The Whole Birth Catalog: A Sourcebook for Choices in Childbirth* (Crossing Press, 1983). *Birth Stories: The Experience Remembered* is her second published book. Janet is now collecting examples of art work and literature for a book on the use of childbirth as a theme in art and culture. Janet lives with her husband Vic and two children, Rufus and Florence, in Saratoga, California.

Jeannine Parvati Baker (a.k.a. Jeannine O'Brien-Medvin) was born in Los Angeles in 1949. She received a B.A. degree in psychology in 1974 and is completing work for a master's in the same subject. Jeannine has been a lay midwife since 1974 and also practices fertility counseling and astrology. She is the author of *Prenatal Yoga and Natural Birth* (Freestone Publishing, 1974) and *Hygieia: A Woman's Herbal* (Freestone Publishing, 1978), and is finishing work on her third book, *Conscious Conception*. A fourth manuscript, *Psyche's Midwife*, is in progress. Jeannine is the founder of Hygieia College, which provides workshops, seminars and a correspondence course on midwifery and women's health, employing the maiutic ("in the manner of a midwife") method of teaching. Jeannine lives with her husband, Rico Baker, and children in Utah. She gave birth to her fifth baby in July,1984.

Cathy Cade was born in 1942 and grew up in the Midwest and South. Since the early sixties she has been active in the Civil Rights, Peace, Women's, Lesbian and Gay movements. Cathy has been a feminist photographer for the last thirteen years, supporting herself with part-time jobs. Cathy lives in Oakland, California with her lover-and-partner and their six-year-old son.

Lee Campbell holds a master's degree in education and is a frequent lecturer and writer on adoption issues. Founder and past-president of Concerned United Birthparents, Lee remains active in the adoption reform movement. Currently Lee is a learning skills coordinator and instructor at the University of New Hampshire.

Peggy Cannon was born on New Year's Day, 1949, in Indiana. She spent her teenage years in Pennsylvania and graduated from Clarion State University with a B.Sc. degree. After two years of teaching English at a junior high in Connecticut, Peggy made her way to Toronto, where she worked for a small publishing company and met her husband Roger. Peggy and Roger's first two children were born in Winnipeg, Manitoba, where Peggy became a La Leche League leader, providing counseling for breastfeeding mothers. The Cannons now live in Oshawa, Ontario, where Peggy continues her work with the League, with a perinatal bereavement group, and as a volunteer at her children's schools. The Cannon's fourth child, a healthy daughter, was born in November, 1983.

Barbara Charles is founder and director of the Long Island Midwifery Service, the only such service with both hospital privileges and the ability to see private patients in Nassau and Suffolk counties. She is assistant clinical professor of nursing at S.U.N.Y. at Stony Brook.

Sadie Harris Crissey was born in Tonawanda, New York in 1894. She graduated from Tonawanda High School, then attended Chautauqua Summer School for three years, receiving a certificate in physical education. Sadie studied physiology at the University of Buffalo and taught calisthenics and dancing at the Larkin Club and the YWCA. She was also a professional singer and sang at church services, weddings, and funerals (receiving $2. per performance). Sadie's current activities include reading, travelling, entertaining, making craft items and needlework. Sadie enjoys her eleven grandchildren and sixteen great-grandchildren. She lives part of the year in San Marino, California with her son John and his wife Alice, and the remainder of the year in her home in Tonawanda.

Lily W. Dinerstein was born in 1897 in Southern Russia near Odessa. Her mother died when she was seven years old and her father emigrated to the United States, leaving Lily and her younger sister Nancy behind with relatives. When he was established and able to send for them, Lily and Nancy made the voyage to New York alone, at the ages of twelve and nine. Lily grew up in New York City and married Samuel Dinerstein in 1918, at the age of twenty-one. She has two children and four grandchildren. Lily lives in New York City.

Jennifer Crissey Fisher was born in Philadelphia in 1951. She completed high school and more than two years of college and received childbirth teacher training at Parenting Services Center in Whittier, California. Jennifer has taught childbirth education classes for five years and is a senior labor coach with Birth in Harmony Labor Coaches. She is also vice president of the Board of Directors of Adoptions Unlimited, a licensed adoption agency. Jennifer likes reading, cooking, gardening, music, and of course, children. She lives in Orange County, California with her husband Lief and their children: Brett, ten; Christian, eight; Eric, six; and Megan, three; and Elizabeth Melanie Sony Hee, four months.

Sarah Franklin was born in New York City and raised primarily in Pasadena, California where her father is a professor of Applied Mathematics at the California Institute of Technology and her mother teaches high school. Sarah is an only child. She attended the University of California at Los Angeles, majoring in Pictorial Arts. Her favorite jobs have included commissioned art work, cooking, working in a ballet studio, working for a silk importer, and work with nutrition and herbal remedies. Her current "job" is raising Benjamin. Sarah volunteers her time as a "doula" at the birth center where she delivered and assists as a labor coach at her local hospital. She is a certified childbirth instructor for Informed Birth and Parenting, a national childbirth education organization. Sarah lives in Palo Alto, California.

Faye Grunow Gibson has worked for seventeen years as a hospital nurse: ten years in obstetrics and seven years in emergency room nursing. She is a certified ASPO/Lamaze instructor, has worked in a free-standing birth center, and has practiced as a lay midwife for three years. Faye is currently in a private practice partnership with a certified nurse-midwife. She also provides counseling, classes and labor support for couples having a vaginal birth after cesarean. Faye is the mother of three teenage children. She lives in Northern California.

Sharon Glass was born in Los Angeles in 1958. She received a bachelor's degree in women's studies (with a focus on health care) in 1982 from the University of California at Santa Cruz. She is a lay midwife, certified by the Oregon Midwifery Council and a certified childbirth educator with the Natural Birth Association. Sharon has worked in women's health for many years, including four years with the Santa Cruz Women's Health Collective and work in four different prenatal clinics for low income women. Sharon currently lives in Portland, Oregon with her husband and daughter, but will soon be moving to Los Angeles where her husband plans to begin medical school. Sharon practices as a lay midwife and teaches childbirth education, prenatal yoga and the ovulation method of fertility awareness. She is also taking pre-nursing courses in preparation for becoming a certified nurse-midwife.

Helen Dinerstein Henkin was born in 1922 in Brooklyn. She married her husband Norman in 1942, at the age of nineteen, just before he left to serve in World War II. Helen received a master's degree in mathematics from Columbia University and worked as a statistician until her first child was born. As her children were growing up, she became involved in civic affairs and political work and served as Brooklyn campaign manager for Elizabeth Holtzman's 1980 Senate campaign. Helen now serves as chair of her local community board. She and Norman have lived in the same house in Brooklyn for the past thirty years.

Lolly Hirsch was born in 1922 and was "badly educated" at Grand Rapids Michigan Junior College and through a brief stint at Antioch College, Yellow Springs, Ohio. Lolly married, in 1941, and eventually birthed "five citizens, all functioning, beautiful and intelligent to this day." Lolly became a "born-again-feminist" in 1969 and she devoted the seventies to gynecological self-help, lecturing and giving self-help demonstrations. Lolly published *The Monthly Extract: An Irregular Periodical*, a newsletter on women's health, the *Witch's Os*, a booklet on women's health, and organized the First International Childbirth Conference in Stamford, Connecticut in 1973. In 1981 Lolly was divorced and since then has been living in Stamford, Connecticut, "self-supporting for the first time in my life and establishing *my* Matriarchy on *my* half acre in *my* home of twenty-six years."

Alice Munro Isaacs was born in Los Angeles in 1921. She attended the University of California at Los Angeles, receiving an elementary teaching credential in 1945. She taught first grade for most of the next thirty years, returning to graduate school in 1973 for a master's degree in special education from California State University at Long Beach. Alice now works as a resource specialist at Caroldale Avenue school in Los Angeles. In her free time she enjoys travelling (recent trips have been to Spain, Mexico, Thailand, Great Britain, and China) and working with feminist women's organizations, including the Women's Political Caucus. Alice lives with her husband John in Long Beach, California.

Jean Chisholm Isaacs was born in Pittsburgh, Pennsylvania on Christmas Eve, 1888. Jean and her husband John had three sons: James, John Jr., and Robert. In 1931, John Isaacs, Sr. died of skin cancer, leaving Jean the sole provider. She sold corsets in a department store and also made and sold orange marmalade to support herself and her family through the Depression. In 1936, Jean, her mother Emma, and two youngest sons, drove across the country to resettle in southern California, so that the boys could take advantage of California's system of free state college education. Jean worked cleaning houses, then during World War II worked on the assembly line in a defense plant. After the war Jean worked as a nursery school teacher and eventually came to teach first grade in a Baptist church school, where she remained for many years. After retiring she continued to live on her own until she was past ninety. Jean died in August 1982, at the age of ninety-four.

Bill London, his wife Gina and daughter Willow are still living happily in the same log cabin. They have formed a partnership free-lance writing business.

Jonathan London was born in 1947 at the Brooklyn Navy Hospital, the second son of a career naval officer. Jonathan attended high school and college in San Jose, California, receiving a master's degree in social sciences from San Jose State University in 1970. As a conscientious objector, he did his alternate service for two years with the Department of Social Services, then spent much of the next several years travelling in Europe and South and Central America. He met his wife, Maureen Weisenberger, while travelling across Canada in 1974. Since 1978 Jonathan and Maureen, a nurse, have lived north of San Francisco. Jonathan has worked as a journeyman display installer and is working toward an elementary school teaching credential. He is a poet and short story writer with work published in numerous magazines.

Sonia Margulis was born in Omaha, Nebraska in 1908, the daughter of Russian-Jewish immigrant parents. She lived most of her life in New York City. Sonia graduated from Hunter College (B.A./music, 1930) and during the Depression she worked as a remedial reading teacher under the WPA. When her first child was born in 1937, Sonia became a "hausfrau," raising three children: one son is now a chemistry professor at the University of Massachusetts, another is a free-lance musician, and her daughter is a family counselor in Oakland. There are five grandchildren. For twenty years Sonia and her husband ran an antique shop, then retired and moved from Mount Vernon, New York to the West Coast, where Sonia studied creative writing at the Senior Center in Albany, California. Sonia died on April 2, 1984.

Marian McDonald is a political activist and poet living in the Bay Area. Born in Ohio in 1948, she became involved in the anti-war and women's movements in the late sixties and began working in women's health in the early seventies, in the abortion rights movement and in health worker organizing. She was active in work to adopt federal sterilization guidelines in 1978, and was a founding member of the Massachusetts Childbearing Rights Alliance in 1979. Marian served as editor of the Childbearing Rights Information Project's book, *For Ourselves, Our Families, and Our Future: The Struggle for Childbearing Rights* (Red Sun Press, 1981). Her poems and articles about women and in solidarity with the peoples of Asia, Africa, and Latin America have appeared in numerous publications, including *The Guardian, Puerto Rico Libre!, Getting Stronger, All Our Lives: A Women's Songbook,* and *Boletín Nacional.*

Florence Scriven Munro was born in Plainfield, New Jersey in 1886. As a young woman she studied art at the Cooper Union art school in New York City, going there on the train each day. She was active in the women's suffrage movement, and marched in the street wearing a banner, "Votes for Women." In her early thirties she married James Munro, a stone mason, and they moved to Los Angeles after the war, raising their two children during the Twenties and the Depression. Florence worked as an artist throughout her life, producing oil paintings and watercolors of California scenes and painting on china. After the death of her husband in 1964, Florence lived on her own until she was past ninety. In her last years, she was cared for by her daughter, Alice. Florence died on February 9, 1983, at the age of ninety-six.

Martin Paule was born in 1946 in England and raised in South Africa, coming to the U.S. as a teenager. He and his wife Rose have two children, Willow and Braden, and live in Burkittsville, Maryland, near Baltimore. Martin and Rose work with The Birthing Circle, a consumer childbirth organization, and are also part of the Deva community, which supports itself by making and selling natural fiber clothing by mail order. Deva is a home-based network of some thirty families and their business/community helps support the members' commitment to "whole-hearted parenting." Martin has also been learning about the art and science of homeopathy for the past five years.

Deborah Regal was born in 1958 in Dearborn, Michigan, and currently lives in Ann Arbor with her husband, Randy, and three active young sons. Besides tending to the needs of her family, Debbie enjoys gardening, vegetarian cooking, and aerobic exercise. Debbie's struggles through her own birth experiences have helped to fuel her current career interests. She is a consumer-oriented childbirth educator, attends births as an assistant on an occasional basis, and is pursuing a career as a lay midwife. Debbie plans to establish an Ann Arbor chapter of the Cesarean Prevention Movement, a national organization devoted to cesarean prevention and education.

Marcie Rendon was born in 1952 in a hospital near the White Earth reservation in northern Minnesota. Her mother and grandfather were born on the same reservation. Marcie is a single mother, a midwife, and a recovering alcoholic. She is active in Native women's health issues including chemical dependency, incest, co-counseling, home birth, and alternative health care. Marcie holds two B.A. degrees, in criminal justice and in American Indian Studies. She has been attending births since 1978 and has been writing poetry since the age of eleven. Her poetry has been published in several books and in the Moon Cycle calendars published by Women's Dance Health Project, a Native American health organization. Marcie lives in Minneapolis.

Chandra Lee Rowe was born in 1965 in Sacramento, California. She graduated from high school in 1983, having worked as an office clerk at her school for a year and a half. She continues to live with her mother and care for her son, now two years old. Chandra's boyfriend Juan will graduate from high school in 1984 and plans to go to college. Chandra and Juan plan to marry in a few years.

Gayle Smith was born in New York City and raised in Boston by her maternal grandmother. Her mother died when Gayle was five years old. Gayle attended the University of Massachusetts at Amherst. She has worked as a bank teller for the past four years and will soon begin nursing school, in preparation for becoming a lay midwife. Gayle works with a community group which teaches women about birthing alternatives and is completing teacher training and certification with Informed Homebirth, a national childbirth education organization. In her spare time Gayle likes to read and do needlepoint. Gayle and her husband Noah live in Boston with their two children, Kaliis and Gabriel.

Abby Joan Sylviachild (a pseudonym) was born in 1945 in New York and attended Barnard College, where she majored in American History and "minored in the peace-in-Vietnam movement." She received a master's degree in American History from a university in the midwest, concentrating on progressive reform, and women's history. Since the late sixties Abby has been a member of the feminist and women's health movements, working with an underground abortion clinic (before 1973), a family planning clinic, the YWCA, in Democratic politics, and as president of her local chapters of N.O.W. and Resolve. Abby's family of four lives in an older suburban neighborhood, where they have planted many fruit trees and a large garden.

Louise Henkin Wejksnora was born in 1951 in New York City. She has taught English composition at Baruch College of the City University of New York and is hoping to teach that subject again at the University of Wisconsin-Milwaukee, where her husband is now on the faculty. Louise is finishing graduate work in medieval English literature, working on a doctoral thesis on Chaucer's *Troilus and Criseyde*. She is active in WisSAC (Wisconsin Association for Safe Alternatives in Childbirth), has begun to write for publication, and tends an organic vegetable garden during Wisconsin's pitifully short growing season.

About the Poets

Ellen Bass has published several books of poetry, including *Our Stunning Harvest* (New Society Publishers). She is co-editor of *I Never Told Anyone: Writings by Women Survivors of Child Sexual Abuse* (Harper & Row) and travels nationally offering workshops for survivors, training seminars, and creative writing workshops. Since writing "For My Husband's Mother" she has divorced, come out as a lesbian, and now lives with her daughter in Santa Cruz, California.

Barbara Crooker has had over 170 poems published in large circulation magazines, small press magazines, and anthologies. She has published two chapbooks, *Writing Home* (Gehry Press, 1983) and *Moving Poems* (Golden Argosy Press, forthcoming). Barbara teaches writing at Cedar Crest College in Pennsylvania and writes articles about herb gardening and canoeing. She is an elected member of the Poetry Society of America and is listed in *A Directory of American Poets and Fiction Writers* (CODA). Barbara is the mother of four children: infant David, two months; Becky, six; Stacey, thirteen; and a stillborn girl who would have been fourteen.

Joan Joffe Hall was born in New York City, attended Vassar College and Stanford University, and teaches creative writing and women's studies at the University of Connecticut. She has published two chapbooks, *Cutting The Plant* (1977) and *The Aerialist's Fall* (1981), and a book of poems, *The Rift Zone* (Curbstone, 1978).

Joy Harjo was born in Tulsa, Oklahoma, in 1951. She attended the Institute of American Indian Arts and later received two degrees in creative writing: a B.A. from the University of New Mexico and an M.F.A. from the Iowa Writers' Workshop. She has attended the Anthropology Film Center in Santa Fe, New Mexico. She is the author of two collections of poetry: *The Last Song, What Moon Drove Me To This?* (I. Reed Books, 1979) and *She Had Some Horses* (Thunder's Mouth Press, 1983). Joy is the mother of two children and is currently working on a screenplay and a new collection of poetry. She lives in Denver with her daughter, Rainy.

Kate Jennings grew up in Richmond, Virginia and graduated from Marymount College in Tarrytown. She has published fiction and poetry in numerous magazines and her work appears in several anthologies, including the 1980, 1981 and 1984 editions of *The Anthology of Magazine Verse and Yearbook of American Poetry, Thirtieth Year to Heaven* (Jackpine Press, 1980), and *Critical Reading and Writing* (Longman, 1983). Her first collection of poems, *Second Sight*, was published by Iron Mountain Press in 1976. Kate lives in Geneva, Switzerland with her husband, a U.N. economist, and three children: David, nine; Anne, five; and new baby James.

Notes

The following notes are based on professional and popular reference sources which are listed at the end of this section. The notes have been checked for medical accuracy by Faye Gibson, R.N.

Introduction

1. *Childbirth Alternatives Quarterly*, a 20-page newsletter, is available for $10.00 per year or $3.00 for a sample issue from *Childbirth Alternatives Quarterly*, c/o Janet Isaacs Ashford, Bin 62-SLAC, Stanford, CA 94305. Write for a sample issue. *The Whole Birth Catalog* is available for $14.95 plus $1.00 shipping from The Crossing Press, P.O. Box 640, Trumansburg, NY 14886.

Uremic Poisoning

1. Judging by her description of her symptoms (edema of the face and extremities, high blood pressure) my grandmother's "uremic poisoning" was probably a case of pre-eclamptic toxemia of pregnancy (see glossary entry for "toxemia").
2. This may be a reference to artificial rupture of the membranes to induce labor (see "induced labor" in the glossary) or may perhaps be a reference to the use of a "bougie," as described in the 6th (1931) edition of *Williams Obstetrics*. A bougie, named after the French city of Bougie in Algeria, is defined in the dictionary as either a wax candle, or a "tapering cylindrical instrument for introduction into a tubular passage of the body."

Childbed Fever

1. *Williams Obstetrics* (1980) provides the following background: "In the great influenza pandemic of 1918, the disease, particularly the pneumonic type, was a serious complication of pregnancy."
2. "Childbed fever" is a common term for a puerperal ("after birth") infection, which can develop when lacerations in the birth canal or the placental site in the uterus become infected by bacteria introduced from within the vagina or from the outside. Puerperal infection is not common in the U.S. today (about 6% of births) but has been historically a major cause of maternal death and still is in many parts of the world.
3. Influenza infection during pregnancy is considered to be a cause of miscarriage, fetal death, prematurity and occasionally anencephaly or meningomylelocele (neural tube defects), but there is no conclusive proof that influenza in pregnancy causes birth defects.
4. Blockage of the fallopian tubes (which carry eggs from the ovaries to the uterus) may result from a puerperal infection, causing infertility.

My Sister Jen, The Doctor

1. Pituitrin, or post pituitary extract, is a form of oxytocin, the hormone which causes the uterus to contract during labor. Pituitrin was first used in obstetrics in 1909 and is prepared from animal glands. The substance was later refined into

Pitocin, an oxytocic which is commonly used today to induce or augment labor.

2. Chloroform is a toxic fluid used as a general anesthetic. Chloroform is no longer used in obstetrics but it was once a popular anesthetic, particularly for home births.

Birth in My Family

1. Even as late as 1946, the 5th edition of *A Textbook of Gynecology* by Arthur Hale Curtis, had this to say about contraception: "The indications for such control must often be a moral one, influenced by religious belief as well as by legal restrictions."

2. "Dry birth" is a colloquial term for premature rupture of the membranes (before the onset of labor), derived from the incorrect belief that labor and delivery would be more difficult in the absence of the amniotic fluid. However, premature rupture of the membranes can be a cause of infection if labor does not begin fairly soon after the rupture or if bacteria are introduced into the vaginal canal through vaginal examinations.

3. Examinations to determine cervical dilation are sometimes done by inserting fingers into the rectum and palpating the cervix through the tissue which separates the rectum and the vagina. This is done to avoid the possibility of introducing bacteria into the vagina, which could cause a puerperal infection.

4. Headache following the use of spinal anesthesia is presumably caused by the leakage of cerebrospinal fluid from the site of the needle puncture, which diminishes the total volume of fluid and allows traction on pain-sensitive central nervous system structures.

Saddle Block and Forceps

1. It is possible that my mother does not remember her labor experience because she was given scopolamine, an amnesic drug commonly used in obstetrics. Under the influence of scopolamine the mother is conscious during labor (unless under the influence of some other drug) but her memory of the labor is obliterated.

A Happy Surprise

1. Anovular means "without ovulation." An anovular menstrual cycle is one in which no egg is released from an ovary.

2. Apparently the doctor thought that the hardness he felt in his patient's abdomen was due to her tense abdominal muscles, but was in fact her enlarging pregnant uterus.

3. X-radiation is today considered harmful to the fetus, causing an increase in mutations and later development of malignancies, particularly leukemia. As recently as 1971 it was considered safe to x-ray potentially pregnant women during the first fourteen days of their menstrual cycle, the average period before ovulation. However, it is now known that the developing ovum is also at risk and there is no "safe" period for abdominal x-ray examinations.

4. Nitrous oxide ("laughing gas") is a gas used for general inhalation anesthesia.

Surrendering My Baby

1. Concerned United Birthparents can be reached at P.O. Box 573, Milford, MA 01757. 603/749-3744.

Birth With "La Partera"

1. "Borderline" is a term often used by physicians and midwives to describe a pelvis with internal measurements which are very close to the minimum size needed for a baby to pass through. Evaluation of the size of the pelvic outlet (and the size of the baby's head) is subjective and very often a woman with a "borderline" pelvis is capable of a normal vaginal delivery.

2. Jesusita's self-professed excellent record is consistent with studies of midwives, both self-trained and nurse-trained, who usually have lower infant and maternal mortality rates than physicians, even though midwives often practice with low-income, rural, or disadvantaged women.

Walking Out of the Hospital

1. Marginal placenta previa is a condition in which the placenta implants and grows low in the uterus, very near the cervical opening. As the cervix begins to efface and dilate early in labor, the placental tissue may be torn and begin to bleed. This type of bleeding can often be contained and does not always pose a threat to the mother or fetus. However, in cases of complete placenta previa, where the placenta completely covers the cervix, the consequent bleeding is a serious complication which can lead to the death of the fetus or mother or both. Cesarean section is often done in cases of complete placenta previa. Placenta previa is associated with breech presentations and may prevent engagement of the presenting fetal part.

2. Shepherd's purse (Capsella bursa-pastoris) is an annual plant of the mustard family used as an herbal remedy for hemorrhage in childbirth. Bayberry bark is derived from the root of two trees of the genus Myrica (Myrica cerifera and Myrica carolinensis) and is used in traditional medicine as a tonic and astringent.

Infertility and Adoption

1. Charting basal body temperature (taken immediately upon waking in the morning, before getting up) can help determine when ovulation occurs, as the BBT goes up slightly at this time. A special thermometer marked in tenths of degrees is used to measure the BBT. Keeping a monthly record of BBT changes, along with changes in cervical mucus (the Sympto-Thermal Method) is used as a tool in "natural family planning" either to avoid a pregnancy (abstain or use contraceptives on fertile days) or to achieve a pregnancy (have intercourse without contraception on fertile days).

2. RESOLVE, Box 474, Belmont, MA 02178.

3. It is beyond the scope of these notes to discuss in detail the various treatments for infertility mentioned in this story. For information consult the literature recommended by RESOLVE (no. 2 above).

4. Many areas have adoptive parent groups which help prospective parents learn about adoption. An excellent one with national outreach is The Adoptive Parents Committee, Inc. (A.P.C.), 210 Fifth Avenue, New York, New York 10010. (212) 683-9221.

A Lesbian Birth Story

1. For more information on lesbian mothers and donor insemination see "Lesbian Mothers" in The Whole Birth Catalog by Janet Isaacs Ashford (Crossing Press, 1983).

2. Sometimes a "lip" or edge of the cervix remains over the baby's head even when the rest of the cervix is fully dilated. This lip is often "anterior" (toward the

mother's front). A midwife can sometimes push back a cervical lip by gently pressing on it during a contraction.

3. Cephalopelvic disproportion (CPD) refers to a condition in which the baby's head ("cephalo-" means "head") is too large to fit through the mother's pelvis. The diagnosis of CPD has increased in recent years and is a major factor in the rising cesarean rate. CPD is often given on medical charts as the reason for a cesarean, after the fact, but it is not clear whether many cases of apparent CPD could result in a vaginal birth if handled differently; for instance, by having the mother squat to push and by allowing more time for the pushing stage of labor.

4. A "posterior" position is one in which the back of the baby's head faces the mother's back, rather than her front ("anterior"), which is more usual. If the baby moves through the birth canal in a persistent posterior position, its passage will be more difficult and slow and it will eventually be born face up, with a characteristic "cone-head" molding of the soft bones of the head. A "missed" or undiagnosed posterior could account for an unusually long pushing stage of labor.

5. Meconium is the greenish material in the bowel of a fetus. It is usually expelled after birth as the first bowel movement. Occasionally a fetus will pass meconium during labor, sometimes in response to stress. If the meconium is inhaled into the lungs during birth it can cause respiratory difficulties or pneumonia.

Unexpected Forceps

1. See *Nutrition for the Childbearing Year* by Jacqueline Gibson Gazella (Woodland Publishing, 230 Manitoba Avenue, Wayzata, MN 55391, 1980).

2. The Lamaze and Bradley methods are described in the glossary. ICEA is the International Childbirth Education Association. For more information contact ICEA, P.O. Box 20048, Minneapolis, MN 55420.

Angry and Happy at the Same Time

1. Nisentil (alphaprodine hydrochloride) is an amnesic narcotic analgesic. Vistaril (hydroxyzine pamoate) is a tranquilizer which also acts as an ataractic (analgesic potentiating drug), which enhances the effects of analgesics.

2. In order to make sure that no piece of the placenta has been retained in the uterus (which could lead to later bleeding or infection), an obstetrician may sometimes pass an entire gloved hand up through the vagina and into the uterus to manually explore and remove pieces of retained placenta.

Toxemia and an Induced Labor

1. See *What Every Pregnant Woman Should Know: The Truth About Diet and Drugs in Pregnancy*, by Gail Sforza Brewer and Thomas Brewer (Penguin, 1979); *Metabolic Toxemia of Late Pregnancy* (Second edition), by Thomas Brewer (Keats Publishing, 1982); and *The Brewer Medical Diet for Normal and High-Risk Pregnancy*, by Gail Sforza Brewer and Thomas Brewer (Simon and Schuster/Fireside, 1983).

2. Phenobarbitol is a long-acting barbiturate sedative.

3. Magnesium sulfate is an anti-convulsant drug used for the prevention or control of eclampsia.

4. A diuretic is a drug which increases the flow of urine. Diuretics have been used in obstetrics to prevent or manage pre-eclampsia by attempting to reduce edema (swelling caused by retention of fluid in the tissues). However, both *Williams Obstetrics* and Jenson, Benson and Bobak state that there is no clear evidence showing that the use of diuretics in pregnancy is beneficial, and their use may be harmful.

5. Magnesium sulfate (see no. 3 above) may be given along with pitocin to manage oxytocin-induced uterine tetany (extremely prolonged uterine contractions).
6. A feeling of rectal pressure and/or a need to defecate can be caused when the baby's head is in the birth canal and presses on the rectum through the tissue which separates it from the vagina.
7. It is a violation of the concept of patients' rights to give any medical treatment or drug without the express permission of the patient. To force a treatment without the patient's consent could be grounds for a charge of assault. However, the well-established concept of "informed consent" is often overlooked in medicine, particularly in obstetrics, where patients may be assumed not to know what is in their own best interest.

The Birth of Willow

1. Effluerage is light, circular stroking of the abdomen done as an aid to relaxation and comfort during labor.
2. The "standing squat" position spontaneously assumed by the mother in this story is similar to one commonly used by mothers giving birth in Pithiviers, France at the clinic directed by French surgeon Michel Odent. For more information on Odent's work see *The Whole Birth Catalog; Entering the World: The De-medicalization of Childbirth* (translation of *Bien Naitre*, 1976) by Michel Odent, Marion Boyers Inc., publisher, The Scribner Book Companies, U.S. distributor, 1984; and *Birth Reborn* by Michel Odent, translated from the French by Jane Pincus and Juliette Levin, (Pantheon, 1984).
3. Gelsemium sempervirens (yellow jasmine) is a homeopathic remedy derived from the root of the yellow jasmine, which grows in Asia and the southern United States. It is used as a remedy for flu, head colds, and tension headache.

Sixteen and Determined

1. Contrary to some popular beliefs, the pain of labor contractions during first stage labor is felt in the area of the cervix (the neck of the uterus), low in the groin, as with menstrual cramps. Sometimes the pain is also felt in the lower back, opposite the groin, as in "back labor." Generally, there is no sensation of pain in the large body of the uterus unless there is an abnormal condition, such as abruptio placentae (premature separation of the placenta away from the wall of the uterus) or rupture of the uterus during labor.
2. Chandra Rowe was well within her legal rights as a hospital patient in refusing the medical treatment suggested by her doctor. See note no. 7 under "Toxemia and an Induced Labor," above.

Home Birth After Two Cesareans

1. Once the amniotic membranes have ruptured, the barrier to infection is also broken. If labor does not begin fairly soon after premature rupture of the membranes (PROM), there is a danger of infection of the mother and/or fetus from bacteria passing through the vagina to the uterus. This danger increases as the time between PROM and delivery of the baby increases. However, there is uncertainty about what is a "safe" amount of time to wait after PROM, before taking steps to initiate labor. Some practitioners feel it is safe to wait 24 hours; some less.
2. The incidence of uterine rupture is about .5%, much less than most people believe. Of that percentage, not all are previous cesarean mothers; many cases of uterine rupture are caused by the use of oxytocic drugs to stimulate labor.

3. "Total spinal blockade" is a serious complication of spinal anesthesia such as the epidural block, which occurs when the spinal needle insertion is performed incorrectly or when too much anesthetic drug is injected. Spinal blockade causes respiratory paralysis, hypotension (lowered blood pressure), and apnea (lack of breathing), and can progress to cardiac arrest and death.

4. A reprint of papers presented at this conference, "1981 Cesarean Update" (36 pages) is available for $2.50 from BIRTH, 110 El Camino Real, Berkeley, CA 94705.

5. Nancy Wainer Cohen (10 Great Plain Terrace, Needham, MA 02191) provides workshops and counseling for vaginal birth after cesarean (VBAC). Her book, *Silent Knife: Cesarean Prevention and Vaginal Birth after Cesarean* (with co-author Lois Estner) is published by Bergin & Garvey, South Hadley, Massachusetts.

6. Teas made from red raspberry leaves (Rubus ideaus) and comfrey (symphytum officinale) are considered beneficial during pregnancy by some herbalists. Red raspberry is said to relax the smooth muscle of the uterus and intestine and to lead to shorter, less painful labors. Comfrey (also called "knitbone") is often used in a poultice applied externally to help promote healing of injured tissue (as for instance, perineal lacerations). However, internal use of comfrey during pregnancy is discouraged by at least one source: *Healing the Family, Volume I (Pregnancy, Birth and Children's Ailments)* by Joy Gardner, (Bantam, 1982) because comfrey's active ingredient, allantoin, has been found to be carcinogenic (cancer-causing) in tests with animals. Neither red raspberry nor comfrey is on the Food and Drug Administration's list of plant materials which are "generally recognized as safe" (GRAS).

7. Acupressure is a traditional Chinese method of healing by applying manual pressure to specified points on the body. It is related to acupuncture, which involves the insertion of needles into specified points on the body.

Katy Jane: Anencephaly

1. Anencephaly (along with spina bifida) is a neural tube defect, which comes about when the neural tube, which contains what will later become the brain and spinal cord, fails to fuse completely in the first month of pregnancy. In anencephaly (which means literally, "without brain") the brain and skull fail to develop, so that the baby is born without a large portion of its brain and without the overlying skull. Seventy percent of anencephalic babies are female. The defect is "incompatible with life" and most anencephalic babies die within a few hours or days of birth. It has recently become possible to detect neural tube defects during the first half of pregnancy through maternal blood screening for alpha-fetoprotein, followed by amniocentesis and ultrasound (see *The Whole Birth Catalog*, listed in the bibliography, for more information). However, AFP screening is not recommended as a routine part of prenatal care for all women because of the possible harmful effects of the amniocentesis and ultrasound tests which are needed to confirm a diagnosis.

2. Polyhydramnios, or excessive amniotic fluid, is frequently associated with fetuses with birth defects, including anencephaly. The resultant increased uterine size and pressure may stimulate an early onset of labor, though many other factors are involved in the initiation of labor.

3. Syntocinon is a synthetic form of oxytocin and is used in the same ways as Pitocin, a natural form of oxytocin.

A Grandmother Welcomes and Remembers

1. The term "acushurka" sounds like the French term for a birth attendant, "accoucheur," and perhaps this usage is a result of the influence of the French language upon 19th century Russia. For a vivid fictional portrait of a Russian-trained, emigrant midwife practicing in New York City at the turn of the century, see *The Midwife*, by Gay Courter (listed in the bibliography).

Miscarriage: The Silent Wail

1. Marian McDonald belongs to a large health maintenance organization which includes a statewide system of hospitals and clinics. Members who need care can call an advice nurse, who will evaluate their symptoms over the phone and recommend whether to come in to a clinic or the hospital.
2. Poor eating habits and inadequate weight gain can adversely affect the fetus, especially later in pregnancy when fetal growth is rapid, but it is unlikely that this would cause a miscarriage in the first three months. Likewise there is no known association between a "busy schedule" or vigorous exercise and miscarriage. About fifty percent of miscarriages are caused by genetic abnormalities in the fetus and the other fifty percent by a variety of known and unknown factors, including hormonal deficiencies, uterine abnormalities, infection, exposure to environmental and workplace hazards, radiation, drugs, and severe malnutrition.
3. See "D & C" in the glossary.
4. *The Whole Birth Catalog* by Janet Isaacs Ashford (Crossing Press, 1983).
5. Endometriosis is a condition in which tissue from the endometrial lining of the uterus migrates to other parts of the abdominal area, where it responds to the hormones of the menstrual cycle, developing and bleeding as with a menstrual period. These "tumors" or "growths" can cause pain, infertility, and other problems. For more information contact the Endometriosis Association, P.O. Box 92187, Milwaukee, WI 53202.

A Native American Birth Story

1. Usually the placenta implants and grows in the upper portion of the uterus, but sometimes it implants low, either near or actually covering the cervical os (opening of the cervix). This can lead to potentially dangerous bleeding during labor, when the cervix opens. Also see note no. 7 under "Walking Out of the Hospital," above, and "placenta previa" in the glossary.
2. As the uterus contracts during labor the upper (active) portion becomes progressively thicker and the lower (passive) portion and cervix become thinner, so that at the boundary between upper and lower segments there forms a ridge on the interior uterine surface, called a physiologic (normal) retraction ring. However, in cases where labor is prolonged or obstructed (the fetus cannot move down) the ridge may develop into a pathologic retraction ring, also called Bandl's ring. In this situation, the lower uterine segment is stretched and thinned excessively and is in danger of rupture.

At the Birth Center

1. *Spiritual Midwifery*, by Ina May Gaskin, is described in the bibliography.
2. The term "doula" was first used by Dana Raphael in her book *The Tender Gift: Breastfeeding* (Schocken, 1976), to describe a woman companion who helps to "mother the mother," helping the newly-delivered woman as she establishes a breastfeeding relationship with her infant in the first days and weeks after birth.
    The birth center in which Sarah Franklin gave birth has expanded the concept, defining the doula as a woman who helps "mother the mother" in labor. The birth center doulas are trained by the staff, meet regularly to share experiences, and volunteer their services. Often they are childbirth educators or former birth center clients.
3. Blue cohosh (Caulophyllum thalictoroides) and black cohosh (Cimicifuga racemosa) are herbs which have been traditionally used to induce abortion and to facilitate labor.

4. "Laborade" is an electrolyte-balanced drink (like Gatorade or Pedialyte) developed by midwife Cat Feral and first published by the Association for Childbirth at Home, International. The drink is intended to help the laboring woman maintain fluid and electrolyte balance during labor, so that she does not become dehydrated or overly fatigued.

Lushness, Magic, Mystery and Work

1. "Station" is a term used to describe the position of the fetus' head in relation to the mother's pelvis. The hypothetical zero station (0) is at an imaginary line drawn through the ischial spines of the pelvis. The head is considered "engaged" when its biparietal diameter (the largest transverse diameter of the head) reaches zero station.
2. In the books by Carlos Casteneda about the Yaqui Indian shaman he calls "don Juan," don Juan describes himself as a warrior in his pursuit of knowledge, a warrior who travels the "path of the heart" (*The Teachings of Don Juan: A Yaqui Way of Knowledge*, by Carlos Casteneda, Ballantine Books, 1969).
3. Nisentil (alphaprodine hydrochloride) is an amnesic narcotic analgesic.
4. In California, certified nurse-midwives are licensed to provide care for normal childbearing women, under the "supervision" of a physician. This does not mean that a physician must be present at each midwife-attended birth, but some hospitals require this, nevertheless. This type of requirement can be considered part of the general effort by the medical profession to restrict or hamper the practice of nurse-midwifery.
5. According to the Lamaze method, as it was developed in this country beginning in the 1960s, mothers were encouraged to push as long and as hard as possible during second stage labor. That recommendation has been revised recently however, in light of new evidence showing that the flow of oxygen to the fetus is diminished when the mother bears down for longer than five or six seconds at a time. Mothers are now encouraged to bear down gently, to not hold their breath for long periods, and to generally push as feels most comfortable to them.

References:

Gardner, Joy. *Healing the Family, Volume I, Pregnancy, Birth and Children's Ailments*. New York: Bantam, 1982.

Jenson, Margaret Duncan, Ralph C. Benson, and Irene M. Boback. *Maternity Care: The Nurse and The Family*. St. Louis: C.V. Mosby, 1981.

Korte, Diana and Roberta Scaer. *A Good Birth, A Safe Birth*. New York: Bantam, 1984.

Pritchard, Jack A. and Paul C. MacDonald. *Williams Obstetrics* (Sixteenth Edition). New York: Appleton-Century-Crofts, 1980.

Webster's Seventh New Collegiate Dictionary. Springfield, MA: G. & C. Merriam Co., 1965.

Williams, J. Whitridge. *Obstetrics: A Textbook for the Use of Students and Practitioners* (Sixth Edition). New York: D. Appleton and Co., 1931.

Other Crossing Press titles which may be of particular interest:

THE WHOLE BIRTH CATALOG: A Sourcebook for Choices in Childbirth
edited by Janet Isaacs Ashford

NATURAL BIRTH, poetry by Toi Derricotte
(The Crossing Press Feminist Series)

RECLAIMING BIRTH: History and Heroines of American Childbirth Reform
by Margot Edwards and Mary Waldorf